Love Strong as Death
Lucy Peel's Canadian Journal, 1833 – 1836

J.I. Little, editor

Studies in Childhood and Family in Canada

Wilfrid Laurier University Press

WLU

This book has been published with the help of a grant from the Humanities and Social Sciences Federation of Canada, using funds provided by the Social Sciences and Humanities Research Council of Canada. We acknowledge the support of the Canada Council for the Arts for our publishing program. We acknowledge the financial support of the Government of Canada through the Book Publishing Industry Development Program for our publishing activities.

National Library of Canada Cataloguing in Publication Data

Peel, Lucy, fl. 1833-1836
    Love strong as death : Lucy Peel's Canadian journal, 1833-1836

(Studies in childhood and family in Canada)
Includes bibliographical references and index.
ISBN 0-88920-373-3 (bound)

1. Peel, Lucy, fl. 1833-1836 — Diaries.   2. Frontier and pioneer life — Quebec (Province) — Sherbrooke Region.   3. Pioneers — Quebec (Province) — Sherbrooke Region — Diaries.   4. Sherbrooke Region (Quebec) — Biography. I. Little, J.I. (John Irvine), 1947- .   II. Title.   III. Series.

FC2949.S47Z49 2001   971.4'6602'092   C2001-930463-3
F1054.5.S55P43 2001

Cover design by Leslie Macredie. Cover image based on "The Junction of the St. Francis and Magog Rivers (Sherbrooke)" from W.C. Bartlett, *Canadian Scenery Illustrated* (London, 1842). Courtesy of Bishop's University Archives FC 72.W5.

Printed in Canada

To the memory of Robin Burns, 1944-1998

Set me as a seal upon thine heart, as a seal upon thine arm: for love is strong as death.   — Song of Solomon 7:6

Contents

Acknowledgements xi

Introduction 1

Frequently Mentioned Names 19

Book One 23

Book Two 71

Book Three 173

Notes 209

Index 227

Acknowledgements

In many ways, this publication has been a co-operative effort. I would like to begin by thanking Dr Hugh Kinder for permission to publish his ancestor's letter-diary, as well as for his kind responses to my questions about his family. I am also grateful to the Eastern Townships Research Centre for their faith in me as an editor; to Dr Juliet Harrison, who transcribed the journal to the word processor; to Stephen Moore and Jack Corse for their research assistance; and particularly to Monique Nadeau-Saumier and Rina Kampeas, who worked hard to make this publication possible. In addition, I wish to thank Sandra Woolfrey, formerly of Wilfrid Laurier University Press, for her initial encouragement; Carroll Klein, who took over the project with equal enthusiasm; the anonymous readers for the Press and the Humanities and Social Sciences Federation for their helpful comments; and Barbara Tessman for her painstaking copy-editing. My research was assisted by funds from the Social Sciences and Humanities Research Council, and publication was made possible by a grant from the Humanities and Social Sciences Federation of Canada. Finally, as always, I wish to thank my family for their patience and support.

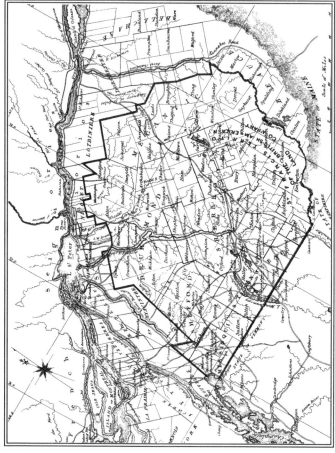

Map of the Eastern Townships, 1833. This map, first published by the British American Land Company the year it was established, gave a misleading impression of the region's accessibility from the St. Lawrence Valley and the United States. Source: DeVolpi and Scowen, *The Eastern Townships: A Pictorial Record* (Montreal, 1962).

Introduction

Lucy Peel's journal, sent at regular intervals to her transatlantic relatives, presents a remarkably complete narrative of her Canadian sojourn with her husband, Edmund, who was a half-pay officer on leave from the British Navy. Lucy's entries begin with their departure as a newlywed couple from the shores of England in 1833 and end with their decision to return home three and a half years later. Such letter diaries, which first appeared in the eighteenth century, became an important means of personal communication between gentry families in the British North American colonies and their relatives in the mother country. Similar documents by Elizabeth Simcoe, Anne Langton, Mary O'Brien, Anna Jameson, and Catharine Parr Traill have been published as journals or diaries.[1] Although Robert Fothergill defines a diary or journal as "serial autobiography" written "of oneself, by oneself, for oneself," rather than as part of a reciprocal correspondence, Felicity Nussbaum has written more recently that by the nineteenth century the diary was "both a private and a public document, no longer confined to secrecy."[2] Nussbaum's definition is more applicable here, and we will use the term journal and diary interchangeably.

The Peel journals, which include occasional additions by Edmund, have survived as a transcription written in two different hands in three bound volumes entitled "Letters from Canada." The journals were recently discovered in a descendant's house in Norwich.[3] Even if whoever did the copying subjected the original document to a certain amount of editing or censoring, these changes would still reflect the values and attitudes of the early nineteenth century, for the transcriptions were probably made shortly after Lucy's instalments were received so that they could be circulated to various members of the family. Moreover, Nussbaum reminds us

---

Notes to this section start on p. 209.

that all types of autobiographical texts issue "from the culture as much as the individual author."[4]

The early nineteenth century was an era when women's diaries still focused on the semi-public world of family and community rather than the private world of the individual psyche.[5] Just as the journals of half-pay officers' wives, such as Susanna Moodie's *Roughing It in the Bush*, provide the best descriptions we have of everyday life and cultural mores on the Upper Canadian frontier, so Lucy Peel's evocative writing fulfills the same role for the Sherbrooke area of Lower Canada's Eastern Townships.[6] While it is necessary to remember that journals such as Lucy Peel's reflect the experiences and views of a small, privileged sector of society, their authors were nevertheless sharp observers of their social and natural surroundings, and they provide valuable insights into the ideology and behaviour of the families who dominated the Canadian colonies socially and politically during the pre-Rebellion era. Furthermore, they give a voice to women, a voice that is rarely heard in the official records that constitute much of the historical archives.

Because of their literary talents, these well-educated diarists and correspondents have also attracted the attention of literature scholars, and Lucy Peel's journal deserves to be included in this rather restrictive canon.[7] Harriet Blodgett refers to diaries as "literature subjectively interpreting life," though not to be confused with "the novel or public autobiography in which life has been retrospectively shaped into a coherent, self-valorizing fiction."[8] Even though Lucy Peel's journal was written with the deliberate "literariness" that Fothergill claims emerged in the early nineteenth century, it is without the artifice of chronicles self-consciously produced for publication.[9]

One cannot expect a diary written as correspondence to be entirely candid, and indeed Blodgett's extensive study of English women's personal journals prior to the First World War found that few such women had much to say about their own problems.[10] Yet, Lucy Peel's journal is far from a colourless chronicle of mundane events, and it clearly came to provide her with a degree of emotional support, just as more private diaries did for their authors.[11] Helen Buss nicely summarizes the function of the letter diary for pioneer women when she writes that it would become "a public record of travel and settlement, a private record of their own development in the course of the new experiences offered them in the new land, and a letter home to family and friends in the old country, and, fortuitously, a history and literature of women's pioneer Canadian experience."[12]

As a prelude to the strongly romantic and intensely domestic world the reader will enter into with the Peel journals, this introduction will briefly explore the natural, economic, social, and political environment in which Lucy was writing, then conclude with a few observations on what the journal suggests about the nature of the genteel family. First, however, we will examine the Peels' family background in an attempt to situate them within the English society of their day, and to understand what brought them to the Eastern Townships in the first place.

Family Background and Social Status

Edmund Peel was born in 1801, the descendant of a powerful English manufacturing family. His great-grandfather, Robert "Parsley" Peel, had been a partner in one of the country's largest textile companies; Robert's son William (Edmund's grandfather) operated a calico manufacture at Church Bank, which no longer exists on a map. Edmund's great-uncle Robert Peel had become one of England's richest cotton manufacturers by the end of the eighteenth century, and was knighted during William Pitt's administration. Robert's son, also named Robert, was prime minister in 1834-5, and again in 1841-6.[13] Lucy's journal reveals that Edmund's father, also Edmund (first cousin of the prime minister), carried on the manufacturing business at Church Bank until he sold it in 1835, presumably because none of his sons was willing to take it over.

Edmund's branch of the family appears to have been comfortably off, but not wealthy. Even though he was the eldest son, there is no indication in the journal that Edmund's income increased substantially when his parents died in 1836. He could afford to pay £150 in cash for a 200-acre lot near the village of Sherbrooke,[14] to build a fine house with five bedrooms, and to hire two or three servants as well as seasonal labourers to help clear his land, but he and Lucy also had to work hard themselves on tasks that would have been beneath their class status in England. In addition, brother Thomas struggled as a bachelor settler on a nearby lot before preceding Edmund and Lucy back to England in the fall of 1836.

Little is known about Lucy's own family, the Meeks, though references in the journal suggest that they had some sort of business connection to Ceylon, and had suffered a reversal of fortune. Allusions to the health of Lucy's father, Richard, suggest that he may have been an alcoholic or depressive.[15] In one letter (26 October 1833) Lucy thanks her brother-in-law, whom she always refers to as Mr Mayne, for being "the guide and gentle counsellor of our family, when the temptations and

dangers of riches smiled on every side . . . and its steady friend and cheerful consoler when comparative poverty and sorrow surrounded it." At
least one of Lucy's sisters appears to have married a professional, one
brother and his family spent a winter with the Peels in Lower Canada
while considering where to purchase land in North America, and her
other brother became a surveyor during these years.

Lucy's journal refers frequently to her own elevated social status in
contrast to the "vulgar" Yankees who surround her. Indeed, she wrote
that she was the only lady on board the emigrant ship to New York, and
she noted that some of her neighbours in the Eastern Township referred
to her as Lady Peel. Lucy's preoccupation with her status may suggest
some social insecurity on her part, but it is more likely that, as with counterparts such as Susanna Moodie, she was concerned about cultural "con-
tamination" by the lower orders. Although Lucy and Edmund did not
come from landed backgrounds, they did belong to that stratum of society defined broadly by Amanda Vickery as the gentry. Among the families
who described themselves as "polite," "civil," "genteel," "well-bred," and
"polished," Vickery includes those headed by lesser landed gentlemen,
attorneys, doctors, clerics, merchants, and manufacturers. According to
Vickery, these people did not use the terms "upper," "middle," and
"lower" class, and they occupied a somewhat ambivalent status between
the nobility and the petite bourgeoisie.[16]

Natural and Economic Environment

Lucy and Edmund Peel chose to leave England not out of economic
necessity but in order to avoid the long absences from each other that
Edmund's naval career would have entailed, and to acquire an affordable
estate on which to establish their future family. While they were clearly
imbued with a sense of romantic adventure, they were not entirely naive
about the challenges they would face on a settlement frontier. In language
that was not gender neutral, yet made it clear that she was an active partner in the process, Lucy wrote on 8 November 1833, after their first
summer in the colony:

> This is a country where the active and industrious must prosper, the
> idle starve; there is on every side endless room for improvement and
> even our small farm would take thousands to make it look anything
> like an English Estate; Mr Peel and I, think it is this very thing which
> makes it interesting, for every little change is the effect of our heads
> and hands, every step it advances in cultivation, a proof of our care and

industry; the worst is, that one man's life is too transient to receive much benefit from his labour, for after all he can only put things in training for those who follow; we sow, what another generation will reap.

Why the Peels chose to live in the Sherbrooke area is not clear, but their political and social conservatism precluded settlement in the United States, and the Eastern Townships had certain attractions for people of their social class, which had been particularly imbued with the English agrarian myth.[17] Though the Eastern Townships lay within Lower Canada, its land was held in freehold tenure, and the southern part of the region, bordering on Vermont and New Hampshire, had passed the frontier stage, having been settled by Americans as early as the 1790s. But development had been slow, and there were still only 7,000 settlers in the vast county of Sherbrooke as late as 1831.[18] While the hilly and economically isolated region was not considered to be a good poor man's country, its picturesque scenery, inexpensive farms, and freedom from the malaria and cholera that plagued Upper Canada made it an attractive area for the British gentry, and those who aspired to that status.[19] The colonial authorities' mistrust of the region's American majority also led to the establishment of a politically powerful British elite who actively recruited genteel families such as the Peels.

Like the English women diarists who settled in Upper Canada, Lucy commented frequently and effusively on the natural beauty of her surroundings. She wrote on 18 August 1833, for example: "Oh Mamma it is worth all the horrors of a sea voyage to be in the verandah at Bellvidere at seven this evening to witness the sun-set. The sky is a beautiful blue and large *golden* clouds are passing quickly over it, the woods in the distance are tinged in the most lovely manner, and the fields sloping down to the house are exactly the colour of a sovereign just from the mint." In a symbolic sense, the presentation of the Eastern Townships as a landscape, which was echoed in the testimonials published by the British American Land Company during the same time period,[20] was a colonizing act in itself. This way of seeing the world reinforces subjective control over an objective environment, and, like the local scenes William Henry Bartlett was painting during these years, it stamped the region with an unmistakably genteel British identity.[21]

The Italian Renaissance concept of landscape had been translated into the British idea of the picturesque by William Gilpin's travel accounts of the English countryside during the 1780s. In contradistinction to Edmund Burke's categories of the sublime (inspiring sensations of fear and awe) and the beautiful (evoking pleasure and tenderness), Gilpin used the term *picturesque* to describe landscape scenes that embodied roughness and irregularity.[22] Lucy Peel, like most of her Upper Canadian counterparts, was more attracted to the the beautiful than to the sublime.[23] On 21 August 1833, she wrote: "Give my love to Mary Jane and Louisa, . . . how delighted they would be to watch the lovely little Humming Birds in the verandah and to gather the wild flowers, and to ride through the Woods, I think also to see our pretty Villa at Dunstall." Yet she also displayed an appreciation for Gilpin's rough and irregular landscape. Rather than seeing wild nature as the enemy, as Northrop Frye's garrison thesis has argued was typical of early Canadians,[24] Lucy depicted it in poetic terms, evoking the picturesque. Thus, she wrote on 8 November 1833: "I am sure you would like to ramble with us over our rude and romantic *Estate*, the greater part as nature formed it, with here and there, such stones as would even defy the power of Samson to dislodge from their deep, snug, and mossy bed; and large stumps of trees which have been cut down, gradually and slowly mouldering away, and enriching the earth as they scatter themselves around." This appreciation of a stump-strewn landscape was hardly characteristic of Canadian settlers, but it does echo Gilpin's praise for the "withered top" and "curtailled trunk" of trees as "splendid remnants of decaying grandeur that speak to the imagination in a stile of eloquence."[25] And Lucy's reference to unmovable stones, hardly the farmer's friends, reflects the fact that the early nineteenth century had brought a reaction in England against the artificially manipulated garden landscapes of Capability Brown. The challenge of the landscape gardener became to "enhance but not alter the accidental beauties of nature in all its roughness, irregularity and variety."[26]

Lucy was particularly rhapsodic after returning from her first walk through the snow on 29 November 1833:

> had you been with us dear Edith, . . . how largely would you expatiate upon the romantic winding road through the woods, the well beaten down snow forming an agreeable walk, the immense trees on either side bearing on their branches countless shapes of snow, the old stumps crowned with *Bridal* Cakes, the sun shining gloriously, not a breath of air to be felt, the sky a clear blue, all nature seemingly at rest, not a sleigh is heard for they pass with noisless [sic] rapidity leaving you almost doubtful whether it were a reality or a vision which flew before you, what would not my country men give for such weather in England.

A more prolonged experience with the Canadian winter would sorely test this romantic vision, which contrasted with the sublime as found in

James Thompson's very popular *The Seasons* (1730).[27] But, unlike Susanna Moodie's *Roughing It in the Bush*, Lucy's journal does not become more pessimistic about nature after the initial enthusiasm of the early months.[28] Her descriptions inevitably grew less effusive with time, but she never expressed the sense of entrapment found in the journals of some of her Upper Canadian counterparts,[29] if only because of the active social scene among her fellow English gentry settlers. Although Canadians are said to have reacted more negatively to the wilderness than did Americans, because its disorderliness threatened their British sense of law and order, etiquette, and social stratification,[30] the British colonial gentry clearly expressed a deeper aesthetic appreciation for Nature (albeit it in an idealized guise) than did their American-born neighbours.

The British genteel sensibility may have excluded the working elements of the countryside, or the idea of farming as an economic enterprise, as Michael Bunce claims,[31] but Lucy's journal makes many references to the details of domestic economy. In October 1833, for example, she noted that she had paid her servant "half her month in salt pork, rice and soap, this is a mutual convenience for these things are too dear in Sherbrooke for the poor people to be able to buy them, and the higher orders have a winter's stock from Montreal which is much cheaper, so it is better for us to pay in kind than in money." In her next journal (number 7), Lucy wrote: "You ladies in England who fancy you have a great [*sic*] to see after, do not know what it is to keep house in such country as this where you must cut and contrive; where perhaps you can only get meat once in three weeks, and where all the workmen you have must be fed three times a day on meat, potatoes and milk."

The limits of the local economy quickly became apparent to the Peels, and Lucy noted on 31 March 1834:

> This is not a country for grain, and supposing it were, there is no one to buy it, each petty farmer growing enough for his own consumption, and we are too far from the market towns to make it answer to send it there; at present this is only a country for a Gentleman who wishes to live quietly and cheaply, without an idea of accumulating money. Land is low enough but the expense of clearing is very great for a gentleman; a labouring man with a family of Sons might soon clear a number of acres.

While wheat sold at $1.00 to $1.10 per bushel in Montreal, transportation costs from the Eastern Townships were 40¢ per bushel during the winter, and 70¢ in summer. Even cattle, which could be walked to market, lost approximately a quarter of their weight en route, lowering their selling price by $5.00 a head.[32] But the British gentry were attracted to pastoral farming rather than to grain growing, in part because it conformed to improved agriculture's emphasis on nurturing the soil. Since most of the gentry felt that a worthwhile profit from a small farm was impossible even when the land was devoted to cash grains, they concluded that farmers should at least strive to live well while preserving the fertility of their land.[33]

Three years after their arrival, Lucy continued to express satisfaction with their farm, writing on 29 March 1836: "Pray do not for a moment suppose I am tired of Canada, it would be a dreadful change to leave a house & farm of our own, give up horses, Cows, and carriages, for a humble cottage in Wales, where perhaps we could only afford some lean mutton once a week; No, dearest Mamma, though sometimes half frozen in the winter, I am very happy, and get more attached to this place every day."

Her tune began to change in the fall of that year, after the wheat crop had failed and prices for produce were inflated with the arrival of settlers who were attracted by the newly established British American Land Company.[34] By 5 December 1836 the Peels had decided to return to England. As Lucy wrote: "Edmund is, after four years hard labour, convinced that nothing is to be done by Farming in Canada; the land here produces too little to pay the labour requisite to cultivate it." Hard as Lucy and Edmund had worked, they had continued to require the labour of servants and farm workers, paying £110 per year in wages and keep. Such a sum was clearly unsustainable in an economy that would become integrated into the market only with the construction of mills and factories in Sherbrooke in the late 1830s and early 1840s, and the arrival of the St Lawrence and Atlantic Railway at mid-century.[35]

Social and Political Environment

Bunce argues that, while the idealized English countryside evolved within the framework of agricultural progress, it was a form of progress constrained by the entrenched hierarchical structure of a rural society in which agrarian objectives were often subordinate to the requirements of gentrification.[36] But while commerce may have been beyond the pale, many of the British gentility had to engage in the manual labour normally considered beneath their status. Dunbar Moodie referred to the task of clearing land as "disgusting,"[37] but Edmund Peel seemed to enjoy the work. Lucy wrote to her brother-in-law on 26 October 1833: "I often wish you could see my excellent husband, how much you would admire his never ceasing industry, his hand is ever ready to do all in his power either on the land or in the house, and though some people may be of a different opinion I am sure you will agree with me in thinking that a man may dig in the fields without being a clown, be his wife's lady's maid without being effeminate and make his own coat without looking like a tailor."

Yet the merchants and manufacturers of Sherbrooke remained too close to the retail and artisanal level, too American, and too politically liberal to be considered entirely respectable by the British officers and professionals. The genteel social activities engaged in by Sherbrooke's tory elite, a number of whom lived in the surrounding countryside, helped set them apart from their less-educated but often more economically successful neighbours. This social elite could thereby justify to themselves their resistance to democratization and their monopolization of the spoils of office, making the region a modified colonial "contact zone," to use Mary Louise Pratt's term.[38] As Sara Mills has observed of the narratives produced by late nineteenth-century British women in India, "rather than the empire being a thoroughly masculine place, it seems that it also had a feminine identity; the production of a type of moral knowledge by females seems an essential part of the justification by the imperialist power of its own presence."[39]

At the centre of the elite circle in the Sherbrooke area were William Bowman Felton and his Minorcan-born wife, Maria.[40] Felton had held the very lucrative patronage-distributing post of "agent victualler" for the British fleet at Gibraltar during the Napoleonic Wars. When his promised consulship failed to materialize in 1814, he decided to emigrate to British North America with several members of his family, including his brother John, who had been a naval lieutenant before his court martial for losing a ship, and his brother-in-law Charles Whitcher, who had been a naval purser. Their proposal to the Colonial Office was to spend the impressive sum of £20,000 in the wilderness of Lower Canada in return for a 5,000-acre land grant. When they arrived in the colony in 1816, Colonel George Frederick Heriot convinced the Felton clan to move to strategically located Ascot Township, about sixty-five miles up the St Francis River from his new military settlement of Drummondville.

William Felton eventually accumulated 25,000 acres of Crown land, independent of what his brothers and brothers-in-law acquired. As the colony's first commissioner of Crown lands (his brother John became the local Crown lands agent), William was in a good position to recruit settlers to purchase land from him, but his development projects were frustrated to a considerable extent by the region's inaccessibility to markets. Lucy Peel's journal nevertheless reveals that Edmund was far from the only half-pay naval officer to settle in the Sherbrooke area during the 1830s, and that one of William Felton's brothers-in-law, William Henry of Montreal, acted as Felton's agent in establishing these settlers.

In response to concerns about widespread smuggling and counterfeiting activities along the American border, William Felton and Charles Whitcher had both been appointed peace commissioners by 1821, the year Felton also became lieutenant-colonel of the Fifth Battalion of the Eastern Townships militia. Felton's position at the head of a regional oligarchy was confirmed by his appointment to the Legislative Council in 1822, enabling him to ensure that the Judicial District of Saint Francis was established a year later, and that Sherbrooke became the site of the courthouse and jail. This was a boon not only to the struggling village, but to Felton's family as well. Felton's brother Charles became the prothonotary (chief court clerk), while Charles Whitcher became sheriff. In 1829 Felton was able to arrange for Whitcher to become the district's first deputy grand voyer, in charge of overseeing construction and maintenance of the region's neglected roads.

The American-born majority were effectively shut out of patronage distribution; the imperial government remained suspicious of their loyalty, despite having invited them to settle the region in 1792. Consequently, as the following excerpt from a local newspaper in 1826 reveals, there developed widespread local resentment against the introduction of "foreigners, unacquainted with our habits, manners and customs, to fill and execute every official function, thereby declaring, in language too unequivocal to be misunderstood, that no confidence was to be placed in a native born American."[41] Three years later, when the Eastern Townships finally gained political representation in the legislature, only pro-reform candidates were elected.

Though Edmund Peel was not interested in a patronage position, it was only natural that he and Lucy would gravitate towards the local British elite. Indeed, they stayed in the large and hospitable Felton home, Belvidere, while their own Dunstall Villa was being built, thereby saving the couple from living in a primitive log cabin as experienced by most of Lucy's published counterparts in Upper Canada. Lucy's journal provides a detailed and lively account of the social behaviour of this small and exclusive frontier elite. Particularly revealing is her 8 November 1833 portrayal of the "clever and entertaining" Judge John Fletcher, whose harsh and arbitrary judgments against the local Americans greatly exacerbated political tensions in the region:

> He is very tall, very stout, and has a corporation, his hair a dingy grey, long and combed back hanging down behind; his hands large, fat, & his fingers inclined towards the wrist, a fat face and three chins, he generally wears a cotton dressing gown with a huge pocket on one side, which is a receptacle for all kinds of things, he never rides out without a man on horseback before him some yards to clear the way and he always carries with him a brace of loaded pistols.[42]

Not all the local gentry were so eccentric, and on 1 September 1833 Lucy wrote of a gathering at the Feltons: "last night I wished some of our friends in England who fancy we are I believe almost amongst savages could have entered the drawing room, we were fifteen of us, all the gentlemen sensible and well bred, and ladies, goodlooking and pleasing, a large handsome room, music and dancing, diversified with intelligent, and constructive conversation." With William Felton absent for long periods of time on official business, his lively wife, Maria, emerges as the central figure in the social world of Sherbrooke. It was clearly not women's role exclusively to domesticate the environment, but under frontier conditions they did have a crucial role to play in creating islands of European civility and maintaining class boundaries. By describing the formal dinners, music recitals, anniversary celebrations, and other "civilized" activities organized by Maria Felton in particular, the Peel journal illustrates clearly how genteel women managed "that open-handed hospitality that was still crucial to the maintenance of social credit and political power."[43] While the Peels were more reclusive, particularly after their first child was born, Lucy's skill at the harp won her widespread admiration, and visiting dignitaries to Sherbrooke often asked to hear her play.

The carpenter who built the Peels' house was not included in this privilege, for Lucy's seventh journal describes how, "to give you an example of Yankee equality and impudence, instead of standing till he was paid, he drew a chair to the fire, sat down, began to hawk and spit, and concluded with asking me to play a tune on the Harp, I looked very savage and felt more so, and soon leaving the room remained away till Mr Haskell took his departure." Lucy's sense of social superiority is reflected in many similar descriptions of the "vulgar" behaviour engaged in by the tobacco-chewing Yankees. Yet despite Lucy's obvious disdain, the local American-born majority was consolidating its political power. Its MLAs joined forces with the radical French-Canadian Patriote party to establish grievance committees against the region's office-holding elite. The debt-

ridden Charles Felton resigned his office in March 1835 when he learned
that such a committee would examine his character and conduct as a public officer. The following year, the Assembly sustained a committee report
drafted by the Stanstead MLA Marcus Child, which recommended that
Sheriff Whitcher be dismissed due to corruption. This motion was not
sustained by the Colonial Office, but William Felton was less fortunate. A
grievance committee chaired by the local MLA, B.C.A. Gugy, demanded
his dismissal on the grounds that he had sold Crown lots as his own
property and acquired more Crown land for his children than they were
entitled to.

Lucy Peel blamed this "inquisition" on the local Yankees, whom she
characterized in an entry on 13 December 1835 as "a spiteful set" who,
rather than wishing "to overthrow the English," ought to be greatful to
them "for they are the only people from whom they get money, they
never see the colour of each others dollars." The political situation in the
colony was rapidly getting out of hand, and the British government had
no desire to see the Eastern Townships join forces with the French Canadians in any armed conflict. Governor Lord Gosford (whom Lucy described
on 11 September 1836 as "a mean looking man, nothing noble in appearance") was therefore willing to sacrifice Felton, and he was dismissed as
Commissioner of Crown Lands in August 1836. After losing a libel suit,
the Sherbrooke patriarch died of unknown causes in the spring of 1837.[44]
Despite the Peels' lack of interest in politics, their decision to return to
England at this time was undoubtedly influenced by the bleak prospects
facing the local office-holding elite, if not the region and colony as a
whole.

Domesticity

As with most middle-class English women's diaries of the past, the chief
theme to emerge from the Peel journals is not society, economy, or politics, but family love and duty.[45] It was the closeness of Lucy's ties with
her parents and siblings that motivated her to continue writing her carefully crafted entries even under the most trying circumstances.[46] She was
clearly anxious to maintain their approval by presenting herself as a good
wife and Edmund as a loving husband,[47] but the intensity of the relation-
ship she describes with Edmund and her children is entirely convincing.
Alan Macfarlane has traced the companionate view of marriage back to
the fourteenth century or earlier, but the eighteenth century brought the
rise of the romantic novel in England and strengthened the belief, in

Vickery's words, that "the union of man and woman offered the greatest happiness this side of the grave, that mutual love would bear couples up through the trials of life."[48]

While conveying Lucy's devotion to her husband, the journals also give ample evidence of Edmund's concern and support for his wife. Describing Edmund's role during the birth of their first child, for example, Lucy wrote on 8 January 1834:

> Poor Edmund was quite overcome with distress but, perhaps fortunately for him, he had not time to give way to his feelings, he was constantly and actively employed either nursing me or the baby, oh Mamma when I saw him fondling his child and looking so happy that all was safely over, I felt rewarded for everything I had endured. I shall not enter into particulars of my dear husbands unceasing and affectionate attentions to me, my heart is too full, and my pen too feeble, to do justice to them.

Lucy's description of the birth, and of the many false alarms that preceded it, does not conform to Helen Buss's statement that "in patriarchal cultures the subjects of pregnancy and labour are not fit subjects for the public discourses that are centred on men's activities."[49] And Edmund's own addition to the journal on 19 December 1833 also runs counter to Jane Errington's generalization that Upper Canadian men were rather indifferent to the process of birth, and that husbands were "banished from the delivery room."[50]

> I was present all the time to support Lucy and I was much distressed to witness her agonies. I thought it the proper place for a husband at such a moment, considering it nothing more than a false delicacy which would make a man absent himself at a time when his presence and support are most required, it is a fearful thing to see a woman in her pain, I could not have believed it possible they had suffered so much, at times I felt quite distracted, as soon as the child was born I staggered into an adjoining room and cried like a child until I again saw Lucy smiling and free from pain, her face last seen was distorted with pain, the impression made on me will never be forgotten.

The love so warmly described here was tempered with deep sadness when their firstborn, Celia, died, for Lucy and Edmund had clearly been influenced by the romantic notion of childhood as linked to innocence and nature, which John Tosh sees as central to Victorian domesticity.[51] Lucy's optimistic spirit changed noticeably at that point, and she and Edmund became less sociable and more religious. On 13 December, a few days after the death, Lucy wrote that Edmund "seldom cries except when alone with me; but he sits like a statue, talks of nothing but Celia, and, when any one but I, am present, never speaks from morning till night. He looks pale as death, and ten years older since Celia died."[52] As for Lucy herself, she wrote on 3 September 1835, eight months later:

> I dwell, when sitting alone, even with pleasure upon the bliss she is enjoying, and consider her in the light of a guardian Angel. And perhaps . . . she may have been taken away in mercy to myself, for I did love her too dearly, and constantly found myself saying, I could not do without her, however I was to be taught otherwise. I hope, dearest Mamma, you will not pronounce me an enthusiast. I am no such thing. I know I am more serious and less fond of gaiety than I used to be, and, I hope, think more before I act, but I keep my opinions to myself.

Such spiritual introspection was characteristic of the growing evangelical movement within the Church of England, and the Wilberforces and other genteel Anglican evangelicals of Clapham Common had already provided the most visible model in England of a child-centred society.[53] Lucy's journal never takes on the obsessively religious and moralistic tone of the true evangelical, but the Peels' spirits clearly failed to recover fully when their second and third children were born in rapid succession, if only because their sickliness caused constant anxiety, given the sudden death of Celia.

When the family returned to England, it was with clear misgiving. Lucy was deeply distressed at the prospect of abandoning the grave of her daughter, and Edmund would be absent for long periods at sea. Lucy would miss him greatly, for they had never been apart since their marriage. She wrote on 18 August 1835: "the separation of husband and wife must be dreadful, for the love between them is, or ought to be, 'Strong as Death' and the longer they live together the harder it would be to part, at least I feel it would be so, for much as I loved Edmund when I married him I have treble the affection for him now."

Lucy Peel's journal does not ressemble those American women's diaries and letters examined by Carroll Smith-Rosenberg in which "men made only a shadowy appearance," and female rituals "rigorously excluded male kith and kin."[54] And, while we can assume that Lucy's journal concealed any quarrels she had with Edmund, her unwavering enthusiasm for her marriage at the very least illustrates the strength of the romantic genteel convention.[55] Furthermore, the same image of companionate marriage emerges from Lucy's portrayal of the Felton, Fletcher, and Hale couples. Writing of her prolonged stay with the Feltons, Lucy claimed on 8 November 1833 that "all the time we were there I never heard one disagreeable word pass between any of the members of this amiable and united family, and I think that if there is a house without a *blue chamber* it is Bellevedere."[56]

While Lucy unfairly depicted local Americans as cold to their wives and indifferent to their offspring, the British elite emerge from her journal with the strong emotional bond between spouses and nurturant attitude towards children that Lawrence Stone defines as characteristic of the modern bourgeois family.[57] Another characteristic of the modern family noted by Stone is its change "from a porous and outward-looking institution to a closed and inward-looking one."[58] Certainly, one can detect what is perhaps a generational difference between the gregarious Feltons, whose spacious home was always open to outsiders, and the more self-contained Peels. The rather taciturn Edmund clearly preferred the company of his own domestic circle, and Lucy wrote several times that socializing was as much a duty as a pleasure. On being promised a ball if they would visit Edmund's cousin in Sorel, for example, Lucy declared (18 January 1834) that "I need scarcely say we shall decline the invitation, I would rather nurse my darling Baby than go to the gayest ball in the world." She did welcome lengthy stays by Edmund's brother Thomas and her own brother Charles with his family, so that they too could become established in the new world. Lucy was also clearly fond of the "neighbour's girl" who served as her domestic for most of these years,[59] but her attention remained strongly focused on her own family.

Davidoff and Hall have associated the strengthening of English domesticity with the rise of the evangelical petite bourgeoisie in the early nineteenth century, much as Nancy Cott, Mary Ryan, and others have done for New England and New York.[60] The notion that domesticity was the product of the middle-class home emerging as a refuge from the pressures and anxieties of the competitive marketplace is clearly of limited value for understanding the Peels. Edmund did not leave home on a daily basis to engage in "demoralizing" or "corrupting" work and Lucy's journal reflects the intensity of emotion that Philip Greven associates with the genteel parental temperament that pre-dated industrialization.[61]

Lucy's journal also challenges many of the assumptions drawn from the separate-spheres paradigm by suggesting that the barrier between classes was higher than that between genders. As Vickery notes, "genteel wives took it absolutely for granted that their husbands enjoyed formal ascendancy in marriage,"[62] still Edmund was intimately involved with household chores as well as the raising of their children. And, while life on a homestead may have called for more resourcefulness than in a developed environment, it appears that Edmund performed these "feminine" tasks out of pleasure as much as necessity. In short, nowhere does Lucy suggest that the frontier had a deeply transformative impact on Edmund's gender identity, and the same might be said for her. Her diary also reinforces the impression left by counterparts such as Catharine Parr Traill that genteel women were better prepared for their role in the New World than Canadian historians have assumed.[63]

Anthony Fletcher states that "the very essence of the companionate marriage . . . was the subordination of women," and that "romantic love proved to be patriarchy's strongest bulwark,"[64] but Lucy does not emerge from the pages of her journal as a wilting violet. Although Lucy was too conservative to be seen as a prototypical feminist, Nussbaum suggests that by recording the "trivial" details of lived experience, women's autobiographical writing "helped to shape and resist the dominant cultural constructions of gender relations and to substitute alternatives."[65] The domestic details Lucy included in her letter diary were doubtless even more important to her family members (both male and female) in England than were her descriptions of the physical and social environment, thereby implying a valued and respected role for women, albeit one in which they remained closely identified with domestic life defined in a broad sense.[66] From the colonialist perspective, Lucy's journals illustrates, in Mill's words, that imperial knowledge was more than "the statistics and manners and customs descriptions of other countries and their inhabitants," and that "descriptions seen as seemingly trivial, because of their association with the domestic and women's spaces [are] just as important in the analysis of colonial discourse as the 'heroic' adventures of male travelers."[67]

What the future held in store for the Peel family after they moved from the Eastern Townships is impossible to say in any detail, but we do know that Edmund became a naval captain, that daughter Flora survived to give birth to twelve children, that son Richard became a captain in the merchant service, and that three other sons were born in England.[68] We also know that the deeply conservative Peels left Sherbrooke at a good time: the social, economic, and political transition of the 1840s would create a world in which they would not have felt at ease. Sherbrooke's merchant-entrepreneurs would triumph politically and economically with the rise of the modern state in the form of elected local councils and responsible government, and the industrialization and commercialization stimulated by the arrival of the railway. The resulting forces would overwhelm both the radical agrarianism of the region's American-born farmers and the British elite's competing vision of a rural landscape dominated by large landed estates.[69]

A Note on the Text

In the interest of clarity and readability, this transcription of Lucy Peel's journal includes some minor changes to the entries as they appear in the Peel letterbooks. Each new day's entry begins on a new line, with a dash added after the date, and long entries have been broken into paragraphs. Commas have been inserted sparingly, with periods occasionally replacing commas, and capitals added at the beginning of sentences. Spellings have not been corrected, but the use of *sic* has been avoided in most cases. A question mark in square brackets follows words that may not have been deciphered correctly in the original transcript.

Frequently Mentioned Names

Lucy's Sisters and Brothers

Rosa – wife of William Birch, who was possibly an apothecary

Sarajane (or Sarah Jane) – wife of Mr Mayne, a wealthy but sickly patron of the Meek family; mother of Mini

Louisa – wife of Charles Oldershaw, who was perhaps a missionary; Lucy is clearly much less close to her than to her other siblings and exchanges no letters with her

Charles – married to Kate; they leave England in 1836 with the intention of settling in the United States

Sturges – younger brother who remains at home with his parents

Edmund's Brothers and Sisters

Johnathan – chosen as godfather to Celia

Thomas – follows Edmund and Lucy to settle on a nearby lot

George – accompanied Edmund to Sherbrooke in 1832, and visited again briefly in 1836

Elizabeth (Bessy) – Lucy's second journal is addressed to her

Sydney – joins his brother Tom in 1836

Mary – mentioned only once (7 June 1836)

William Bowman Felton and Maria Felton's Children (marital status as of 1846)[1]

William Locker Pickmore – oldest son; becomes a local lawyer and politician, marries Clara Lloyd

Eliza Margaret – marries the politician Thomas Cushing Aylwin in 1836; dies of cholera in Quebec in 1849, shortly after her husband is appointed chief justice of the St Francis District

---

1 The age ranking is based on that found in Lucy to My dearest Mamma, 27 May 1833; and Sherbrooke Historical Society, P21 5, Assignment and Partage between Mrs Anna Maria Felton and William L. Felton and others heirs of the late Hon. William B. Felton, 13 October 1846.

Charlotte Julia – unmarried

Fanny Lucia – marries Joseph Hunt, a Quebec notary

Maria Antonia – marries Percy Arthur Cunningham; living in Dieppe, France, in 1846

Octavia Sophia – unmarried

Matilda Catalina – marries Lieutenant Richard Burnaby of the Royal Engineers

Edward Pellew Murray – a minor in 1846; becomes a local notary

Isabella Monica – minor

Narbon (Norborn) Orlando – minor

Other Characters

Edith Bourne – friend and correspondent of Lucy

Captain Guy Colclough – Edmund's Eastern Townships contact on his first visit to Sherbrooke in 1832; became an agent of the British American Land Company by 1835

Lucius Doolittle – Anglican minister living in Lennoxville

Charles Felton – brother of William, and prothonotary of the district court

John Felton – brother of William; local Crown lands agent

John Fletcher – judge of the district King's Bench

Edward Hale – land agent and speculator; son of Receiver-General John Hale, and grandson of Colonel John Hale and General Jeffrey Amherst; succeeded William Felton as the most politically powerful person in the region after the latter's death in 1837

William Henry – husband of William Felton's sister, Charlotte Sarah Felton; Montreal-based land agent, and former fur trader with the North West Company; due to errors in transcription, he is referred to as Mr. Theney in much of Book 1.

Mary Lyon – friend and correspondent of Lucy

McReadys – neighbouring Irish family whose daughter, Ellen, was Lucy's most valued servant; a wide number of spelling/transcription variations on this name are found in the journals

Parkes – the Peels' indispensable farm servant, leaves and is replaced by Patrick Macarty in November 1835

Edmund Peel – cousin who lived in Sorel, Lower Canada

Theney — see William Henry

Charles Whitcher – brother-in-law of the Feltons; district sheriff and deputy grand voyer in charge of the district's roads

William Wilson – English doctor who arrives in the area in summer 1833.

Book One

No 1

My dearest Mamma

The morning after I sent off my last letter to you, which was Saturday the 30th of March, I was awakened at five oclock with a great noise. Edmund was soon up, and found that a steamer which the Captain had hailed, was along side. This steamer, most fortunately for us, was going to Drogheda,[1] so would be able to take us much further than any other. On Sunday we passed Holy head,[2] it was a most beautiful day but sadly too calm to make any progress. We have been a fortnight to day on board and are not more than a third of our way to New York. The weather is fine and quite warm. I walk upon deck without any shawl. We have had only two days quick sailing and then we got on pretty well, but I begin to be heartily tired of this slow work and I wonder any one can find charms on the sea, I shall be delighted to find myself once more on shore.

Edmund is as kind and attentive as possible, and indeed it requires all his affectionate care to make up for the many disagreeables on board a ship, which when contrasted with the comforts of Mount Cottage, and the present company with those dear friends I have left and have thought so constantly of since I parted from them, are doubly hard. The Captain is all attention, I being the only Lady am well taken care of. The Captain ordered a large basket of oranges to be put into our Cabin and said he had bought them at Liverpool on purpose for me, he hoped I would accept of them, I did most thankfully, and when I was unwell they were the only things I could eat. Everything we have on board, to drink, is excellent, particularly porter, but the meat and fowls are all spoiled with being stuffed with onions, the fish does not escape. The bread is very sour, the biscuits excellent.

Sturges, I often wished for you when the ship was pitching about, I wanted some one to make me laugh, and I feel convinced you would not have been two minutes together on your legs. I could not stand alone and was quite afraid of moving. My work box, books and candlestick, bearing the table cloth with them came constantly to the ground. I was obliged to twist my legs to those of the table to keep myself on my chair. At dinner the gravy out of the dishes flew about, the milk jug was emptied into my lap, plates were broken & my wine glass just as I set it down was sent to the other end of the Cabin and broken. This was amusing for a short time, but the inconvenience of knocking about soon made it

Notes to this section start on p. 215.

exceedingly disagreeable. The steerage passengers are a great annoyance. There are a great many children and they cry and shout till Edmund is almost out of patience, some of the people appear in a wretched state and look half starved, seventeen sleep in a birth, Men, Women and children, there are two or three respectable looking women and how they manage I know not.

April 25th – We have been on board dearest Mamma a month to day, and have made only 49 degrees of Longitude, having still 24 to make. We all begin to feel melancholy at our long voyage, even the Captain looks gloomy and says he never made so bad a passage; since my last date I have never been able to write to you, I feel better to day. Edmund has been ill too, he was in bed three days and lived upon sago[3] and rice – To day he has been on deck, and he enjoyed some chicken broth which I got the Steward to make for his dinner. I began almost to dispair, my husbands illness, myself constantly sick, the bad weather and the knocking about of the ship, you would have been sorry for your child. I wished I could be near you, yet I used to say to myself much as I should like to see dear Mamma, I would not have her here for the world, for I feel convinced, what with the noise of the Captain and Mate giving orders, the shouting of the men as they obeyed those commands, the roaring of the sea, the pitching of the Vessel, the cracking of every bit of wood in the ship and also of the ropes which never cease, the crying children and noisy steerage passengers, you would never live even to see blue water.

The day before yesterday was so dreadful that we were obliged to have the dead lights[4] down and had candles all day, the waves washed over the deck, the Captain and Mate were up all night, and the poor sailors were reefing for four hours. In the morning the sea went down and we had quite a warm day, however at night there was another gale and in the morning at five oclock we had a dreadful storm accompanied with thunder and lightening, which the Captain did not quite like as the Vessel had once been struck, four men knocked down and one remaining blind four days. I did not mind the storm so much, as the ship was pretty easy and I could be quiet in her, but the night before I durst not try to sleep for fear of falling out of my birth. I was obliged to hold by the wood to keep in. Edmund, who was in the top birth had many narrow escapes, every thing in the Cabin fell down, I never saw such a place as it was the next morning.

There is a little doctor amongst the second class passengers, he was so frightened that he went on deck in his shirt and told the Captain he thought the ship was on her beam end and that he was cutting away her masts, he begged to be made useful. The Captain told him there was no danger and that he had better go below and dress himself or he would take cold, he did so, but came on deck again as he dared not remain below, so he left his poor wife and child to take care of themselves. The little Man, Kirk by name, when he had been up some time lost his hat which blew off into the water, he looked after it in despair, it was the only one he had. I am very sorry for him, for though I often hear him chattering too much to his companions, I think he is a well meaning man, he is so kind and attentive to the sick steerage passengers, and when the Captain said he would, upon his arrival at New York, willingly pay him for his attendance, he said No, he would not have anything, that he considered it only an act of christian duty to be of service to his fellow creatures.

The young Yankee on board is vulgar, seems to have travelled and read a good deal, and he chews tobacco and spats every instant. We have in the Gentleman's Cabin a Mr Freeman and Son, they look like retired blacksmiths. I heard the old man tell some one on deck that he was taking his son to America and that he was desirous to do a great deal with a little. The old man professes to be a bit of a wit. His son is a quiet, and appears a sensible man, unpresuming, yet always ready to oblige, and it is with his ink I am now writing to you. When I had left the dining Cabin yesterday, Sturges, the old man filling his glass to the brim with Champagne, said he would give a toast; he wished that all the devils in hell would break loose and murder each other. Poor man he is quite undone for he has lost his spectacles, and has drank all the ale there was on board. We are now convinced that the beginning and not the end of March is the time to sail, we shall know better another time. Our Captain has had so many accidents with his ship, that I believe dear Mamma between ourselves he is a little bit of a coward and does not make the most of the few fair winds we have, besides which he has sadly too few hands, I mean working hands on board.

Last Sunday but one was a beautiful day, Edmund and I were walking on deck when a young man whom I had often noticed as being clean, quiet, and respectable looking, came up crying to the Captain and told him, that on Saturday night he went to his box, and took a pair of white trousers which were quite at the bottom out of his box to see if five pounds were safe, he found the money & returned it with the trousers into the same place under every thing else, that on Sunday morning going again to his box for a clean shirt he found the white trousers at the top and four sovereigns gone, the box was locked therefore some person must have a key that would open it. He said he should know one of the pieces for he had marked it in a particular manner, and that he suspected a young man who had seen him count his money. This young man, tall and thin and though not at all like a gentleman, looks very superior to the rest and we call him the half pay Dragoon, he was examined by the doctor, the First Mate and young Mr Freeman, he firmly denied the charge, said where he came from and that his father gave him 21 pounds before he left home, he was obliged to show his money and one sovereign was found with a mark upon it. This was taken out, the person who had been robbed had a shilling given to him that he might make a similar mark upon that to the one he had made on the piece of gold, he did so, and it was exactly the same as the mark on the sovereign found upon the Dragoon; he still denied taking it, but willingly gave up four pounds to remain in the Captain's hands till they arrived at New York when the thing is to be settled. I cannot think the young man innocent, he is avoided by most of the passengers. I don't envy the Dragoon, for innocent or guilty, the remainder of his passage cannot be agreeable.

Our Captain is a little fat man with a little Corporation,[5] a red & good looking face, fine black hair and eyebrows and dark sparkling eyes, when he was young he was in Paris a year, and during that time was confined in eighteen different prisons, in some suffering a good deal, however in one they were not so severe and allowed him to go out on his Parole. He got taught to dance Quadrilles & to Waltz. In learning the latter his Master used to prop him up against the wall after whirling him round till he could not stand – The first and last time he waltzed in public, he and his partner both fell down to the great merriment of the company. I wish you could hear the Captain tell his own tale.

May 6th – Since my last date we have kept creeping on in spite of bad winds and another so bad a day that we were obliged to have the dead lights shut again. I have been only one day tolerably well. To our great joy to day at two oclock we saw land, the poor Irish shouted with delight and I felt quite inclined to do so also. A nice wind freshened up and at three a beautiful pilot boat came alongside and put us a Pilot on board, the afternoon was fine, the sun out and we were told we should be at New York at eight. We sailed along and I was astonished and charmed as we proceeded with the scenery. On the right, Long Island and on the left the High Lands, farther on Statton Island, on the left the Fort Washington and Fort Diamond, on the right the fields looking green, the trees coming out, the beautiful wooden cottages, the smoke curling from the chimneys, altogether I never was more pleased. Several News Boats came along side, but we had no news. The South America which sailed from

Liverpool the tuesday after we did arrived at New York last friday. Then followed a boat and the doctor came on board, all the Irish passengers had to be examined by him before we were allowed to go up to New York.[6] It is now seven oclock dearest Mamma and we are nearly there, but it is not yet certain whether we shall sleep on shore to night. Not much time will be lost in your having this letter, a packet will sail next Wednesday.

Tuesday 7th – Webbs Mansion House, Broad Way, New York. We landed this morning and are comfortably accommodated in this house. I have walked a good deal to day and am delighted with this beautiful City. I have not room to say a word about it, but shall give a full account to — — by the next packet. I feel almost too happy to night, though rather tired. I have a splendid Piano all to myself. Oh that you were all here to enjoy the beauties of this place. I am equally pleased and surprised. I am surrounded with every comfort and the people amuse me much. Dear love from us both to you, Papa and Sturges.

ever your attached child
Lucy Peel

[No number][7]

To Miss E. Peel
New York   May 9th, 1833

My dear Bessy

It would be quite impossible to find words to express my delight at being once more on shore, only those who have suffered as I have done for more than five weeks can enter into my feelings; during the whole voyage there were only three days I felt tolerably well and the constant sickness I had to endure would have reduced one almost to despair had it not been for the never ceasing attention of the best of husbands. Webbs Hotel, where we are staying, is very comfortable, it is in the grand street called Broadway, where all the best shops are. On Tuesday, the day we arrived in New York, Edmund having seen me safely here, set off with Capt. Toubman[?] to the Consul and after some little trouble procured from him a permit for all our boxes to be taken out of the Vessel unopened, and without paying any duty, this is a great thing for us as it saves us much trouble and some expense.

When he returned we walked into the Town, we returned and dined at five, then walked in the Battery gardens which are exceedingly pretty, broad level walks and most beautiful weeping willows in abundance, there we saw numbers of Gentlemen and Ladies, the former remarkably well dressed and look more like gentlemen than any I have seen in Manchester or Liverpool. The Ladies dress well and have good figures. Many have pretty faces and feet, but they cannot walk, they all waddle like ducks; we returned to our Hotel about half past seven when it began to rain, thunder & lighten very much, it was exceedingly hot all day. The rooms here are beautifully furnished in the french style, the one we have, which the Landlord hoped we could manage with, being the only one at liberty, is a good size & lofty, papered handsomely and carpeted. It contains a neat french polished sideboard with three large china jars full of flowers and covered with glasses, two silver candlesticks with wax lights. Bookcase, a round table covered with gold and a marble slab at the end with glasses and a china jug full of Rose water upon it, two other tables with marble slabs and white marble pillars, bronze claws, on each a handsome glass lamp and china flower pot with a large rose tree in it. A Piano, one of the very best I ever played upon and in excellent tune, a dining table, sofa, large mirror and two splendid glass lustres, and this is one of the smallest rooms in our hotel.

I am delighted with New York and if it were not for the expense should like to remain some time, there is much to please the eye, every thing is new and unlike what we see in England. The houses are clean looking, the foot paths wide, the shops large and handsome, in short, much as I had heard of this City and much as I expected, I am agreeably surprised and Edmund is equally pleased. Almost all the men servants are blacks, they are quiet and wait uncommonly well, the man we have creeps about so I can scarcely hear him come into the room. The curiosity of these people is unbounded, but I can do with it very well for they do not question you in an impertinent manner, they are civil and the servants though free, are kind and attentive and do not, like some of the pert English servants, *look* a thousand disagreeable things, though silent.

I will give you one or two instances of their curiosity. When I went into a shop the man said, when did you come to New York? Had you a good passage? What ship? What Captain?, and when Edmund went up to two young men to ask his way to some street one having answered him took hold of his seal with his crest on and said to his companion, a devilish pretty seal this, is it not? The chamber maid asked me questions without end, but she smiled and looked so good tempered all the time, and waited upon me so well that I really think any one with good feeling would give all the information they could.

Yesterday Edmund went to Mr Lawes to whom he had a letter of introduction. Afterwards to buy bedding, we gave for a large hair mattress, a straw Do., Bolster and two Pillows, 36 dollars. Capt Toubman dined with us at five. After dinner, under his guidance, drove about to see the different places worthy of notice. The most beautiful buildings which are just finished are those in La Fayette Place, the outside is perfect all marble, the Corinthian order, I never saw anything more chaste. Certainly these Yankees have great taste. The railings in front are iron bronzed, there is a marble pedestal on each side every house door and on these beautiful bronze lamps which at night are lighted with gas.

You would laugh dear Bessy to see some of the curious carriages here. The public ones are greatly superior to our English ones, and a stranger would take them for private carriages, they have all arms painted on them and the numbers are not seen. The coach men are well dressed, the horses, generally speaking, excellent, the carriages have two curtains on each side which in the summer are undrawn, and the linings being good & clean they really look very pretty. The horses look like racers, so sleek and slight, holding up their heads & tails quite in a superior style. The omnibusses are numerous and handsome, most of them have four horses.

Yesterday was very hot, we sat with the windows open till we went to bed. I play on the Piano every evening, I believe I have had many listeners. Edmund is gone to see that our packages are put on board the boat which is to sail this evening and will arrive at Albany about the same time we shall, we intend to leave here tomorrow morning at ten as we have no further business in New York we do not consider it right to remain to lose our time and spend our money, yet I shall be rather sorry to go. I anticipate great pleasure in sailing up the Hudson.[8] When you think of us remember you are five hours before us, for instance, when it is five in the afternoon here, it is ten at night in England.

Saturday 11th – We could not go yesterday the luggage was not ready till the three oclock boat, we must be at the Steam boat by ten and shall arrive at Albany at ten this evening. I am sorry to say it is raining, I hope it will clear up for it will be very provoking not to see the beautiful scenery as we go up the Hudson. Edmund joins me in love to all at Church Bank [where Edmund's parents live] & remember us to the one dearest to you

Dear Bessy your affect sister
Lucy Peel

No 2

Sherbrooke   May 24th 1833

My dearest Mamma

Here we are at last after a most tedious journey. We left New York on Saturday in the ten oclock steam packer. The greatest beauty I ever saw, it had only run one day before, it is more like an Hotel than a boat. You enter it on a very large lower deck covered all over which makes it cool. On this deck there is a promenade from one end to the other, the Capts. office, offices for cooking, two doors leading down to the Gentleman's Cabin and a small saloon for the Ladies. From this Saloon we go down stairs into the Ladies sleeping Cabin handsomely fitted out with every possible convenience. The room for *sick Ladies* made me almost, if I had not been tired with being sick, long to be ill, through this room there were folding doors into a large drawing room beautifully furnished. Sofas all round and two large mirrors. Folding doors again out of this to the Gentleman's Cabin where we dine. 80 persons might sit down with comfort, we were about 50. Through this room there is a kind of Coffee room and Bar, where every thing good to eat and drink may be had, and a good library if you chuse to read. There is an upper deck to walk upon, but no awning was up so few remained long, besides which it is not a very safe place on account of the wood flying about which is used at the Engine. I had a hole burned in my dress and a man came running up and said "look your burnt, your *umbreel*.

In this splendid Vessel my dearest mamma we left New York, and sailing up the Hudson were soon surrounded by the most magnificent scenery. On the right there is New York with its Battery and Castle gardens, on the left Jersey City and Hoboken on the south, a view of the narrows leading to Sandy Hook and a view of the Atlantic 22 Miles from the City. The Pallisadoes, which are more superb than I can describe, begin at Nehanken[9] and extend 20 Miles up the Western side of the river, they are a range of rocks from 20 to 550 feet high, they form nearly an impassable barrier having almost a perpendicular surface.

It would take up more paper than I can spare to describe to you all the beautiful places passed on each side [of] the Hudson, many interesting from the events which happened there. I shall, however, mention a few. *Singsing*,[10] East side, 34 Miles from New York, has a State Prison which looks very handsome as we pass, it contains 800 Cells and is built of hewn marble, the work was done by the convicts. Sleepy Hollow, South East, where Washington Irvin [*blank space*] his tale in the Sketch

Books.[11] Antonys Box, S.E., a rock 1228 feet from the level of the river. Lewis's Dock where are the houses of General Morgan Lewis, formerly Governor of the State of New York,[12] and of Mr James Livingstone,[13] they are both beautiful places, and several members of the latter family have handsome seats further up the river, I scarcely know which to admire the most. The Town of Hudson is a large and important place, it is considered the third City in the State as to its manufacturing importance. There are several beautiful Islands in the river, and one I saw with a house & bridge and garden upon it made me quite wish to live there, I think the name of it is Magdalene Island.

We arrived at Albany about nine, it was raining heavily, immediately as the boat was at the Pier we were assailed on all sides by the *runners*, people sent from the different Hotels, and the cries of "Are you going to the Springs Sir? "To Troy Sir? "To the West?" To what Hotel Sir? put Edmund quite out of patience, and it was all he could do to keep possession of our Luggage. We went to the nearest Hotel on account of the heavy rain, it happened to be one of the best in the Town, we went to bed immediately, we had an excellent room.

At seven oclock in the morning a man came to the door and asked if we would take our seats at breakfast before the bell rang. This is one of the attentions they pay in this country to Ladies and married men, they sit at the top of the table, then the bell rings and it is laughable to see the rush of all the men in the house to enter the room to get seats. They look like a herd of cattle and it is disgusting, particularly to a person not very well, to see them eat, I noticed many with mutton, fish, butter, toast, cheese, and sweets on their plates all mixed up together, and often the addition of eggs.

We were obliged to remain at Albany till the following morning because Edmund could not see the agent about forwarding our packages, this was very disagreeable, we could not have a private room, so we took to our bed room – not a woman servant can you get near you in this country without sending a particular message for one. Whenever I rang my bell, a Man, not only came to the door but opened it and walked in. We sent to know what time they dined the answer was, at two. Edmund took me to walk thinking it would do me good. Albany is a dirty Town but has some handsome buildings, it is the Capital of the State of New York. The principal buildings are the Capitol which is built of stone and cost 120,000 Dollars, a dollar is 4/6 of our money, a Cent the hundreth part of a dollar. The City Hall is a costly Edifice of white marble, the dome is guilded, and is conspicuous at some distance from the City. We returned to our Hotel a few minutes before two and waited as patiently as we could till after three, still no dinner bell rang, we sent to know the reason and were told they dined at one. Edmund was very angry and ordered some dinner to be got immediately. They did not seem very well pleased, but in a short time we had some excellent fish and a tender beef steak.

I was delighted to leave Albany on Monday morning, Edmund had been to see the agent before breakfast who was to send our packages on to Burlington in a sloop. We went in the Mail, rather different to those in England for we drove round the Town for passengers and at one place waited half an hour for a man, they think nothing of this, the Mail holds nine, inside it has three seats which hold three each, fortunately we had one to ourselves, the other two were full of men chewing and spitting, one young man very neatly dressed, good looking and gentlemanly quite disappointed me by beginning to chew. An old Man desired the coachman to set him down at the Arsenal five miles from Albany, the coachman clapped the door to, saying, well sing out when we get to it for I guess I don't know where it is; he did sing out and was set down. When we arrived at the opposite side of the river to Troy we drove down to the side of the water and to my great surprise and alarm we crossed the Hudson, which is here, a quarter of a mile wide, in a horse ferry boat.

Troy is a pretty town, the buildings are principally of brick and are shaded by rows of trees on each side of the streets. The town has seven churches, three banks, a coach House, a jail, and a market. The Episcopal Church is a superb specimen of Gothic Architecture, the population is 11,605. At this place a Dutchman and a young Yankee got into the Mail, all the rest remained at Troy. The Dutchman had travelled over the united states and most parts of Europe, he talks like Mr Lindon, & Edmund and I were kept laughing many miles listening to his conversation with the young Yankee who had never been far from home and appeared a complete child of nature, good looking and intelligent, he had often the best of the argument, and his remarks showed both good sense and good feeling, he did not chew or spit.

At Fort Edward we dined, and at Sandy Hill a few miles further we lost our young and amusing companion, he lives at a pretty house close by the road side, the country is very interesting all about Sandy Hill, there are a hundred houses in the village and 500 inhabitants. Between Fort Edward and Sandy Hill we were shown a wood in which there is a large Pine tree with a Spring at is foot, memorable as the spot where Miss M'Crea was murdered by some Indians, during the revolutionary war.

Perhaps you do not know the story, she was engaged to a Mr Jones an American, Refugee, who was in Burgoine's Army. Anxious for an union with his intended Bride he sent a party of Indians to escort her to the British Camp. Against the advice of her friends she committed herself to their charge, she was placed on horseback and accompanied her guides to the Spring, where they were met by another party sent on the same errand, a quarrel took place between them as to the promised reward which was a barrel of rum, and while thus engaged they were attacked by the Whites, at the end of the conflict the unhappy girl was found a short distance from the Spring tomahawked and scalped. Mr Jones died of a broken heart.[14]

We arrived at Fort Ann about nine where we remained all night, as we were told the roads were so bad owing to the rain, that we could not proceed to White Hall,[15] I was not sorry for I was much tired, almost shaken to death with the rough roads, you cannot possibly form any idea of them, an English Coachman would as soon think of flying up to the moon as attempting to proceed, indeed English coaches and horses would not do here, we were twelve hours going sixty miles, now going up steep hills, now full speed down the other side over immense stones and trees, now over deep gutters across the road, the horses stepping over and the coach following so fast that the wheels had not time to remain an instant in the frightful gap, then over long wooden bridges made of loose planks, several inches between each plank and they rise up on the sides as we whirl over them, then through water in which the mud was so deep it came up to the horses knees. In short you are kept in a continual fright, twice we had to get out that the coach might be carried over the gaps. I thought of you all and we agreed that had Charles and Kate been with us, one would have pulled a very long face and the other would not have gone on. Bessy Peel would never have ceased screaming. Sturges would laugh & you and our kind friend Miss Winter would have died on the spot.

You may suppose I did not feel very comfortable at Fort Ann. We went to bed in a miserable little room, but fortunately a door opened out of it into a large ball room and we made use of that; we found that we might be kept at this wretched place four or five days, and thirty five passengers were waiting to proceed, some going to Montreal on business of importance, this being the case and finding the water so high, they in the afternoon hired a Canal boat and the Captain engaged to take us to White Hall at a Dollar a head which was to be paid by the proprieter of the Coach as we had paid him our fare of seven Dollars from Albany to

White Hall. Edmund was some time, indeed till the boat was ready to set off making up his mind whether to take me, for he well knew there was great danger, and that it was just an even chance whether we were lost or not as we had to pass though some Rapids in the Narrows, where if the boat went the least to one side or the other we must perish, however, the horrid alternative of remaining at Fort Ann and losing so much time decided the thing and we trusted ourselves to the skill of our Captain and his men.

We went, not along the Canal for the banks were broken but through the Creek across flooded fields, sending down fences in our way, under bridges, dodging about, first on one side then another, sometimes over the road, passed by the coaches, then into the river. When we approached the Rapids not a word was spoken, every face looked grave, the perspiration ran off the men's faces with the exertion, had you heard the shout the yell as they called out "All's right! She's off" as we *flew* down the Rapids you would never have forgotten it. Our next adventure was at a bridge, one of the men said we could not get under, the rest maintained it just possible, however as we were going under every one perceived it could not be done. The Cabin below was so small it would not hold six comfortably and now more than thirty men made a rush towards it to save their heads. Edmund seized my hand and hurried me on, there was a man on the steps, hesitating and seemed quite beside himself, Edmund said very sharply, go down, Sir, directly, and he went head first into the Cabin. Edmund saw me safely lodged and then went above, some stooped very low, others jumped on land, the poor Dutchman fell upon some sharp pieces of wood and took all the skin off his legs, he complained bitterly, kept saying, I am not coward, I am not afraid, I *vill* show you that, I *vill* do vot I will do, but let me get out; the men now, by force, pushed the boat under the bridge, they both cracked dreadfully, and some wood was torn off the top of the Cabin.

We arrived at White Hall without any further alarm, it was nine oclock on wednesday morning when we left Fort Ann and it was three when we reached White Hall a distance of only eight miles. We were at a comfortable Hotel and had a nice sitting room up stairs to ourselves, with a Piano in it. The situation of this place is low, but the rocks and the country round interesting, and in England would be considered beautiful, but amidst such splendid scenery it is thought nothing of.

On Thursday afternoon at one oclock we went in a small boat down the river to meet the steam boat, it was a very nice one, and the Captain gentlemanly. The scenery on each side Lake Champlain is most beautiful and the Islands exceedingly pretty, we saw the Lake to the greatest advantage, a bright Sun & clear sky. We reached Burlington at nine where again we were annoyed by the runners, they first came to me, I said I knew nothing about it, when one man said, the Lady has a Gentleman, and away they went after Edmund, he told them he would knock down whoever attempted to touch his luggage. We took a coach and went up from the Lake to an Hotel where we were told that the Mail left there for Stanstead the next morning at four oclock, and that there was not another till Tuesday; I was sorry it went so early, I wished to see something of Burlington which I am told is a beautiful Village. I forgot to say that in Lake Champlain we saw the split rock on the west side, elevated above the level of the water twelve feet, the part broken off contains about half an acre covered with trees, and is separated from the main rock 20 feet. The opposite sides exactly fit each other, through the fissure a line has been dropped to the depth of 300 feet without finding a bottom.

We got into the Mail on friday morning at four, with five companions, and now the roads were worse than ever, the Gentlemen were frequently obliged to get out and hold it up on both sides, the hills became almost perpendicular, often immense trees across the roads which we went over at a great rate, ruts, half way up the wheels, once we could not proceed along the road, and were obliged to turn into a field, go through a hedge and over a ditch; I never saw such steady horses, and the coaches are so constructed that they can follow the horses almost any where. We proceeded in this manner till one oclock when we stopped to dine and afterwards went on in an open waggon as the people at the Inn said the Mail could not proceed without being injured. This waggon had four seats, and nine of us with all our boxes were stuffed into it. This vehicle was very long and low, the roads became worse and worse and I felt so ill that really I was afraid I should not be able to bear it much longer, for though my kind Edmund sat by my side & held me in when it shook so dreadfully, it did not releave me, I dared not look at many places we went up and down, I wonder the people do not mend the roads for the scenery is splendid past description, but who could enjoy it suffering as I did. Many times we went *smack* into the woods for miles and the road chiefly composed of large trees thrown across. I forget the name of the place where we staid all night, we had a small centre bed room, and on one side had three men, on the other an old woman. We had been eighteen hours going sixty miles and were still thirty from Stanstead.

The next morning, Saturday, we again entered a waggon with only a pair of horses and passed through a beautiful country to Stanstead, now in the midst of a grand wood with trees so high it made my eyes ache to look to the tops of them, and then along roads with the land cultivated on each side and pretty frame houses and barns upon the different farms most of them painted white, the people all looking clean and neatly dressed and with such happy countenances I was quite delighted to see them. The roads were now much better though still rough and we reached the pretty village of Stanstead about two oclock.

After dinner Edmund went to call on Mr H m — n — [Hamilton]¹⁶ the custom house officer to speak to him about allowing our luggage to pass without being opened. Edmund paid the *fee* of a dollar and all was right. Mr H. asked us to spend the evening at his house, we went to tea, his wife was agreeable and gave us excellent tea bread and *fresh* butter, the first we had tasted since we left England. Mr H. married for his first wife the daughter of Major Colcough [Colclough was the father of Captain Guy Colclough, who had been one of Edmund's local contacts on his visit of the previous year] – he is very free in speech and manner, too much so for our English tastes, and we were not sorry to leave his house. We met a young Englishman there, he has been in the Army and is now a Lawyer at Stanstead.

Sunday morning we left Stanstead at nine oclock in a hired waggon and proceeded to Sherbrooke thirty five Miles distant, the country all the way quite beautiful, particularly as we got nearer to the Town. The drive is close to the fine river of St Francis. We saw two large encampments of Indians, they looked merry and happy and their hair shone like a well polished table, they are, I understand, a harmless people if kindly treated, honest, and make pretty baskets. I can scarcely express my surprise to you dearest Mamma when we entered Sherbrooke. Edmund did indeed make the worst of it, the inhabitants call it a Town, but I call it a lovely Village and one that we should be proud of in England.

Our Inn, the only one at present, a large handsome one is to be built immediately, is pleasantly situated on a Bank. Out of the dining room you go into a varanda and have a view of the river St Francis just below, some fields and Cottages on the opposite side the river, and here the noise of the waterfall dashing down from Lake Magog¹⁷ into the River. Captain Colcoughs house is near the Inn, and is the best in the place. I admire it exceedingly. There are in Sherbrooke two Churches, one Catholic, a very nice academy, a large jail, and new houses are springing up in every direction, all looks cheerful, and in an improving way. The idea of this being a wilderness, as I believe some of my Lancashire friends consider it, is absurd, and you will soon find that I, already am acquainted with persons

SKETCH of SHERBROOKE and ITS VICINITY, EASTERN TOWNSHIPS, LOWER CANADA.
Principal Station of the British American Land Company.

Sherbrooke, 1836. This panoramic view of Sherbrooke from across the St. Francis River was drawn by Surveyor-General Joseph Bouchette or his son, Robert S.M. Bouchette, and published in the British American Land Company's promotional brochure of 1836. King's Hotel, where Lucy and Edmund first stayed, is (vaguely) identified. Source: DeVolpi and Scowen, *The Eastern Townships: A Pictorial Record* (Montreal, 1962).

Junction of St. Francis and Magog rivers. In the foreground is the bridge crossing the Magog River with the waterfall that deeply impressed Lucy Peel and others. In the background is the recently completed covered bridge over the St. Francis River. Source: W. H. Bartlett, *Canadian Scenery Illustrated* (London, 1842). Bishop's University Archives FC 72.W5.

enough to prevent dullness, and near enough to *Dunstall* to see when we please.

Tuesday 21st – Yesterday morning as Edmund stood at the Inn door Capt. Colcough [Colclough] and his mother drove by in a carriage drawn by a pair of black ponys, they were going to Quebec, they stopped to shake hands with Edmund and welcome him back to Canada, they appeared quite pleased to see him.[18] Soon after Major Colcough, father to the Capt., called upon us. He is a Gentlemanly Irishman and I liked him exceedingly; he sat some time, we then went home with him to call upon his daughter in law, she is a very pretty likeness of Mrs Fielding, has beautiful hair, and appears a kind agreeable woman, she is Irish and has eight children living, four boys and four girls. Her eldest daughter married and lived at Quebec. She died last year. Only one of Mrs Colcoughs girls is at home, she is almost five and a pretty dear amusing child, she took a great fancy to me, and when her Grandpapa told her to cry because Grandmamma was gone, she said no, it is of no use when Mrs Peels here, but some time when she is gone I shall cry. She repeated to me, beautifully. The Colcoughs asked us to tea and we spent a very pleasant evening with them, we met a Miss Lowther, a nice Irish Girl, she is to be married next month to a young Clergyman.

Edmund's agent has been with us all the afternoon, Mr Theney [Henry],[19] he married Mr Felton's[20] sister and lives at Montreal, he is a pleasing man, has a good honest face, friendly in his manners, gives us good advice, I think we are fortunate in having such a man to look after us. Every one speaks well of him. He has had many of the trees cut down and squared for the house. Mr Theney told us Mr Felton was at Quebec, and expected us to go out that way; hoping therefore to bring us back with him.

Mrs Felton her eldest daughter and Mr and Mrs John Felton[21] are at New York, they all return next week and orders were left with Mr Theney to be ready to receive us and say that there was no house where I could have comfortable lodgings and that there would be rooms ready for us at Mr Felton's place, Bellvedere,[22] which he hoped we would take possession of directly and consider ourselves at home till our house was finished. This my dear Mamma is real kindness. I fear you could not find a family in England equally ready to assist a stranger. This speaks a volume in our friends praise. Mr Theney arranged to send for us to day but it is wet and we have had a note to say that the carriage will be here, for us, tomorrow.

Wednesday 22nd – Last night about seven it was beautifully fine and we went a walk, we first passed over a wide wooden bridge across the St Francis at least half over, for in the centre we remained to watch one of the most romantic and lovely sights I ever saw, it was the water boiling up round the corner of a rock from Lake Magog, rushing round a little Island covered with trees, and then with encreased fury dashing under the bridge into the River making so much noise we could scarcely hear each other speak. We passed on down the road to Three Rivers, it is really past description, the River, the rich pastures and the rural fences, forming altogether a scene every one must admire. We thought and talked of Mr Peel & wished he were with us, saying how much he would admire the quiet beauty of the place, it was late when we returned to the Inn.

Sunday 26th Bellvedere – On Wednesday morning Mr Theney drove two of the Miss Feltons to Sherbrooke to have their music lesson from Miss Chambers, a *Cobblers* wife, hers is the only Piano in the place. She keeps no servant, binds the shoes for her husband and teaches most of the young Ladies music. Mr Theney took us to call upon Judge Fletcher[23] and his Lady, they had expressed a wish to see us, and the Lady was old & too infirm to come to me. We found them very friendly and agreeable, Mrs

Fletcher hoped I would never go to Sherbrooke without calling, that she should be glad to see me at all times, and to stay as long as I liked. I was introduced to the High Sheriff Mr *Witcher*,[24] he married a Miss Felton and lives at Sherbrooke, he was in the Navy, is good looking, his wife too delicate to go out, he hoped I would visit them at their Cottage whenever I liked & thinking that we were remaining at the Inn, offered me any thing he had in his gardens. The people about here really bestow favours as if they were receiving them. You see dear Mamma your child will not live among savages.

We arrived at Bellvedere soon after four, their usual dinner hour, I can scarcely give you an idea of this pretty house and beautiful situation. All the rooms are on the ground floor and very large, the dining room and drawing room nearly the same size as those at Church Bank are furnished in the English Style. A large Hall where we generally dine, long wide passages and a delightful Veranda the whole length and round one side of the house 6 feet wide.[25] The house is quite as long in front as Mr Scholes row of houses in Tetlow Fold. I feel quite at home here & like the children, there are eleven of them. John the eldest, Eliza, Charlotte, Fanny, Maria, Louisa, Octavia, Edward, Isabella, and Narbonne two years old a beautiful little boy with dark eyes.[26] Then there is Miss *Mow* the governess, a good natured person, but rather strange looking, the old nurse Mrs Scott has lived in the family sixteen years, she is a Staffordshire woman and lived at Abbots Bromley – She remembers the name of Meek very well.

On Thursday Edmund worked very hard on his land & came home quite tired with rooting up the trees and all the skin off his hands. On Friday I went with him and would not allow him to work so hard. Yesterday, Saturday, Mr Felton came home. He is rather short, very plain but sensible looking and gentlemanly, he welcomed me most kindly and said he considered himself much obliged to me for coming to live for a short time in his large family, that he hoped I should be comfortable. I am sure I shall like him and good Mr Theney grows in favour every day. Mrs Felton and party are expected tomorrow, which being post day I shall be obliged to send this off without seeing her. I am sorry to put you to the expense of a double letter but I can not manage better now, when our packages arrive I shall get larger paper.[27]

I wish you could see & taste the wild Strawberrys and Raspberrys, there is no end to them, they grow all over the fields and woods, excellent fresh when ripe and make very good preserves. The Feltons make their own candles and common soap. The situation of Dunstall is very romantic, I am sure you would admire it greatly. I shall describe *our* house in my next letter, the men begin tomorrow on the foundation. It is Edmund's planning & we all think it will be a very nice one. Dear love to Mr Mayne, Sarajane and all dear relatives and friends. Edmund would like to see Charles Meek rooting up the stumps of trees. I am delighted dearest Mamma with my future abode, and if all my dear friends were only a little nearer I should be perfectly happy. Kiss dearest papa & Sturges for me and believe me

your much attached child
Lucy Peel.

No 3

Bellevedere   May 27th 1833

My dearest Mamma

It rained all yesterday, no one ventured out but Edmund who walked in the varanda. Mr Felton was very agreeable, he is fond of music and quite anxious for the arrival of the Harp that he may hear me play. I made a blunder in telling you the names of this family. The eldest son is called William, and I left out one girl, Matilda, between Maria and Louisa. This morning Edmund went to Dunstall, Mr Felton and Fanny to Lenokville [Lennoxville], four miles from here to meet Mrs Felton, I am sorry to say they returned without her, I say sorry, because I feel the want of her company. All the children are obliging and would do anything for me, but they are complete children in ideas and manners, though Charlotte is nearly seventeen and ought to be able to converse well.

I never see Edmund from soon after eight, for we often breakfast at half past seven, till almost four in the afternoon, this makes me feel dull. I have no useful work about and no harp to amuse myself with. I walked with him to Dunstall and remained to see him dig, but must not attempt it again, for though only two miles and a half from here I was much fatigued when I returned to Bellevedere. I shall be delighted when the house is ready for us to go into, then we shall both be upon the spot, and see all that is going on. We have engaged a man servant upon trial, for a month, he is one and twenty, strong, and has done a good day's work, he seems to understand what he is about. Edmund returned to dinner quite tired, Mr Theney had been with him marking out the ground for the house, and some men are engaged to begin upon it tomorrow. I have been a walk with Edmund this evening.

28th – Edmund as usual at Dunstall. Maria and Matilda to Sherbrooke to have their music lesson. I have been reading till I am quite tired. They have two Guitars here, I am already much improved on this instrument and now the harp is away Edmund likes to hear me play. I have composed several things which are thought pretty. I wish dear Rosa had them. I will write to her soon. I forgot to say, we give our man eight dollars a month and till he can live with us, one dollar and a half for food per week.

I will now give you the particulars of our house. Our friends approve the plan and it is Edmunds. First there is a stone wall all round three feet high to keep out the snow in winter, steps to enter the house. The passage will be six feet wide, to the right the drawing room and a bed room, to the left the dining room & kitchen, these rooms are all 15 feet square. The kitchen at a future time is to be a bedroom, and we shall build kitchens at the back. Next to our bed room a store room 15 by 8. Opposite a small bedroom the same size. Two servants rooms and lumber room above. Cellar 20 feet square the passage will be 38 feet long. The windows to the sitting rooms french, down to the ground and a varanda all along the outside of the house. It will be covered with clap boards, painted a pale pink; this colour is the cheapest I know, it will be a beautiful Cottage when finished.[28]

How many things are wanted to furnish a house, it almost frightens me when I think of it, but no doubt we shall do very well with good management, it is only at first that we shall have to be so very economical. Our house will cost us more than we had calculated upon, labour is so terribly high. Mr Theney is returning soon to Montreal, where he lives, and is to send us a load of things to lay in for the winter, every thing would be double bought at the Sherbrooke stores, he will send flour, rice, sugar, tea, bacon, soap, glass crockery etc etc. We bought our Carpets at New York and a beautiful rug for the Hall. I am sure you and Kate would envy me if you saw it, I gave three dollars for it.

31st – Mr Felton went to Sherbrooke to meet his wife and daughter, and about three they arrived at Bellevedere. Mrs Felton is a very little woman with a nice figure, pleasing countenance, very Lady like and the youngest looking woman of her age that I ever saw. I cannot fancy her the mother of all these great children. Miss [Eliza] Felton is rather taller than Rosa, has a good figure but is rather too thin, fine hair, lighter than mine, pleasing grey eyes, and a sweet expression, too red a complexion, and having been some time at New York, has acquired the Yankee manner of speaking, which you have heard Edmund take off. I think I shall like her. Mrs Felton expressed great sorrow at not seeing us in New York, and welcomed me to Bellevedere in the kindest possible manner, begging I would consider myself quite at home, her foreign accent is very interesting. Mr William Felton is very like Mr Fort is, agreeable and attentive.

It is exceedingly cold, we have fires in both rooms. I wish you could see the sky in this country it is often beautiful beyond discription, if a painter were to excecute such a one, it would be pronounced by an Englishman to be unnatural; last evening when Edmund and I were walking, it was a deep pink and went shading off towards the Orford Mountains in the most lovely manner. This evening it is a deep blue without a single cloud or break.

Sunday 2nd – A wet day never once ceasing to rain, and very cold. Mrs Felton in bed all day, not well.

5th – On Monday I awoke with bad head ache, I could not get up to breakfast, I was quite ill till nearly four, every individual as kind as possible to me. I got up to dinner. Yesterday I felt as usual again. Mr Felton took me at eleven in his *waggon* to Dunstall, he then went on to Sherbrooke and called for Edmund and me on his return. I sat watching Edmund at his work and had some nice rich new milk from our own Cow.

As I am sure you will like to know all our first expences I shall tell them you as they arise so that you will know how we stand when we enter the house, it will be some time before I can tell you what that will cost. We have procured several things cheaper by paying in *money* and ready money, the people here exchange articles, and money is so scarce we are obliged to pay men something in advance before they begin work for us, they have no money themselves to purchase provisions. Our Carpenter is an Englishman called *Hale*.

Sovereigns here pass for 24 shillings currency which gives us many extra pounds in our little property. Our Land 150 acres cost — dollars.[29] One yoke of oxen 50 dollars, one Cow and Calf 22 Dollars. 7 sheep 2 Cents 1/2 per pound, one pig five Cents per pound, 4 lambs 1 dollar each. One Lamb 1/2 a dollar, two of the sheep have to Lamb. This stock cost us in English money £24.19.0 Ten Cents make a yankee six pence and so on to a dollar, 5 shillings to the dollar.

Friday 7th – Our luggage arrived. Mr Felton would have it all here. One package No 4 is lost, containing 2 beds, 4 prs of sheets, 3 Cotton Quilts, 4 Pillows & cases, & 3 blankets. A great loss to us, we shall write about them, but I much fear never recover any of them. Eliza, Charlotte, three others and myself, were all this morning taking the things out of my Harp Case and large wooden box. They were quite wet, the Harp rusty, we were three hours cleaning it. My bonnets were in a sad state, my tuscan [finely braided Tuscan straw; hats and bonnets of such material, *OED*] cannot be worn till cleaned and put into shape, the others I have restored myself. My striped silk dress half of it turned green and can only be worn in an evening, even then, I fear it will be scarcely wearable. All my gloves changed into various colours.

Saturday 8th – This morning we have again been busy airing all Edmunds things. The glass is come safely, the tools rather rusty, but they will not be the worse. Mrs Felton is well again; they are all delighted with my playing, the Harp sounds beautifully. I am very glad to see it again, none of the girls but Eliza had ever seen a Harp, or cup and ball, or Battledores and Shuttlecocks.[30] I wish you had seen their astonishment. Some of the preserve pots were broken, the Hamburgh Beef Mouldy, the Ham, all right, they are hung up in Mr Felton's Kitchen. I have composed a song for the Guitar, both words and music, you may suppose it has some merit for it is admired even when I sing it. Rosa would like it, and how delighted I should be to hear her sing it.

19th – Cold & uncomfortable all yesterday fires in both rooms, I played on the Harp. I think all this family like us, Mrs Felton said to day our coming is quite a *windfall*, and I heard Eliza tell Charlotte she did not know what they should do when we leave them. I have been teaching Maria to play at Battledore. There is one good thing attending this cold wet weather, it keeps off the flies and Musquitos, I had a fortnight ago more than twenty bites, and the flies tease Edmund sadly, he is very much tanned [?]. I have a bad cold, but don't feel so much of the heat burn as I used to do.

Edmund Peel at *Sorel*[31] has not written to us, we see in the paper that he is now at Montreal. Our Pig the last few days has been busy rooting up the newly set potatos and was so wild he could not be caught, however at last we succeeded and put a ring through the gentlemans nose, when the operation was over he cut a few capers in the air and set off into the woods, we have not seen him since, but I dare say he will return soon. I had some excellent tea last night made from the wild black Currant. I never tasted better in England.

Tuesday 11th – Edmund walked to Sherbrooke yesterday and called upon Mrs Colclough. I sent her the buckle I bought for her in England and a note, she admired it much. Major Colclough, her father in law, said that the note & box independant of the buckle were worth keeping. Mr Theney returned here a little before dinner and brought with him a Mr Cook an Englishman, in the army and gentlemanly. He is travelling in this country & is delighted with this neighbourhood and would like to settle here, he is a sensible man and talks agreeably. He staid all night and went off at six this morning. He liked the situation of Dunstall exceedingly and said he envied us the pleasure of building a house after our own plan and having a possession of our own. He says they are very much afraid of the Cholera at Quebec. Two Vessels from Ireland are in strict quarantine there, twelve have died on board one, of Cholera, and seven on board the other.[32] I have given Mrs Felton her shawl she is quite delighted with it, and appeared pleased at the attention.

13th – Yesterday Eliza and I went on horseback to Sherbrooke, we called upon Edmund at Dunstall. I am to ride as often as I like. We called upon Mrs Colclough and at the Judges. I like him very much he is so sensible and amusing. Mrs Fletcher gave us some nice bread and butter. The Judge said he should ride over the first day he could to see me, and hear me play on the Harp, an instrument he is very fond of. He says that he has deeply studied politics for more than forty years, and he feels convinced that in three years more England will have no taxes, no Funds, no Church, no Thing. I wish you could hear him talk.

We had to wait at the Hotel whilst a buckle was put to my saddle, the Landlady came into our room and Yankee fashion sat down to amuse us with her conversation, I am sure she meant to shake hands but we both drew ourselves up and she kept her distance. I certainly did not look pleasant at her. Her dress was a yellow muslin gown, a pink band with pearl buckle, blue & white silk handkerchief, her hair in high bows before and behind and an immense bone comb cut in all shapes, glass broach and fine glass rings, black and white stockings, black shoes all in holes; I never saw such an object of finery and vulgarity. We arrived at home soon after three. Mr Felton went this morning to Quebec for a few days, I have written to Mary Lyon by that Rout and shall to Rosa, let me hear if they receive these letters.

June 15th – Yesterday the nice old Judge came from Sherbrooke to call upon me, he sat a long time and was much pleased with the Harp, he was pleased to call me quite a proficient. We had a letter from Edmund Peel who is at *Sorel*, he does not like that place, and says the farms are all nearly worn out, he wished Edmund to write and tell him if there is land to be had here, there are several places near us to be had, and one nice farm just on the opposite side the road to Dunstall, I think our cousins are nearly sure to come. They were almost seven weeks coming out from England and he unwell most of the voyage. I have found a book in this house which I have long wished to read, I am quite delighted with it,

Orlando Furioso.[33] I remember dear Sarajane reading it loud many years ago at Mr Birches of Barton when Louisa had the scarlet fever. I have just been feasting on a plate of strawberries and rich cream, Sturges, if you and Charles were here you would never be out of the hedges.

Pray write regularly and fully, remember how very anxious I feel about you all, particularly you and Mr Mayne, you are never, dearest Mama, many hours out of my minds eye, I fancy you doing all kinds of things, and if I could only snatch one look and one kiss from you now and then, I should indeed be happy, when I think of what I shall do in my house I endeavour to remember all your economical plans, pray give me some hints and good advice in all your letters. I mean to have my garden very neat and nice, and every flower that springs up will remind me of a beloved parent. Sometimes when I fancy you unwell and no child near you I am very uncomfortable and think I ought not to have left you, but when I see Edmund before me and receive from him daily and hourly encreased attentions I cannot help considering myself a fortunate woman. You would be pleased dearest mamma to see what a favorite Edmund is here, Mrs Felton watches him when he talks as if he were her own son. She is very kind to me, & gives me much useful information. I dare say it will be a comfort to you to know that our medical man at Sherbrooke is clever and much liked by the Feltons. Give my best love to all my relations and inquiring friends. I have not room to mention names. Edmunds best love, ever your warmly

attached Child
Lucy Peel.

No 4

Bellvidere   July 24th 1833

My dearest Mamma

The day before yesterday I sent off a long letter to dear Rosa which I begged her to forward to you immediately. We had dreadful thunder storms all day and night, Edmund came from Dunstall completely wet, his poor neck and arms covered with bites of the horrid black & white flies. He has ordered an iron pot to make a portable *smudge* in, this is the only thing which keeps them off. Oh Mamma had you seen how eagerly I read, and Edmund listened to your letter, you would have been sure how much we love and think of you, I am convinced that marrying encreases instead of diminishes the affection of a child for her parents.

Yesterday I went to Sherbrooke in the waggon with Eliza, Maria, & Matilda Felton, we met Capt. Colclough who said he was just going to drive Mrs Colclough to Bellvedere to call upon me, this being the case I got out & sat an hour whilst the girls went on to Sherbrooke. Mrs Colclough is a quiet pleasing woman. Mrs Peck called whilst I was there, she hoped to see me at her house the next time I go to the Town. It was her husband, the Member, who gave that gay ball at Sherbrooke last year when Edmund & George where [*sic*] here.[34] Capt. Colclough would not let me walk to the Judges where I was to meet the Miss Feltons, he drove me in his waggon & then returned to his wife.

Mrs Fletcher was delighted to see me, the Judge was at Stanstead holding his court.[35] The old Lady was full of his praises, saying he had few equals in knowledge being master of most subjects, and she was sure the more Mr and Mrs Peel saw of him the more they would be charmed with his society, that his lectures on natural philosophy delighted all who heard them. She knew only one thing which he attempted that he did not do well & that was playing on the flute. I believe the little woman is nearly right in her opinion of Mr Fletcher for he is universally considered an exceedingly clever man.

The people at Sherbrooke are talking much of a Mr Wilson who is coming to live there, he has taken a small house in the town for the present intending to look about him before he buys land. He is a Physician from Ripon in Yorkshire and intends to practice as one here, but does not seem very anxious to be employed at all,[36] he was at Ripon twenty years, and had all the best practise in the neighbourhood, but he gave offence to many persons at the passing of the reform Bill. The Ripon people brought another Physician from London and Mr Wilson disgusted with this treatment and thinking his money not safe in the Funds, took out every farthing, and brought his wife and seven children, four girls and three boys, to this place, I hear that he has plenty of money, he has brought out with him letters of introduction to all the great people in Lower Canada, amongst the rest, Mr Felton. Capt. Colclough, with whom he has been staying several days, tells me that he is a gentleman, and that he is evidently a man of sense and information, he has been abroad several times in the early part of his life. Mr Wilson says there are several agreeable English families who are only awaiting his account of the Country to bring out their children, so you see dear Mamma our society and what is of much more consequence, Canada, is likely to improve greatly.[37]

July 7th – our house was raised Wednesday and Thursday, it is a general custom here to have a number of men present who drink as much as they can at the expense of the Carpenter, who has contracted for the job. Our carpenter, an Englishman, wisely kept the thing snug, and only engaged as many hands as were necessary. You may easily imagine, what a piece of work the raising is when I tell you that our house is made of square blocks of wood six inches thick, that these are all put together on the ground, in four sides, and when finished the sides are raised separately to the top of the foundation wall three feet above the ground. It will be a very warm house for besides the lathing and plaistering inside there will be clapboards at the sides and back, inside, and at the front under the varandah which will be seven feet wide, planks with mouldings to hide the piecings, these will be painted pink, and make a beautiful finish to the house. It is a sloping roof covered with shingles, which when painted have the appearance of tiles.

How I shall wish for you dearest Mamma to lay out the beds of my little garden in the front of the house. I have bought 50 pounds of wool to make a sofa we give two shillings a pound. We killed one of our Lambs & made a present of it to Mrs Felton, she gave me a very pretty work basket made by the Indians of different coloured woods.

July 9th – Sturges you should have been with our Man when he was setting potatos with your gun ready loaded, a large bear came out of the wood and sat quietly looking at him, should you have liked a shot at him? Yes, that you would and at the immense partridges and beautiful wood pigeons, which are in such large flocks that they pick up the corn in whole fields in a few minutes.

10th – Mr Felton came home yesterday, he has been all over the back of Shipton about 30 miles from here with the Governor Lord Aylmer,[38] his Lordship is determined to bring this part of the country into notice and intends next summer to travel through all the Towns, having at each an agricultural meeting himself to give the prizes. He left Lady Aylmer at Sorel, where I hear, our Cousin Edmund notwithstanding the poverty of the soil, has taken a farm, we think he will repent. Mrs E. Peel has called upon Lady Aylmer. The Governor and his Lady go to Three Rivers to remain till after the races the 25th of this month. Elisa & Charlotte are going, they will stay with their friend Miss Nelson who is adopted Child to Judge Verleruse [Vallières].[39] Miss Nelson is to return with the Feltons to Bellvedere.

Mr Felton called yesterday at Dunstall to see our building, he admires it and tells me it looks quite large now it is raised, I am quite anxious to see it. Edmund pulled up five stumps yesterday and finished hoeing the potatos, the weeds grow so fast that it has been a long job. We pay two shillings for your letters from New York, & the same with those we send out.

13th – Yesterday we went in the waggon to Dunstall – Edmund was ready to receive me, the rest went on to Sherbrooke – I admire the house exceedingly its only fault I think is, that the roof has too high a pitch, but Mr Felton tells us that what we lose in beauty we gain in utility, for when the snow begins to melt in the spring it all leaves the roof in one mass, and if it do not slant well some of the snow will be left behind & will melt on the top which of course injures the roof.

Lake Memphremagog (near Georgeville). On 13 July 1833, Lucy described the view of Lake Magog from the Peel property. Lake Memphremagog lies a few miles to the south and west. Source: W. H. Bartlett, *Canadian Scenery Illustrated* (London, 1842). Bishop's University Archives FC 72.W5.

I climbed with Edmund half way up the great Rock "Peel Rock" to see the beautiful view, it is indeed grand, we see Lake Magog very plainly – Mr Felton called to take us back to Bellvedere. I think if Mr Clowes were to live in Canada he would fix upon Dunstall for his situation, how lovely he might make it with all his money and he might have rockerys without end. Mr Felton says no place has more capabilities than ours, it is so romantic & quiet, yet close to the road, the house cannot be seen until you are within a few yards of it, we mean to have a drive up through an avenue of the second growth of trees.[40] Mrs Wilson is quite charmed with Sherbrooke, she is getting her small house in order, her youngest child is only three months old, what an undertaking to bring such a large family so far.

17 – Sunday last was very hot, the thermometer 80 in the shade, in the evening dreadful thunder, lightning and rain, and such a hail storm as I think you will never see in England, the hail stones great pieces of ice, in one of the provinces a few weeks ago the hail stones which fell, were six Inches round and pierced the cattle like knives, killing many. Edmund mowed down a field of Raspberry bushes, I hear he is an excellent mower. The Raspberries are now coming in and the wild strawberries going out, there are black Raspberries which follow the red and white. These are considered the best for preserves having a much finer flavour. The veranda is put up at Dunstall. I hope now the men will get on quickly. I am now anxiously expecting a letter from you.

19th – Mr & Mrs Felton and I went in the waggon to Sherbrooke, the roads were in a dreadful state owing to the constant rain we have had, we went to the *Store* for they are not called shops here, Mr Ball had just had all his fresh stock, and really you can get everything here that you want for the comforts of life, but how an English draper would laugh to see the different things that are to be purchased at the same place with Muslins, silks, Tapes and Calicos; the latter article is very cheap and good. I bought some coarse linen to make the first cushions of my sofa.

Edmund met us at the store, having walked to see after some goods which had arrived from Montreal, three loads are come and there is another on the road, we pay seven dollars a load for carriage. The things are all at the hut on our land close to the house, which hut we mean to make a stable of this winter. I am quite impatient to see if all my crockery and glass is safe. I have been making the bolster cases and preparing the rest for my kind husband to stitch up, he having promised to help me. I expect to be able soon to make almost anything, necessity makes many industrious, and I assure you could I have my relations near to see all we are doing I should never feel happier that I do now, I contrive every thing myself.

Sturges will you not laugh when I tell you that one bedstead is to be made by a Coachmaker. They have a custom in America which perhaps you have heard or read of that, the people when they wish to have a new situation to live in, put their houses upon rollers and take them to the desired place, I have not seen one of these removals yet, but shall in a few days. Mr Felton has a large barn which is to be taken from one side of the yard to the other, I am quite anxious to see the removal. When Eliza Felton was at New York last year a gentleman she knows had a large new built [brick?] house, a road was being made or rather a street which would oblige his residence to be disturbed, he got it upon rollers, and with his family sitting in it quite unconcerned, and furniture untouched it was drawn by horses or oxen to another street. Does not this appear to you almost impossible?

Mr Felton & two of his daughters go to Three Rivers tomorrow and Mr Felton will go on to Quebec, I shall send this by him, he says in the summer months it will go safely that way and I have no postage to pay by Quebec.[41] English post days are Tuesdays and Fridays. It is a lovely day I expect Edmund will begin to cut his hay. Yesterday I was introduced to Doctor Wilson, he is a plain man and rather lame, I also saw Capt. Colclough and Judge Fletcher, shook hands with them both, we called at Mr Kimbles[42] to see his beautiful garden and fine show of flowers and fruit, I never saw anything like the currant trees. The kitchen garden is a flat piece of ground, from that you go up a flight of steps to a broad walk with flower beds on each side, then up another flight, walk & beds the same as the first, then up a third which brings you to the top where there is a pretty Alcove covered with hops, flower beds and a walk round, we have an extensive and beautiful view from the alcove. Mr Kimbles is close to the river, the small farms, huts, and hovels on the opposite side looking exceedingly pretty. Now dearest Mamma do I write to please you? Am I circumstantial enough or too much so? Tell me truly. Dear love at Lichfield and Barton and kind regards to all inquiring friends.

Our beautiful little calf is sold for five dollars, I am quite sorry to part with it, the poor Cow had a bell tied round her neck, fearing she might go in search of her *child* and be lost; as soon as she was let out off she went, the sound of the bell frightened her, she cocked her tail & went as hard as she could to some distance. The men were to finish shingling our house to night, it will take about 20 thousand shingles, a dollar a thousand, rather a dear roof to a house. Doctor Wilson dined here to day, he said he had written to his friends in England and told them that as he stood upon the beautiful bridge at Sherbrooke watching the cascade which falls from Lake Magog into the river St Francis, that it was surprising to see with what impatience the Heathen God[43] flew into the embraces of the christian Saint.

Edmund sends his best love to you all, I shall get him to write in my next, but really he works so hard and comes home so tired I can scarcely ask him. We have had two most beautiful days which I assure you we enjoy exceedingly after all the rain. We see the Aurora very often. Though we are not what would be called politicians yet we wish to know how you are going on. With everything that is affectionate from us both to you believe me your attached Child

Lucy Peel

No 5

Bellvedere   July 29th

My dearest Mamma

We sent off a letter to Church Bank this morning I now begin another sheet to you, and I trust that tomorrow I shall be able to say I have received a second letter from our dear friends at Mount Cottage, we feel quite uneasy at your long silence.

30th – No letter from England, however complaints will do no good, and only take up room, that might be more profitably occupied. Yesterday Capt & Mrs Colclough, their newly married daughter Mrs Waller, Miss Miller her sister in law, and little Annabella dined here, they were delighted with my Harp, Mrs Waller had neither heard nor seen one before.

31st – Mr Felton came home yesterday unexpectedly, he left the girls & Mr William Felton[44] at Three Rivers, they are to return on Monday week, accompanied by their friend Miss Nelson. Mr Felton brought the Moreen [wool, or wool and cotton fabric, used for curtains and other items, *OED*] for our bed, it is a beautiful rich colour. I have cut it out this morning and have made one of the Curtains, you would be quite surprised & pleased to see how well I manage things, I never thought I should take so much interest in such matters, but I now really like work & shall feel quite proud to sleep in a bed of my own making. Mr John Felton returned to Bellvedere yesterday.

Our Carpenter is constantly in liquor, and has such a character for not paying his men that none remain with him many days! Edmund has already paid him half what he is to receive, and he told him yesterday that he would give him till this morning to make up his mind whether he would be sober and mind his work or give up the contract. He has not done one days work himself since we engaged him. He is a single man and might have made his fortune. It would be an excellent thing for any good carpenter to come out, I would venture to promise him, if he would resist the prevailing vice of the country, he should be a rich man in a few years. Carpenters & Masons are in constant request.

Sunday August 4th – Mr Hale has given up the contract and Edmund has engaged another man named Haskel, he is steady and finishes quickly what he undertakes; he says he will complete our house in six weeks, so we are now in hopes of soon being settled. It has been very hot all day, and I trust we shall have some fine weather for the Hay. Just as we had finished dinner Judge Fletcher and Mr Hale[45] came to call, the latter is a young Man who wishes to settle in the neighbourhood, he married one of Judge Bocas' [Bowen's] daughters, and is nephew to Lord Amherst, whose secretary he was when he went to the West Indias. Mr Hale is much pleased with the place, he has been married two years and has two children.

5th – This morning, about seven, Mr Felton, Mr John Felton, and Mr Theney set off on an excursion up the river St Francis, to see some part of the country they have not visited, after the two first days they will be quite in the woods and be obliged to sleep there, with not even a log hut to shelter them; they went away in high glee and are to be absent about ten days. They took a large box of provisions with them. It is a lovely day, Edmund is at Dunstall busy in his hay, he mows and makes it all himself, we have only three acres this year.

Sturges did you ever hear the tale of the Methodist Chandler? He said to his servant one evening, poking his head through the small glass window which looked from his parlour into the shop. John, have you watered the brandy? yes Sir, Have you *sanded* the sugar? Yes Sir. Then come into prayers. Mr Felton pressed Edmund very much to join his party on their trip, but like a good husband he remains at home to take care of me and indeed I could not have parted with him just now [Lucy is expecting a baby at the end of the year].

11th – We have passed a very quiet week being a small party, no visitors, and bad weather. I have been fully occupied making my bed curtains, and preparing the wool for my sofa, the children are kind enough to assist me. We had a letter from Edmund Peel of Sorel on friday, he has taken a farm three miles from that Town on the River Rich lieu [Richelieu] and one mile above the Government house, he has 80 acres, 50 of them cleared. He is building and hopes to be in his house next Month, he invites us to go and see them. He appears to like the situation and finds it agreeable being so near Lord Aylmers,[46] he and Mrs Peel have dined twice at Government house. The family are there only during the summer; we do not envy them their great neighbours as we prefer peace and quiet.

Haskel works hard at our Villa, and we mean to go in when one sitting room, our bedroom and the kitchen are ready, which will only, I hope, be a month.

Tuesday 13th – Mr & Mrs Witcher came to call upon us, she has been ill, or would have called sooner, she is a pleasing Lady-like woman completely English, and seems to regret her native land not a little; I played to her, she is fond of music, and appeared much pleased, she said it reminded her of old times. Yesterday Mr Felton and his party returned home quite delighted with their trip and all they had seen, they say the country is most beautiful, and that it is impossible to describe the loveliness of the flowery banks of the St. Francis; however I think they were not sorry to find themselves at home again, they were tired with so much walking. Tell Mrs C. Bourne that Mrs Felton knows Capt. Battersby, she knew him both as a Lieutenant and a Capt., and she has often heard of the handsome Richard Battersbea and the several noble and generous actions of his in the Peninsular War.

Fanny, Matilda, and I went on horseback yesterday to Dunstall and we tired ourselves with making hay; we regaled upon new milk, Raspberries from *Peel Rock*, and biscuit. We got home about three, Edmund soon followed us. Mrs Felton says I must not make hay again, I felt so unwell all evening after my exertions. It is very tiresome that I cannot bear fatigue, as I have much that must be done now we are so soon to be in our house, and I cannot afford to be idle. Mrs Felton is so kind as to send to Quebec for the things I shall want for your expected Grand child and she will cut everything out for me. She has very prudent ideas, and will not advise me to make more than is necessary, she wisely says if children are neat and clean it is all which is requisite in this place.

Thursday 15th – I have finished my Moreen curtains and they look well, the wool is all pulled for my sofa and Edmund and I are very busy fastening it down in the seat; Mrs Felton has given me a lesson in bed-making, it is not disagreeable but rather hard work. Edmund puts the large needle through with string and I put in the knots of wool, we half finished it yesterday after dinner; you cannot think how well we manage, as to Edmund he is never idle many minutes, I don't know what I should do if I had not a husband who could and would assist me, we are so dependant upon one another here. I have finished my rocking chair this morning, stuffed & knotted it myself, Mrs Felton admires it so much she intends making one, and has asked me for the paper pattern which I first cut out. I shall be so good an Upholsteress that if I return to England I shall even rival Miss Falkner.

Sunday 18th – On Friday Mr Felton & two of the girls went down to Sherbrooke in the waggon, Fanny and I on horseback, I rode Mr John Felton's black, he is so kind as to beg I will use him as often as I please. I never saw a kinder hearted man in my life, he is always the same, polite and attentive without being officious. Fanny and I called at Mr Witchers, it is a beautiful place close to the river side and half a mile from the Village, we staid about half an hour and then rode home calling at Dunstall for Edmund who walked by our side. Riding does me good for I cannot walk far, and I never go off the walk when on horseback.

Yesterday we had unceasing rain, Edmund remained at Bellvedere and we finished the seat of the sofa, it has been a long piece of work, to day it has rained till five, and has gradually cleared up all evening; Oh Mamma it is worth all the horrors of a sea voyage to be in the verandah at Bellvidere at seven this evening to witness the sun-set. The sky is a beautiful blue and large *golden* clouds are passing quickly over it, the woods in the distance are tinged in the most lovely manner, and the fields sloping down to the house are exactly the colour of a sovereign just from the mint, it is indeed a splendid sight, how I wish you could see it.

Monday 19th – 13 men were taken up the other day and put into the prison at Sherbrooke for counterfeiting, they will be tried when the Judges come up.[47]

Wednesday 21st – Yesterday I received your letter No 2. but my joy at seeing it was soon turned into sorrow, when I read all that my dear relations have suffered. Papa, kind, excellent Papa, surely by this time you have ceased to be an anxiety to Mamma and your friends; how fortunate that you, Mamma kept well & that Miss Cresswell was with you, I have not room to *say* how much I feel but you may easily imagine; I shall be most anxious for your next account. Sarajane, Mr Mayne and Rosa I shall think much of you all. I am glad to hear Mr M. Lyon is going to be married, indeed I conclude he is married by this time, I am convinced it is the most happy and rational state if properly entered into. Mr Mayne's opinion of my letters gratifies me exceedingly, I know I may believe it, for he never flatters those he loves, what a trial to Sarajane to part with dear Mini.

Give my love to Mary Jane and Louisa, I shall be glad to receive their promised letters, how delighted they would be to watch the lovely little Humming Birds in the verandah and to gather the wild flowers, and to ride through the Woods, I think also to see our pretty Villa at Dunstall. Mr Felton was there yesterday and quite delighted with the place, he admires the plan of the house. It is indeed a romantic spot. Tell Williamson and Maria I shall not forget them. I wish I had the latter here, and if Williamson had such a beautiful cooking stove as I have she would never like to cook by a fire again; it is the most perfect thing I ever saw. I suppose you are greatly pleased at the idea of seeing the Oldershaws, I shall much like to read their letter and hope Mr Atkinson will make his appearance soon. Dear love to Charles and Kate, what trouble if they have to move again.

Maria & Matilda have caught some young trout in the brook to day, they cooked them themselves & brought them to me for my lunch; they were excellent, and I thought how nice it would be if I could have you by my side to partake of them. I did not forget Rosa's wedding day, and we shall drink your health the 9th of next month but I fear not at Dunstall. We are expecting Miss Feltons, Miss Nelson and Mr William's friend, Mr Black on Tuesday, we shall have quite a house full. The Judges will most likely come to Sherbrooke at the same time. I am pleased that all my friends inquire about me, I shall never forget any of them.

We have now very hot weather & I suffer from the bites of the Muschittos, my left leg is so stiff I cannot walk without pain. They are as bad to me as a blister. Our house gets on well, our present Carpenter is an expeditious workman, we have used 40 thousand feet of boards some of them 15 Dollars a thousand, the pine boards for the Floors, so you see, even wood which is so plentiful cannot be had for a trifle. Dear love to our relations at Church Bank and else where. I cannot spare Edmund room to write this time. Ever your attached

Lucy Peel.

[No number]

To Mrs Peel of Church Bank

Belvidere   August 23

My dear Mrs Peel [Lucy Peel's mother-in-law]

Yesterday we sent off a long letter to Mamma, and I shall therefore address this to our dear friends at Church Bank of whom I assure you we frequently think and talk; from a letter we received last Tuesday from Tetlow Fold we had the satisfaction of hearing you were all well at that time and that you have Miss Peel once more at home, how delighted you and Bessy must be to see her again, she is so lively amusing, and in fact I think as nearly perfect, as mortality will permit, pray give our best love to her and say how much I should like to see her at Dunstall Villa, I am afraid she would not be happy long in so quiet and retired a spot but every thing would have the charm of novelty, and I flatter myself she might spend one summer here without dying of ennui, as for myself I like the place better every day, and when we can take possession of our house which is now making rapid progress, I shall be indeed delighted. I have finished my bed curtains and sofa covers, both look very nice, and I hope could you see my handy work, that I should receive some praise from you; I am convinced that we are never so happy as when fully and usefully occupied, and that there is much more satisfaction in the quiet rational life I now spend, than that when gayer scenes took up so much of my attention. Dear Bessy you were beginning to change your mind about Balls and parties when I left England, and when you are married believe me you will, if you love your husband as I do, think all those things very foolish indeed.

Sunday 25th – On Friday last Eliza and Charlotte Felton accompanied by their friend Miss Nelson and escorted by Mr William Felton arrived from Three Rivers. Tell George I do not admire his taste if he call Miss Nelson pretty, she seems a good tempered laughing girl, but nothing particular in any way; Mr William Felton is good looking and gentlemanly and I am told clever, but rather too conceited, he is however a very young man and I daresay will grow wiser, as he advances in life, he is made so much of by his new family that he does not at present know himself; we are quite a large party now at Belvidere, we are eighteen not including servants.

Yesterday Maria, the quickest and most promising I think of the family, fourteen years old, rode on horseback with me to Dunstall, I was pleased with the progress in the house; and the oftener I go the more impatient I am to be in it; nothing can be kinder and more gratifying than the attentions we daily receive from our friends at Belvidere, still there is always a restraint in another person's house which is not agreeable for so long a time; and quite unsuited to Edmund. Last night I played for the rest to dance a quadrille; there was also waltzing and several songs from Miss Nelson. I often think if you were here that you would never leave the house in the evening, the frogs are so large and so numerous, I never saw such great creatures, and their croaking scarcely ever ceases, I believe even Bessy would scream at them.

Sunday, September 1st – We have had very wet weather all last week, Judge Valliere came from Sherbrooke to dine here on Wednesday and remained all night; and he and Judge Boen [Bowen][48] came yesterday and will stay till tomorrow. Judge Boen is a very gentlemanly man and a stout pleasing likeness of Mr Jere [?] Hulding [?], he has thirteen children, and his eldest daughter who is married to a Mr Hale is coming immediately to live at Sherbrooke, I hear she is a nice little woman. Last night I wished some of our friends in England who fancy we are I believe almost amongst savages could have entered the drawing room, we were fifteen of us, all the gentlemen sensible and well bred, and the ladies, goodlooking and pleasing, a large handsome room, music and dancing, diversified with intelligent, and instructive conversation, we think Mr William Felton improves upon acquaintance, he never talks nonsense, and I have never heard him say an ill natured thing of anyone, he is an admirer of Miss Nelson,[49] and I think the kind feeling is mutual; I hear Miss Kemble[50] is turning the heads of all the people at Quebec, she is equally admired on the stage and in the drawing room, she is now gone to Boston, I think they cannot be good judges of theatrical talents, to give so much praise to this lady.

Wednesday 4th – We lost Miss Nelson, Mr William Felton and the Judges this morning, it has never ceased raining the whole day so I think they would not have a very agreeable journey. Yesterday was very fine and Mr John Felton was so good as to drive me in his gig to Dunstall, I took Narbon, the youngest child with me, he is about two years old, and would be a most delightful child if he were not so dreadfully spoiled, I do not think any boy could bear with temper the treatment he meets with, he is first boxed[?], and then kissed, I am the person he most attends to, he does every thing I tell him and I am sure is fond of both Edmund and me, you would be much amused to hear him talk, the other morning when he went to walk with us Edmund put some seeds of grass down his back, the little child went on a short way and then stood still looking up to Edmund with a very grave face and said you *putted* it in and you must take it out, he eats bread and butter from morning till night, and when it is refused him he says *any* body might give me bread; he was quite pleased at Dunstall Villa, we gave him a large bason of bread and milk and Edmund made him a wooden spoon to eat it with.

I was delighted to see how far our house is advanced, it will certainly be very pretty outside and comfortable inside, not an inch of room is lost, we hope to be in it in three weeks, I wish you could see what a nice store-room I have fitted up with a dresser and shelves, I really feel childishly anxious to begin housekeeping and to be in a place of our own, Miss Felton has promised to try to draw our Villa, so if she succeed you will all be able to have an idea of the house as I shall get her to copy it in one of my letters, we shall have five comfortable bed rooms and can make another if we please, two on the ground floor and three above which is the lightest and most cheerful part of the house.

Mr John Felton has kindly offered to take me to Dunstall whenever I like to go, and begs that when I wish to go and stay the day to unpack and put things by, that Edmund will take me in his gig and keep it till we return to dinner; what should we have done without the attentions of this excellent family, Mr Peel would I am sure be much pleased with Mr Felton he is so well informed and agreeable, how delighted I should be if he would venture across the Atlantic, if he do you must make up your mind, dear Mrs Peel, never to see him again for I am sure he would be too much pleased with the place to wish to leave it again. Give our love to our brother Jonathan and say we have made our doors high enough to admit of him coming in with his hat on without stooping.

Wednesday 11th – This morning I found the dresser and places for our shelves put up in the store-room, and Parkes very busy about the shed, the mason goes there to-morrow with four men to begin plastering, he says he shall finish in four days; the three bed-rooms up-stairs are done, and very nice ones they are, we can make another when necessary, and still have a large lumber[?] place, these rooms are not plastered, but are finished with planks made of pine and ribs to hide the piecings, they look exceedingly cheerful, and neat, tell Sydney that if he should determine to come out I shall have one of these pretty rooms ready for him, I am sure he will like his quarters, the window looks out upon our beautiful rock which rock we mean to clear in time and have fruit trees upon it.

Thursday 26th – We had a letter last week from Mr E. Peel of Sorel, he says he is very busy reaping and his wife is staying at Colonel Craigs' at Quebec, he is under Secretary, he and his family only came out last year from England. Give my best love to Mr Peel and Bessy and believe me to remain my dear Mrs Peel your very affectionate daughter in law.

Lucy Peel

My dear Mother

As I am such a poor writer Lucy has engrossed nearly the whole of this sheet, her account of our transactions will amuse you more than mine would have done, the house will be ready for our reception in two or three days, it will be I think a very comfortable one. Every possible precaution has been taken to make it warm as it is in an exposed situation commanding a very extensive view of the country, we both look forward with great pleasure to inhabit a house we can call our own, not that we have any cause to complain of our present abode, for all the Feltons have been truly kind to us, but home is home be it ever so homely as the man said, then I shall feel so proud to be the possessor of a *Villa* as they have named it here, in every aspect I feel perfectly happy, blessed with an amiable and affectionate wife, good health and sanguine hopes of the future, I should be unreasonable not to be content, that you and all the family may be the same is the prayer of both Lucy and your affect. son Edmund Peel

No 6

Many thanks dearest and best of Mamas for your last long and entertaining letter, I am indeed glad you did not wait for the provoking box for I should have been most anxious about you all, it is exceedingly tiresome of Mr Atkinson sailing without it as I am obliged to make many of my little things with the few and not particularly nice patterns of Mrs Felton, for she tells me she is sure I shall be confined in November from what I tell her, I am too great a novice in these things to feel at all certain. Your praises of my letter writing delight me but I sadly fear you are a partial judge, I cannot do less for my vanity's sake than continue my journals, now I hear the pleasure they give my dear friends in England.

So Mr Mayne has been again ill; I am afraid we shall always have to think of him with trembling, however he has skill to prescribe for him and an affectionate wife to attend him, if human power can preserve his valuable life, he may still for many years be spared to those he loves, and surely this will be the case; Rosa too and her little children, what a constant anxiety a family is Mama and how few women are fit to be mothers. Dear Papa you say is getting quite well again and Sturges likes to hear my letters read; take care of each other all three of you. Sturges would I am sure nurse you tenderly but I am sorry there was occasion for his attentions. It pleases me to hear of any kindness to you from Mrs Garnett, I hope it will continue. I have written a long letter to Mary Jane[51] which I trust you will have read some weeks ago before you receive this.

This last week Judge Fletcher has been holding his court at Sherbrooke, there were fifty cases to try all civil law, what think you of this? it is next to impossible not having any thing to do with the lawyers, even Edmund could not escape, and the most provoking thing was, he might not to have been brought in, but here, as elsewhere, there is much law but little equity. Our two former carpenters, Hale and Simms, chose to quarrel because Hale did not pay Simms what he owed him for work, so Simms procured a writ from the court desiring Edmund not to pay Hale what was due to him for raising our house, but to be at the court on the 20th of this month and pay the money into their hands; Edmund went on the 19th and Mr Kimball, Simm's lawyer, told them the writ was to be taken out of court and that he was at liberty to pay Hale or Simms, which he pleased; not withstanding this, it was continued in Court and the next day, on Edmund being called, he of course after what had passed was not there to answer, consequently that honest man Mr Kimball made him a defaulter, which subjected Edmund not only to pay the forty dollars due to Hales but seven pounds more to make up the whole of Hales' debt to Simms and also the law expenses which would be no trifle.

Mr Henry fortunately happened to be at Sherbrooke at the time, and when he came home he recommended Edmund to go down the next day and see what could be done, he did so but would have found no possible way of getting off had there not most luckily been a flaw in the writ, so he payed Hale his 40 dollars and came away very well pleased. This is the French law, would they have proceeded thus in England. We sent off a letter to Church Bank this morning so you will have constant accounts of us.

Tuesday October 1st – Yesterday Eliza and I went in Mr Feltons Gig, to the villa, we had two women there cleaning the house, we unpacked the crockery hamper and only found three things broken, a soup plate, a tumbler and a wine glass; Eliza and I washed every thing, dinner set, tea set and glass. There were two stakes put into the ground in front of the house and a bar across from whence hung a large boiler with a fire under it, so that we had plenty of hot water; you would have laughed to see how busy we were in the old hut which is to be our stable this winter; our man Parkes carried the things into the house as we finished them, and before we left I saw them all safely lodged in my pretty store room. I felt very much tired in the evening with my days exertion. Our shed is finished and is [a] very large and useful one, it will be close to the house at the back.

What do you think of rose blankets for a double bed being at Montreal 14 dollars a pair, I wish we had some from England, had I known soon enough I should have asked you to buy us some to have sent in the box we are expecting. Sturges, should you not like to have been with Mr Charles Goodhue last week? he went with an old boat man to the Magog and with flies caught 140 Trout. I wish you Mamma had some of them.

Dunstall Villa Sunday 6th October – At last, dearest Mamma, we are in our house, and though all in the rough feel as comfortable and snug as possible. I have so much to do, an hour seems a minute and I never was so happy before. On Friday evening, it being our last night at Belvedere, I played with all the children from oldest to youngest, Mrs Felton & Miss Mow into the bargain, at all the games I could think of, we had a regular romp and they were all delighted. I think Mrs Felton enjoyed it more than any of us, "All the Muffties" is the favourite game.

On Saturday I parted from my kind friends and Mr Henry drove Eliza and me to Sherbrooke in the Waggon as I had many household things to buy. I also called on Mrs Hale, if you remember I told you she is the daughter of Judge Boen [Bowen]. She, her husband, and two children are to live all the Winter in Sherbrooke and will buy some farm in the neighbourhood in the Spring, they are great friends with the Wilsons. Mr Hale's sister, Lady Dundas, lived near Doctor Wilson before he left Yorkshire and sent out letters to her brother to recommend him to his notice; they mean to purchase land near to each other, Mrs Hale is very young and rather pretty. It was 5 o'clock before we reached Dunstall where Eliza left me with my load of goods promising to come to day to help me, but it is raining and I do not expect her.

That excellent woman, Mrs Felton, sent me two pounds of butter, two loaves of bread and a brace of partridges, knowing I should have nothing in the house, desiring me to let her know if I wanted more, and promising to send me tomorrow a tub to salt my beef in some hops and some yeast. I have been very busy all this morning putting my store room to rights I thought of you dear Mama as I put paper over my jars of raisins, currants, mustard pepper, etc etc and wrote on the top the contents of each. I wish you could see how neat and pretty it looks and could taste some of my rich cream and new milk. We have 110 lbs of beef to salt for the Winter.

I have a servant woman whom I trust will suit us, Sarah Lewison, an Irish woman, her husband was a soldier and she cooked for the Mass [mess], she has lived here some time and has frequently been for months together at Belvedere, she has put out her two children to come to me, Mrs Felton is without a cook and I am sure very much wished to have Sarah but she, never forgetting me and knowing I should want one who could manage alone, as in a short time I shall not be about to do much if any thing, gave her up to me. I give her 5 dollars a month, rather high wages but if she is steady and careful she will be worth that to me, she seems to know what she is about. We are very unfortunate in our furniture which throws us back a good deal; now we come to put up our bedstead we find that notwithstanding the man measured our bedding he has made it a foot too narrow and the sofa a foot too long for the cushions, all this is as stupid as it is provoking.

Monday – Edmund is gone to Sherbrooke to buy some things with Parkes and the rest, he seems quite happy now he is at home and I am sure it will be the study of my life to make him continue so. I have my washing woman here two days Mrs Mountey, she is a nice clean woman and can do any thing, she is cutting out and sewing for me to day, she leaves me tomorrow. You would laugh in England to be called upon to pay people as we do here. I have paid Mrs Mountey half her month in salt pork, rice and soap, this is a mutual convenience for these things are too dear in Sherbrooke for the poor people to be able to buy them, and the higher orders have a winter's stock from Montreal which is much cheaper, so it is better for us to pay in kind than in money.

We have the Ceylon picture over the chimney piece and are anxiously waiting for the basket and caps, how good of you to part with them Mamma!! Give my best love to Charles and Kate, I should much like to see their beautiful baby. Give my love also to Sarah and say when I am more settled I will write to her, indeed you must say every thing proper to all my friends, I cannot mention them separately but they must not think they are forgotten on that account. I am glad Mary Lyon received her letter, I hope Rosa was equally fortunate.

We are more glad every day that we did not attempt to put in any grain this year for we have already more than we can well get through before the Winter, and it would have been more expensive for us to have extra hands for the farm than to buy the little we shall want, the stock of eatables seems tremendous to me that Mrs Felton tells me we must lay in for the winter, I shall get my butter for 7 1/2 a pound. I shall have fifty pounds and I have a nice covered tub to put it in. We give 6 dollars a ton for our hay, 1/2 dollar a bushel for carrots, a dollar a bushel for onions, 1 a bushel for turnips.

I never told you Eliza Felton has begun the Harp, she has a good ear for music and was very anxious to learn so I offered to teach her, being really glad to make some return for the kindness we received at Belvedere. Eliza will soon play very well, I have written to Grospan to order a Harp for her, I hope he will send a good one, it is a present from her brother. Remember us kindly to Mr Hart Ethelston, I am glad he was amused with my letter. I am afraid they will be more stupid now we are at the Villa for we shall have little variety. Edmund is busy making the carpet, it will improve the room when it is down. I find it is a great comfort having a door out of our sitting room into the bedroom, and when I am ill it will be still more convenient, I can see the nice blazing fire as I lie in bed. Edmund sends his best love with mine to dear Papa, you, and *old Sturges*, love to the Maynes and Birches, I shall like to have the Lichfield letters, I suppose you left them to put into the box, believe me your ever dutiful and ever affect child

Lucy Peel.

Pray never spare your advice, I shall always be delighted to profit by it. Remember me to good Williamson and Maria, I hope I shall see them both when I visit England. I have been busy today rendering suet to make candles, and Charlotte has been brewing for me, she and Eliza are now making some little shirts for me, they are very kind

No 7

[October 1833]

My dearest Mamma

We sent off a letter to you yesterday by Quebec and it is the last you will receive till next spring by that route as the river will be closed. We shall have been a week tomorrow in our house and I already begin to feel more at home, the first few days every thing was so new, housekeeping, and all the duties which fall to the share of a wife, that I was rather puzzled but I now manage very well. You ladies in England who fancy you have a great [*sic*] to see after, do not know what it is to keep house in such a country as this where you must cut and contrive; where perhaps you can only get meat once in three weeks, and where all the workmen you have must be fed three times a day on meat, potatoes and milk, I have now in my house 118 lbs of beautiful Beef which I have salted in a large tub and it is astonishing how fast it disappears; besides this I have 4£ worth of Salt Pork for my winter stock, 40 lbs of suet enclosed for candles and a tub of grease to make my soft soap. My woman servant, though an excellent one for this country, is not like an English cook, and I have to see her do most things, she fortunately makes good bread. Edmund, three men, two yokes of oxen and a plough were all yesterday ploughing up the ground in front of the house which is to be the garden, he will fence it this fall and we have indeed no time to lose for last night there was such a frost, a man who is putting on the Clap boards and steps in a shanty close to the house was frozen in bed.

You would be amused to see our cow coming of her own good will morning and evening to be milked, there is always some salt for her at the house and this is the inducement, we have got in 15 bushels of potatoes and shall have thirty in all, if last nights frost has not killed them. Mr Felton has promised to supply me with Turnips. Mrs M'Curdy,[52] a neighbour of ours who with her daughter cleaned our house after the plasterers, filled our two straw-beds, finding the straw, brought me a basket of apples yesterday, and said if I had any old gown to let her have she should like it better than money for what she had done, so I gave her my very old *brown silk* which had yellow spots over it from the damp at sea, I thought of course I should have to give her some money besides, but however it was so much more than she expected, that she said she must send me something in return, so I had the next morning 1 lb of nice fresh butter & two fresh eggs and four cabbages; I think I got my work done very cheaply, I wish I had brought out some more old things, for articles of dress are so dear here, that an old gown is much thought of I assure you.

I am going to amuse you by copying a bill sent to Edmund by a man from whom we have bought furniture, it will do for your Album. "E. *Peall* Esquire *Bot* of R B Killogg 1 Chest of *drawes* 2£. 1 *Beadstead* and *Curtings* 3£. 5s. The *above* amount for E. Peall Esquire. Sir. the *bead wayes* 41 poundes at 1s/3d wash *bowl* and *your* 6s/3d. *Cloas* horse 10s." Is not this a perfect pattern of good spelling? Mr Killogg is a Yankee.

Monday – Yesterday we had for dinner two of our nice little chickens and a piece of your beautiful ham, dearest Mamma you cannot think how much we enjoyed it, for all the hams and bacons are so smoked in this country, Edmund greatly dislikes, I cannot eat them; the Beef we bought is very good, we have had a small piece of it, we have begun upon our beer and it is good. I have window curtains up and my arm chair decked in its cushions, Oh that we could have you to sit in it by our blazing fire, dear Papa, too, who would amuse himself placing the wood nicely on the hearth; and Sturges to laugh with us at the Yankees. We have bought some very good port wine at 4s. a gallon, what do you think of this? but I assure you the low price does not induce either of us to take much, we are very moderate and economical as 'tis fit we should be.

Thursday 17th – On Sunday last my servant Sarah's little boy was taken so ill that they sent her word she must go home, I of course was obliged to consent, however it was so wet all day she could not go, and on Monday morning when I got up, to my great surprise, she was off without waiting to see me and had left every kitchen utensil dirty and I had not half a pound of bread in the house. Ellen M'Ready, whom I had spoken to, to come during Sarah's absence was in the kitchen, she is a nice, steady, clean, civil, well brought up girl of fifteen, willing to do any thing but quite ignorant about cooking or waiting; I could have sat down and cried but wisely thinking that would make bad, worse, I was in the kitchen all day, watched Ellen clean every thing and put the things in their proper places, cooked the men's dinner, boiled my hops and made my barm of them and then prepared our dinner. You may imagine I was much tired at night but I could not afford even then to be quiet, but plied my needle till bed time, and the last thing put the barm by the stove to rise till morning, I am sure could you see us you would say we earn our daily bread.

On Tuesday I sifted my flour, put the barm to it which has risen beautifully, put in a little salt, got my little *kitchen* before the open fire in the dining room, worked up my bread, and it rose and looked as light as possible, I then baked it in the kitchen, and had Williamson seen the two pretty loaves when they were finished she would have been proud of her pupil, my dear husband praised my handy work at dinner so I was amply repaid had it been double the labour.

Eliza Felton called on her way home from Sherbrooke and brought me dear Sarajane's and Mr Maynes' letters which Mr Atkinson had given her brother at Quebec. I shall write and thank them both for all their affection and I fear unmerited praises. Yesterday Eliza and Charlotte came and sat working several hours for me, and seeing I have more than I can well finish in time they would take some home with them, they have promised to bring it back on Saturday. Edmund was fully employed last night making our bedroom carpet, he finished it; he has also made the rod for my window curtain and is this morning making some rods for the bed curtains. I do not know what I should do if I had not a husband able and willing to assist me.[53] Sturges, Parkes has shot me three partridges and a hare, we have the birds to day in a pie; when I went into the kitchen the night they were killed, I saw Parkes with an apron on very busy skinning the hare and cleaning it, he did it very well save that he cut off the head, the best part I think.

18 – The frost and slight snow we had a few days ago have disappeared, and yesterday was exceedingly warm, I took a stroll with Edmund on our beautiful rock; at night Edmund put up the rods for my bedcurtains and there came on a dreadful storm of thunder, lightening and rain, however it is quite fine this morning. Mr Henry has just called to bring me our Albion, the paper we take, he and a dancing master and two ladies were kept at Mr Charles Felton's[54] in Sherbrooke till two o'clock this morning on account of the rain.

I have made another batch of good bread, but have nearly burned my face to pieces, watching at a large round fire. Sarah is not come back and I care not if I do not see her again, Ellen goes on so well and her wages would suit our pocket much better than Sarah's. Haskell, the carpenter who finished our house, came in this morning to receive his money.[55] Edmund brought him into the *room* where I was, and, to give you an example of Yankee equality and impudence, instead of standing till he was paid, he drew a chair to the fire, sat down, began to hawk and spit, and concluded with asking me to play a tune on the Harp, I looked very savage and felt more so, and soon leaving the room remained away till Mr Haskell took his departure.

Teusday 22nd – Last Saturday Eliza and Fanny came; the former played the Harp and the latter used her needle in my service. Edmund was employed all day painting the chimney piece, doors and skirting board of the drawing room, he had not finished till 11 at night; on Sunday Mr Henry and Edward Felton came to breakfast, they seemed to enjoy the English ham, we returned with them to Belvedere and spent the day, it was as pleasing as it was flattering to see the pleasure expressed at our presence by kind words and smiling faces, the children all crowded round me and formed a circle near me the whole day, they sent us home in the evening.

Yesterday Mrs Felton, Mr Henry, Mr Felton and Major Colclough called, so we were quite gay, I should not like so many people every day for I really have not time to attend to them. My servant Sarah is not coming again, I have engaged Ellen M'Ready for two dollars a month, I am writing to dear Sarah Jane and Mr Mayne by the same post which takes this. I hope they will receive their letter this time. I begin to think the box will never arrive. Parkes killed one of our lambs yesterday, very early, it is only 36 lbs, I wish we could send you some of it, should you not like to eat meat off our land?

Saturday 26th – On Wednesday Mr Felton came on horseback and took back before him half our lamb. He said six years ago he would have willingly gone 12 miles for such meat. On Thursday Eliza, Maria and dear little Narbon came to see me, he went with me into the store room and seeing some unbaked pie crust asked if I would let him have it, I told him it was not baked he then went to the bread and asked if that was baked and when I said yes he looked at me saying "then somebody might give me a piece."

Yesterday Mr Henry called and brought us a note from Mr William Felton, he wrote to tell us that our box is now in the Custom house at

Quebec and as soon as I send him word the contents, speaking generally, he will forward it to us. I cannot express how much I am pleased to hear it is at last arrived but I shall not keep this letter till I see it, for Mr Felton, who has been all this time confined with his leg, goes to Quebec on Monday so I shall send this and a letter to Lichfield by him.

Last night we began about 6 to put up our bed curtains, we have been waiting till now for small nails, we had not finished it till 12, you may fancy with what pride we looked at it, every stitch being put in by our own hands. I wish you could see how pretty it looks, whenever I finish any thing I always end by saying Oh! that dear Mamma could see it. We went up our hill the other day where our sugary is and Edmund pulled up 50 young birch trees which we carried home and planted round the fence of the garden. I thought if you had been more active you would have enjoyed the work, it would remind you of the time when you planted the trees at Dunstall Cottage but Dunstall Villa is a more romantic place than that. I bought a quarter of nice beef yesterday, Parkes has cut it up, it is 70 lbs and I paid 14s. for it, 4 cents a lb, ten cents make sixpence. I must tell you I have risen in rank since I left England, I am called Lady Peel by some of the lower orders; Mrs Felton the same; she had a letter the other day directed Lady Felton. I hope I shall have a letter from Sturges in the box. Oh! that I had his talent for drawing, I could amuse you greatly with different things. Send our best love to Church Bank the same to Papa, Sturges and you, kind regards to all friends who ask after us believe me your affect child

Lucy Peel

Tell Williamson and Maria I am sure the young Canadian will grow double quick time when it wears their presents, they are very good to think so much about me.

Book Two

My dear Mr Mayne

Your affectionate and gratifying letter arrived at Dunstall Villa on the 15th of October just 3 months and 5 days after the date it bears; how shall I thank you for all your expressions of praise and kindness? So flattering to my vanity, so fondly cherished in my heart; which beats with pleasure or throbs with pain as I read the different accounts from England of the happiness or suffering, my dear relatives there alternately experience. I shall not now enter upon the wide field of gratitude, for would it not be endless to one who was the guide and gentle counsellor of our family, when the temptations and dangers of riches smiled on every side? and its steady friend and cheerful consoler when comparative poverty and sorrow surrounded it? however one of this family is now rewarding for the vexation the rest may have caused you, our dear Sarah Jane your companion in health and pleasure, your tender nurse in pain and sickness, is destined to pay off this heavy debt, and does she not amply do it. Yes! I hear you say a thousand fold. I think Mamma ought to consider herself a most fortunate woman in marrying her daughters to four such men as you, Mr Peel, William Birch, and Charles Oldershaw, to be sure we are all poor in the worldly acceptation of the word, but we are rich in happiness, our means are small and the wants of sensible people are simple; 'tis only a vitiated taste makes them otherwise. I sigh – not for a more splendid lot and I dare say my three sisters will say the same.

I thank you for your present, be it what it may, it is evidently a pair of something, the rest is left to conjecture. The young stranger shall early be taught to love the kind friend, who has so early thought of it, and it will be my delightful and interesting study to bring it up, should its life be spared, so that you and all my family may be proud of their Canadian relation. I often wish you could see my excellent husband, how much you would admire his never ceasing industry, his hand is ever ready to do all in his power either on the land or in the house, and though some people may be of a different opinion I am sure you will agree with me in thinking that a man may dig in the fields without being a clown, be his wife's lady's maid without being effeminate and make his own coat without looking like a tailor, as for myself I never felt so deserving of the love of my relatives as I do now, for I was not till now so useful or so active, we

---

Notes to this section start on p. 219.

know not what we are equal to till tried, we are now completely thrown upon our own resources, and I feel convinced that if we do not succeed, that idleness or extravagance will not be the fault.

Our house has been so long in being built and the season so short, that we have not time this year to do any thing to the land except plough-ing a little for next year's crop. We have had beautiful open weather the last week but are told we may now expect snow any day. I think you would be much amused seeing Edmund working away at the stumps and large stones, when I am tired with walking I sit down and watch him, he pulled up two yesterday and many great stones; we have had a bonfire the last two days of shavings and cedar stumps; which sent forth a delightful perfume round our Villa, it is a pity we cannot send some of these trees to England instead of destroying them. The Indian corn has failed this year. Mr Felton's was all rusted. I do not think we shall ever attempt much of it. If we had a thousand pounds to spare we could make this place beautiful, and as it is I would not change it for any I have seen on this side the Atlantic; the only inconvenience is being so far from either Montreal or Quebec, but we have many other advantages which compensate for this, and one very great one, less temptation to spend our money. Edmund sends his kind regards and best thanks for all your kind offers of advice and assistance. I assure you that you only do him justice when you say that you think he will not undertake any thing without rea-sonable hopes of success.

Thursday 31st – On Teusday last we received Mama's nice long journal No 4. She does not give very good accounts of you, pray take care of yourself, how busy and gay Mama is, she is grown quite young again now all her daughters are married, it is delightful to hear she is so com-fortable and happy, and has so many young friends ready to attend upon her but who can help loving that knows her, I shall now have no more fears about her. We shall receive our box next Teusday but I shall send this off before then as I know you and Sarah Jane will like to have it. I feel quite anxious for Teusday to come that I may see my little presents and read my letters from so many dear friends. I fear winter is setting in, we have had snow on the ground several inches deep for several days and frosts at nights; it is now snowing a little, but frost and snow are far before a *melting sun*, *bugs* and Mosquitos; our house is very warm and I do not dread the winter in the least; I have just made an excellent batch of bread, how proud should I be if I could send you one of the beautiful little loaves.

Believe me ever
your affect. sister
Lucy Peel

To Mrs Mayne

My dearest Sarah Jane.

You will I hope like the march I composed before I left our kind friends and have written out for you; it is not executed in an elegant style, but I have done my best, and it will I trust reach you unimpaired by the briny main. Your letter to me replete with expressions of affection and kind wishes, is duly appreciated by your far distant sister, how good of you to devote time which I know is precious to you, in working for me, I shall value the little robe, contrived by your head, and made by your industrious fingers more than the most costly gift you could have purchased because I flatter myself almost every stitch you plied you thought of me and mine. I am glad I did not know how ill you were after leaving Mount Cottage till all danger was over, distance always magnifies illness, and I should have fancied a thousand melancholy things, it must have been a trial to part with Mini, but you would know she was well taken care of at Fisherwick. Give my love to the dear child, I dare say she will be a woman when I see her again, and she will not remember me, but I know you will teach her to love Aunt Peel.

I dont know how you would like the housekeeping in this country, I begin now to manage pretty well, but it is endless trouble. I have a nice girl, very young, Irish but tall and lanky as a Yankee, she walks quite upright with her elbows tucked close to her sides, and waddles away; none of the servants in this country wear caps, and Mrs Felton said I should not be able to make them, however mine is preparing some and I made my first woman Sarah use them, I have no idea of giving way to such people. I taught one Yankee manners this morning, he came to the front door, and he was not attended to until he went to the back, I think they will not take any liberties here, and if every one would act as we do, they would soon know their place. I really believe all they do is from sheer ignorance, without any wish to offend, for they are kind hearted people and the lower orders will lodge and board travellers from the old country, without wishing for any thing in return, they have also another

rather extraordinary trait in their characters, they will take their neighbours children if they wish to part with them, bring them up and give
them a cow, and feather bed when they marry.

We mean to kill our pig this next month, he is a rusty gentleman, and
it took three men to catch him the other day and fasten him up, he is so
wild he would never get fat at liberty, though fed with hot food twice a
day, we have put him in the shanty, a kind of wooden tent, and he grunts
away sticking up his bristles, looking most provokingly thin, the people
here never kill their pigs till after Christmas.

Sunday – Mrs Goodhue[1] called yesterday and sat some time, she is a
pleasing kind hearted woman, she brought me a basket of cranberries and
a glass of jelly, and said she would endeavour to persuade my husband to
purchase them; I do believe that for ready money they would some of
them sell their last coat. We have now made our lot of land complete, by
buying 50 acres more adjoining ours and thus securing ourselves from
troublesome neighbours.[2] Our estate consists of 200 acres part of it excellent and rich land; our pretty villa is the most romantic part, where comfort, plenty, and harmony, reigns; and kind friends at hand to occasionally
enliven the scene, we could not in England rent such a place, for the
money the whole has cost us to make it our own for ever, and as the land
company of this Lower Country will certainly make large purchases here
next year and consequently bring numbers of emigrants to the Townships, our place will become more valuable every year.[3]

The more I see and think, the more I am convinced that a settlement
in this country if managed with prudence, is the most judicious and comfortable plan we could adopt, and some years hence I am much mistaken
if many who now perhaps consider us amongst savages, will not gladly
follow our example, the wise will make up their minds quickly for as the
demand of land increases, its price will rise accordingly, and I think even
next year will make a great difference, I consider myself amongst the
most fortunate of emigrants, and in a few years when more skilled in our
various pursuits we shall be as able, as we are now willing, to assist those
that may follow our steps.

Edmund is keeping the most exact account of what our house has cost
building, this may be a great assistance to others, for I am sure none can
have an idea of the trouble and expence, there are so many after things
which are not at first considered, you read in books that a house may be
built for £80 with five or six rooms below and others above, but these
authors should add that this is only the carpenter's work, then there is
cutting the timber, drawing it from the woods, the chimneys, brick

boards of which we had more than 40 thousand feet many pine at 12 dollars a thousand. Clap boards for the outside, shingles for the roof plastering lime etc etc, besides a shed to put your fuel in for the winter and a stable for cattle, a barn for hay. I am glad we did not know all our difficulties before we came out for it might have been the means of our remaining in England, and now the thing is over, which we have endured appears nothing and we have double pride in having surmounted so much.

When you have an opportunity give any kindest regards to my friends at Elford, Upfield, and Fisherwick. Edith shall have a letter from me this Winter as you think it will please her. I am sure I wish all my old friends to remember me with affection, of course my inestimable husband is first, last, and every thing to me, but I have abundance of love left for those who care about it, and there is no fear of me forgetting any one I have ever cared for. Give my affectionate love to Rosa and her family, I hope she has written to me in the box, may you all prosper and be as happy as

your very affect. sister
Lucy Peel –

Edmund sends his best wishes and kind regards he is not fond of writing and says I tell you every thing. We drink your health with that of other friends every day after dinner in a bumper of excellent port wine at 4 shillings a gallon. Kiss dear little Mini for me. Tell Mama we pay 2^s 1^d for all letters from England, 1.11^d for those we send to England by New York, and 9^d for those we send by Quebec –

No 8

Dunstall Villa   Oct 31-1833

My dearest Mamma.

I sent off a letter to Sarajane this morning, and I had your long one on Tuesday. My house keeping goes on very well, I like my servant Ellen, she learns every thing very quickly. Edmund is just gone out with his Gun to shoot me some Game, I wish you dear Sturges, were here to accompany him, should you not like to come and shoot the Deer this winter.

$Nov^{ber}3^d$ – Yesterday Eliza and Charlotte Felton came about twelve and stayed working for me till four, they took some home to finish, they wanted us very much to go to Bellvedere to day and would send for us, but I declined for I am much better quiet at home, particularly as I have not been quite well the last few days. Edmund is the most attentive and patient of creatures when any thing is the matter, and I am sure it must be very trying to him to be disturbed at night after working hard all day as he does, I am happy to say that the snow has all taken its departure and the sun is now shining cheerfully. I expect Mrs Felton to call, she says she will come if she even have to walk. We have the book shelves up in the drawing room which you gave me, they look very pretty, the Ceylon picture hangs over the chimney piece. Oh that I had you in the red case, dear Sturges will you send it me the first opportunity? I promise to return it to you when you cannot see Mamma every day as you do now, think what a pleasure it would be to me to have it.

6th – Fancy my disappointment dear Mamma, yesterday we sent the cart and Oxen to Sherbrooke for the box and a quarter of beef, the Stage was so full the coachman was obliged to leave several boxes behind at Shipton thirty miles from here and ours amongst the number. Parkes told him to be *Sartain* sure to bring it on friday and I must wait as patiently as I can. The Cow too, or the creature as they call it, was not killed, so our team came back empty. Eliza & Charlotte Felton walked here yesterday and staid till four. Edmund has made me a side board, he sets his hand to anything.

Friday – another trial for my patience – no box, and the stage driver says it is not at Shipton. I know it has been more than a fortnight at Quebec. We have now had several fine days, I walked with Edmund part of the way to Sherbrooke yesterday and enjoyed it exceedingly, but was rather tired. Mr. Theney [Henry] and the four eldest girls called this morning on their way home from Sherbrooke where they walked yesterday and remained all night, they had quite a party at Mr. Kimballs, the Lawyers, Mr. and Mrs. Hale, and Doctor Wilson's daughters were there, they played at speculation. Give our best love to dear papa and tell him we have bought a handsome Leicestershire Ram from Mr Felton. Edmund has made a dressing table to day for the spare room, I assure you he saves us many dollars by being so industrious.

10th – yesterday was so warm we were obliged to let out the fire and open the windows. Parkes went with the team for some Potatos, he left here about eleven in the morning and had to go about 5 miles, in the evening it poured with rain, seven, eight, nine, ten oclock came and no Parkes, so we gave him up for the night, however soon after 11, as we were preparing for bed he arrived, he found the place much farther than he expected and returning the oxen were so tired having a heavy cart and twelve bushels of potatoes, they lay down, our man turned back to a house on this side [of] Sherbrooke to borrow some cattle, but the owner refused to lend *them* so he had to coax one oxen up which he did with some trouble, but after going a short distance they lay down again and were nearly lost in the wood, Parkes called at another farmers who was more civil and said he might have his cattle if he could find them, which he did, and putting them before ours at last reached home, looking as good tempered as possible, and this morning he has cut me up 160 lbs of Beef for salting, we shall kill our pig as soon as the box arrives. I must tell Sturges the melancholy fate of my poor fowls, the handsome cock was found dead in the field, the best hen and her four fine chickens were eaten the other night by a fox, and the last hen looks so dejected I shall have her shot and stewed for soup. Am I not unfortunate?

11th – So warm to day it is quite extraordinary, we have all the doors open and the blinds down to keep out the sun; Edmund and Parkes are busy ploughing the garden with their coats off.

13th – Mrs Felton, Mr Henry and three of the girls called yesterday in [*sic*] their way to Sherbrooke, Octavia remained with me till they returned, she is a nice child of nine years old. To day is dear Sarajane's birth day, we are keeping it. Eliza and Charlotte Felton come to dine and stay all night, we shall drink her health in bumpers after dinner.

17th – Eliza & Charlotte left me on friday, it was a beautiful day and when they were gone, I walked with Edmund to a piece of ground that he is clearing on one side of the house, he had a bonfire and I sat by it some time, we had thunder several times and the next morning the ground was covered with snow, and to day much remains, is it not a strange climate? Our beer was excellent to the last, I hope you all like it as well as we do. Fat Geese are now selling at 15^d a piece, I have sent for one to day. No box yet, I begin to dispair about it. Edmund made me a music stool yesterday, we stuffed the top with wool, and covered it to the ground with print, the same as our curtains. Our Pig is a constant plague to us, no cord, no wooden wall even, will keep him fast many hours, he knocked down the side of the Shanty the other night.

19th – Snow – Snow – Mr. Henry has brought me a letter from England. Thank you dear Sarajane, Rosa, William, and darling Sturges for your agreeable additions, how gay you all appear to be to us quiet people, it always raises my spirits many degrees to read your interesting and delightful letters and to hear how much you think of us. Mr. E. Ethelstan overrates my head piece, you know I never had any talent for figures. I am not surprised that our brother Johnathan wishes us back, he is so much attached to Edmund, but as you say dear Mamma not at present. I really shall like to see more of this country before I return to England, besides it is useless thinking of an event which is so far distant.

21st – Winter is really setting in, it is cold but the sky as clear as possible, the sun shines beautifully but has not heat enough to melt the long thick Icicles which hang from our Veranda, and by moonlight have a splendid appearance. I am having a stone oven built we find it so very troublesome baking by the open fire only two loaves at a time. Tell Rosa I took her lecture as it is meant in kindness, but it came too late to be of use. Edmund is painting the dining room, I wish you could see our pretty rooms.

I have thought of dear Papa the two last mornings, we have had some beautiful cold pork for breakfast and we wish for him to partake of it. Edmund is as fond of it as my good parent and as he cuts piece after piece to make all straight, he says this is the way Mr Meek does. My husband has began his Flannel waistcoats this morning and he finds it rather ticklish but very comfortable & warm, he had one & I am making him two more, the one I have finished fits well, I am becoming quite expert at cutting out, I dare say you remember the trouble I gave you by being so helpless that way. Eliza & Charlotte Felton and Mr Henry have just called in the sleigh covered with fur, & bells to their horses necks, that looked so nice and comfortable, they are coming soon to take me a drive if I keep pretty well.

Sunday 24th – A deep snow and yet it was so warm yesterday we had scarcely any fire and the hall door was open, to day it is not cold but rather gloomy looking. I hope you will all remember to drink my health tomorrow, what a difference one short year has made in my fate, we shall be quite alone but not lonely, at present we are not tired of each others society and I trust we never may, for something must be wrong at home when you have to look abroad for happiness.

25th – Yesterday about 11 Mrs Felton, Mrs Henry, Eliza, Charlotte, Fanny, Maria, and Isabella came in a Cutter and a Sleigh, they would make us return with them to dinner so we went and remained till six when Eliza & Charlotte brought us home in the Cutter, it was quite warm and I enjoyed my ride. I wished you could all have seen us flying through the snow in the midst of the woods. I am sure Sturges would have liked to have been with us, there are three sorts of snow carriages, Sleighs which are low have round bodies; sometimes one, sometimes two seats and drawn by one horse. Carrioles also low, but two horses and two seats, Cutters higher, larger, square bodies, two seats, two horses. Edmund has made me two nice boxes for my hams and bacon, the hams I am curing from Rosa's receipt, our pig was killed on Monday.

To day the 29th is beautiful, I wish you could be here and see the clear heavens and bright sun shining upon the snow & icicles. Eliza Felton and Norton [Narbon?] came last Wednesday to see me, I taught Eliza to raise Pork pies, we made seven, I sent two to Bellevedere, they are excellent, I wish Papa could have one for his breakfast, Eliza brought me a very pretty little robe that she has made for me & I have just finished one which if you could see I think you would admire and praise my ingenuity.

Yesterday we had 109 lbs of beef put into a box also a goose and some Pork to keep fresh for the Winter, we put on no salt but first a layer of meat then one of snow, so on till the box is full, this is kept out of doors and freezes. Yesterday Mr Henry and two of the girls called in the Cutter and took me down to Sherbrooke. I called upon Mrs Colclough and Mrs Fletcher, the last lady I found very unwell sitting in her night cap, she appeared much pleased to see me, kissed me and gave me some excellent bread and butter and some delicious cordial of which she said she had only two bottles and kept for particular occasions, she put it away as soon as I had finished saying, "I expect three or four more here presently and I do not mean to give this to every one," soon after the girls called and we returned home. Sleighs full of eatables, poultry, meat, etc. are now coming in from all quarters to be sold for winter stock. We bought a fine fat sheep for £1 6^d what do you say to that dear Papa? geese 15^d each; I was introduced at Sherbrooke to our new clergyman Mr. Doolittle,[4] he is a Yankee but apparently not a vulgar one, there is service to day, the Feltons offered to take me to church but I thought I was better at home.

Wednesday 4th – No box but we have heard it is on the road between this and Quebec so we shall I dare say receive it on Friday, tomorrow is post day so I shall send off this letter as I am sure you will be anxious to hear as it is more than a month since I wrote. I had your and S. Jane's letter on Tuesday, the accounts of yourself dearest Mamma are delightful. I hope my next letter will be finished by Edmund to tell you that you are GrandMamma to a little Canadian. In the Spring we have to build a barn which though only of wood will cost more than £50 sterling and then we have to fence the land. I am glad Johnathan likes our letters and wish he could see how happy and comfortable we are. Two Sleighs came from Bellevedere to day full of kind friends to take me a drive. I went home with them, sat a few hours and Mrs Felton brought me back to the Villa. They come again tomorrow and I shall go with them to take this letter to the post office and call upon Mrs Wilson. Old M'Ready came here to day and touching his hat to Edmund said "Sir I have a proposal to make, you have no horse, I have and when Mrs Peel is taken ill if you will send over to me, I will ride for the doctor though it be in the middle of the night." I need scarcely say his kind offer was thankfully accepted, his wife will come to nurse me. I am sure I shall have good attendance so do not be uneasy about me. Open your next letter carefully for should the baby be born I shall enclose some of its hair. Edmund unites with me in love to you, Papa & Old Sturges. Edmund has finished half the Verandah to day, braiding with wide planks & ribbons, it looks very nice & has saved us 12 dollars – believe me

Your attached child
L. Peel

No 9

Dunstall Villa,
December 6th 1833

My dearest Mamma

Mrs. Felton and Eliza called to take me to Sherbrooke yesterday, but I was too unwell to go, I was up [a] great part of the night. I feel pretty well to day, I sent your letter by Mrs. Felton to the Office, I hope it will have a quick passage, or you will be anxious about us. My dear Sturges, in your rumbles through the romantic streets of Manchester have you ever had the good fortune to meet the *Man with the [blank space]*, he is now on his travels in England, he says he has seen the glorious sun rise in Persia, and sink like the scarlet lillies; In Greece like the ball on St Pauls newly gilded; In Arabia like a copper tea kettle, and at the North Pole like a Globe of silver. You will know the Man with *the* [blank space] from his being dressed in *Canvas*, look out for him and ask your friends if they have seen him.

8th – I was so ill on friday night that Mr Barnard was sent for but I got better in a few hours. I am tolerably well to day. You would have laughed to have seen our Man Parkes on friday night, he did not go to bed again after getting up but lighted his lanthern and chopped wood all night. Mrs Felton has been to see me to day and is gone on to Sherbrooke to see if she can prevail on old Mrs Fletcher to part with Mrs Salt to come to me for a few days, I hope she will, for I find Mrs M'Reidy a poor creature, how you would love your kind, and excellent Son in Law did you see his attentions to me, he supported my body when in pain and cheered my spirits, I would suffer ten times as much for such a husband. Mrs M'Reidy said, "Well Mrs Peel, you have something like a husband how kind he is to you!" Sturges how amused you would be to hear my servant Ellen talk, she said to me, Ma'am it *frized* so last night that the barme has not *ris*. And then she says she never *sawed* a thing. I shall try to teach her better.

9th – I was ill again last night but am going about this morning, and am busy brewing, I want to keep well till Wednesday that I may see my beer finished, and read my letters, for surely the box will come by the stage tomorrow.

10th – You will be glad to hear that I have Mrs Salt here, she is a most kind attentive nurse and takes great care of me. I was ill again last night, Mr Barnard was sent for. I disappointed them all, it is very tiresome for all parties but worse for me. Mrs Salt amused us last night with a most romantic account of her first year in Canada, seventeen years ago, few women would have remained to suffer as she did, she was often left whilst her husband and Sons went to the different Villages, in the woods by herself in a Camp and nothing but a fire to protect her from the Wolves and Bears; and when her wooden house was built, she during the absence of her Male protectors was visited by nine Indians who remained all night and slept in the same room separated from her only by a blanket, each having a scalping knife and a Tomahawk, however they departed in peace the next morning having bartered sugar for flour. Another time whilst living with Mrs Felton at Bellevedere, she was on horseback taking a basket with a couple of live fowls in it, a Hawk flew down and pecked at them and tried to carry them off.

12th – Ill again last night, had Mr Barnard sent for again. I have been very unwell all to day, it is hard work dearest Mamma. Mrs Fletcher has sent up twice to inquire after me, the kind old Lady has sent me Oatmeal and desires I will ask for anything I want and be sure to inform her when all is over. Mrs Hale has also sent with similar offers, so you see dear Mamma what kind and attentive friends I have. Edmund tells me if I were a Duchess I could not be made more of. Mrs Felton has refused to go and meet her husband at Three Rivers entirely on my account. She is indeed an invaluable friend. Do write to Caroline Loaden as soon as you receive this to tell her the news for I am sure she will like to hear about me.

16th – Since I last wrote I have not been many minutes free from pain, and at times my spirits begin to fail me I suffer so much, Mr Barnard has been five times, still I disappoint them. Yesterday I was never out of bed, Mrs Felton was here all night, she slept upon the Sofa and my dear husband was up with me most of the night – Mr & Mrs Hale called on Saturday, I was up and being pretty well at the time, saw them, they were very pleasant. Cap^r. and Mrs Coclough have been to enquire after me to day, I did not see them. Mr Felton is coming home tomorrow, surely he will bring our box. Mrs Felton twice after seven oclock in the evening has entered her open Sleigh and driven to the Villa to see how I was going on, how few ladies in England would think of even turning out on a cold winter night and a deep snow, in a close carriage on such an occasion.

A tale for Sturges – Mrs Salts husband some time ago went out to chop wood, the Axe slipped and cut off his toe at the first joint. Judge Fletcher persuaded him that if he had it Sewed on it would grow. Mr Salt could not get any one to perform this simple act of kindness, so he took a needle and thread and did it himself, however the joint would not unite and the poor old man was obliged to have it taken off again. I should like to keep up till after tomorrow that I may read my letters and enjoy opening the box.

18th – Written by Mr Peel – To day Lucy is much better and in higher spirits. At last the long looked for box is arrived, Mr Felton found it at Three Rivers where it had been left by neglect. Lucy and I, send you many many thanks for your nice presents.

19th – It is with great pleasure I have to announce the birth, not of a Son and Heir to Dunstall Villa, but of a little girl, both Lucy and myself wished for the former yet still feel thankful, it was a long severe and painful illness – and at one time very critical. Fortunately the Doctor was a very clever man. I was present all the time to support Lucy and I was much distressed to witness her agonies. I thought it the proper place for a husband at such a moment, considering it nothing more than false delicacy which would make a man absent himself at a time when his presence and support are most required, it is a fearful thing to see a woman in her pain, I could not have believed it possible they had suffered so much, at times I felt quite distracted, as soon as the child was born I staggered into an adjoining room and cried like a child until I again saw Lucy smiling and free from pain, her face last seen was distorted with pain, the impression made on me will never be forgotten.

20th – Lucy is very well but weak, the Doctor has just called, he appears quite satisfied and says she is doing very well, but keeps her on low diet. The baby is thought a fine large child, something like me Lucy thinks, but I cannot see the likeness, it has light hair and large blue eyes; I assure you I feel quite proud of it being every thing the fondest wishes a father could desire. I hasten to conclude that Mr Henry may take this to Montreal, I expect him every minute to call, give my best and kind respects to Mr Meek and Sturges, and believe me dearest Mother to remain yr affec[t]

Son Edmund Peel.

Enclosed you will receive some of the childs hair, it's name, by Lucy's desire is to be Celia, quite romantic and novel, at least, in the Peel family. Lucy wishes my brother Johnathan to be Godfather.

To Miss Edith Bourne
Nov[r] 8th 1833.

My dear Edith

I shall have great pleasure in amusing you to the extent of my ability with some of our proceedings in this wild, grand, and new country, where I shall most likely, pass the greater part of my life, and if all my friends in England are as happy and comfortable as I am, they can have no reason to complain. I think could some of my young friends see my house and the beautiful view from our noble rock they would envy me the possession of such a mansion and still more envy me the possession of its excellent and unequalled owner, the best & kindest of husbands. I am sure you would like to ramble with us over our rude and romantic *Estate*, the greater part as nature formed it, with here and there, such stones as would even defy the power of Sampson to dislodge from their deep, snug, and mossy bed; and large stumps of trees which have been cut down, gradually and slowly mouldering away, and enriching the earth as they scatter themselves around.

We have two *Sugaries* and intend this winter to try our skill in making sugar. This is a country where the active and industrious must prosper, the idle starve; there is on every side endless room for improvement and even our small farm would take thousands to make it look anything like an English Estate; Mr Peel and I, think it is this very thing which makes it interesting, for every little change is the effect of our heads and hands, every step it advances in cultivation, a proof of our care and industry; the worst is, that one man's life is too transient to receive much benefit from his labour, for after all he can only put things in training for those who follow; we sow, what another generation will reap, but when we consider

Scene on the St. Francis River near Sherbrooke. This scene, like the others depicted by Bartlett, minimizes the settlement of the region, as does Lucy's journal. Source: W. H. Bartlett, *Canadian Scenery Illustrated* (London, 1842). Bishop's University Archives, FC 72.W5.

that those most likely, who are near and dear to us will be the gainers, we proceed cheerfully for our amusement and their advantage.

My housekeeping is a constant source of occupation to me, and I find that I daily improve in this art on which our comfort so much depends, but I must confess I am more interested in what my husband is doing either on the land, or in the carpenters line, for he passes many hours in a cold day making different little things that are wanted for the house, and which I look at, and use with double pleasure being his handy work. My Harp is not neglected, for I assure you I am not like some women satisfied with gaining the affections of the man I marry, but I wish to retain them as long as I can, for ever if possible, and I am convinced that did the generality of wives think the same and act to that effect, there would be fewer neglected ones.

Our kind neighbours & friends the Feltons often come to see us, their attentions are as undeviating as they are considerate; not an opportunity is lost either to oblige or assist us, and when we were at their house a dozen little hands were ever ready to wait upon me. The reception I have met with from Strangers in a foreign land is as flattering and pleasing as it is uncommon, I fear, that few in my own country would have taken two persons perfectly indifferent to them into their house and treated them as we were treated for five months; scarcely under any circumstances, but particularly when there was an Inn near at which they might have taken up their abode. All the time we were there I never heard one disagreeable word pass between any of the members of this amiable and united family, and I think if there is a house without a *blue chamber* it is Bellevedere.

The Yankees appear to be a cool calculating set, and the lower orders of Irish and English, when they have been a short time in this country are worse than the natives; the only way is to be as distant as possible, I dare say they will think us proud. I hope to have an opportunity of seeing some of the higher orders, I should be sorry to judge of the Americans from those I have at present seen, the few families we know are chiefly English and Irish. To give you an example of the little feeling amongst some of the people, when their young children die they lock them up in a drawer without the tribute of a sigh or tear, till the day they are to be carried to their last home.

Louisa Bourne would be delighted to watch the beautiful little Squirrels running in the woods and hopping from branch to branch, they are very small and I hear are excellent eating. I think some of our acquaintance would please and others amuse you exceedingly, the most eccentric character about here is Judge Fletcher, clever and entertaining, you have only to keep your eye constantly upon & to listen attentively, then he is satisfied and you instructed. His fault is making too much of every thing, and like many eloquent people using six words when two would express what he wishes to say. He is very tall, very stout, and has a corporation, his hair a dingy grey, long and combed back hanging down behind; his hands large, fat, & his fingers inclined towards the wrist, a fat face and three chins, he generally wears a cotton dressing gown with a huge pocket on one side, which is a receptacle for all kinds of things, he never rides out without a man on horseback before him some yards to clear the way and he always carries with him a brace of loaded pistols. Mrs Fletcher is some years his elder, a little woman whose head nearly rests upon her shoulders, it is curious to hear how the Judge speaks of her when she is present. One day speaking of handsome people he pointed to his wife and said, that was a fine woman when I married her rather gone by, but she was a fine woman. He always buys things by the gross he has a gross of flutes, a gross of watches etc etc.

Mrs Felton is a delightful little woman and a second mother to me, she is a native *Mahon*[5] and Speaks English in an interesting manner, she is anxious to have an English governess for her children. Mr Felton is an honorable, a Colonel, has a seat in the upper house and is commissioner of the Crown Lands, for which latter Office he has five hundred a year. He must have been a Man of spirit scarcely equalled to have begun and accomplished all he has. He came to Canada fifteen years ago with his Wife, two children, two brothers, a Mother and three sisters, when for thousands of miles round the then little Village of Sherbrooke which only contained three or four miserable frame houses, not a tree was cut down, he settled his party in the best of these abodes, bought ten thousand acres of land made a road from Sherbrooke five miles through the woods into the country to the Site he had fixed upon for a house, cut down trees till there was space enough to build; erected a large and handsome square Log house which cost him a thousand pounds and which in England would be considered as unique as it is pretty, with a veranda eight feet wide and 83 feet long, merely along the front of the house.

He brought with him from Italy beautiful furniture, doors, window frames, oil paint figure and ornaments of Italian marble, and other things to the amount of four thousand pounds, these were put into a Store at Sherbrooke till wanted. One night the Store was set on fire and burned to the ground, not one thing being saved. Not in the least daunted by what would have disheartened most other Men, Mr Felton consoled himself with thinking that had his furniture not been distroyed it would soon have been all spoiled by the careless and wretched servants of the country, he replaced his loss with neat painted wood furniture from Montreal. When settled in his house he cleared and cultivated a thousand acres of land, which is now repaying him for his trouble, the remainder of his property is still all wood. Our little Estate was his. What surprises me most is, that Mr Felton says he should like to part with Bellevedere, go farther into the woods and begin again.

29th – I am just returned from a walk with Mr Peel, had you been with us dear Edith, you who can so ably use your pen might have sat at your desk when at home more than an hour describing the beauty of the scene, as novel as interesting to a stranger, how largely would you expatiate upon the romantic winding road through the woods, the well beaten down snow forming an agreeable walk, the immense trees on either side bearing on their branches countless shapes of snow, the old stumps crowned with *Bridal* Cakes, the Sun shining gloriously, not a breath of air to be felt, the sky a clear blue, all nature seemingly at rest, not a sleigh is heard for they pass with noisless [*sic*] rapidity leaving you almost doubtful whether it were a reality or a vision which flew before you, what would not my country men give for such weather in England. It invigorates your body, clears your head, cheers your spirits and enlarges your ideas. This is certainly the climate for health.

Tell Mr Charles Bourne the farms and farming in this country would astonish him, the Slash fences composed of entire trees, cut down and raised one upon the other would appear very slovenly to an English eye, we are at present obliged to follow the Yankee fashion to keep out our neighbours cattle & secure our crops, whilst we look about us and form plans for a more lasting and a neater enclosure. The summers are so short the farmer has little time for improving his property; it is all bustle to get his winter stock in his barn before the winter overtakes him, and for more than five months, nothing but chopping can be done so that the land has small chance of being highly cultivated.

Jan 17th – My dear Edith a most important event has taken place since I last wrote, for I am a mother, how much is comprised in that short and endearing name, This being the latest account I have sent to England tell Mamma she will hear from me soon, but I have now little time to write. I wish you could see my little Celia, I am sure you would love her, and indeed you must do so, for my sake. Tell Mamma if she have not letters regularly from me she must conclude they are lost on the passage not that I neglect her, for I do, and shall write once a month, I love her too well to disappoint her . . . ever your affectionate friend –

Lucy Peel –

No 10

January 8th 1834

My dearest Mamma –

It is three weeks to day since my darling little Celia was born, and here I am quite well and strong writing to you. I did indeed for nine days suffer dreadfully and for eight hours before baby entered this world of trials, I suppose few persons have had harder and more severe pains. I am convinced Mamma that no one can form the most distant idea of the agony of child birth but those who have experienced it. Poor Edmund was quite overcome with distress but, perhaps fortunately for him, he had not time to give way to his feelings, he was constantly and actively employed either nursing me or the baby, oh Mamma when I saw him fondling his child and looking so happy that all was safely over, I felt rewarded for everything I had endured. I shall not enter into particulars of my dear husbands unceasing and affectionate attentions to me, my heart is too full, and my pen too feeble, to do justice to them. For a fortnight he never left my bedside for many minutes, he was to me, father, mother, brother, sister, nurse and husband, all these endearing titles comprised in one, am I not fortunate to possess the undivided affections of such a man. I often think I am too happy for it to continue. Celia is the image of her papa, his small mouth, chin and bright blue eyes; every one pronounces her a beauty, and if she be as good as she is pretty I shall be quite satisfied. She is as strong as a child of several months old and sits quite upright, her neck is as stiff as possible her hands are always in motion and wide open, we think she fancies she is playing on the harp.

I am glad to hear Mr Mayne is likely to be at liberty, I am sure he will be better when he has less anxiety. Give my love to Rosa and say I am pleased she suffered so little, what is the name of her baby? My child against hers for a thousand pounds. The accounts from Ceylon are good I hope, you will have them in the spring, how much I should like to see them. My love to Mary Lyon & tell her I am much obliged for what she wrote in Bessy's letter, she knows I like to hear from her; ask her if she will venture across the wide ocean to see how happy I am.

Now let me thank you for the pretty and useful contents of the box, it just came in time for me to enjoy opening it. The little Glass is invaluable, I should not know what to do without it. The tins I admire exceedingly, in short every thing is duly valued. Kate was very kind to think of me, I shall be delighted when Celia is old enough to wear her handsome present and Mr Mayne's pretty shoes. Sarajane what trouble you took to please me, how could you find time to put in so many stitches for your Canadian niece. I think of you and Mini every morning and evening when I attend upon my baby, I dare not trust any Servant here to wash and dress her. Tell Mary Jane and Louisa their notes gratified me much, and I shall take great care of Mary Jane's purse which has been admired by all the Miss Feltons. Mr & Mrs Felton, Eliza & Charlotte are gone to Quebec for a month, they are to be in the midst of gaiety.

12th – I have been out riding and walking several times since I last wrote, my dear baby improves daily, Oh that you could see her. Maria Felton has been staying a few days here, she came to nurse Celia. We bought two Cod-fish 25 lb at 3^d, we have had part of one and it is excellent, they were so hard frozen we were obliged to saw them through. Mr & Mrs Hale called the other day. I was out walking. It is now getting very cold but we are warmer in the house than I ever was in England during winter, we have a large stove in the passage close to our bed room door which we begin to feel very comfortable, the wall is constantly kept warm. I was at Sherbrooke yesterday, the foam from the horses nostrils froze & hung in long icicles.

There was a gay ball at Sherbrooke on New Years day, we had an invitation from the Stewards, the Gentlemens tickets a dollar, Ladies did not pay anything, we did not go. I should like to have been at Bellevedere on Christmas day, they had a very large party, and the day passed off well. Mrs Felton says that she shall have another Christmas day when she returns home that I may be of the party. My new servant is a middle aged woman, careful and a good plain cook, I hope she will go on as she has begun. Ellen is nurse and appears fond of the baby, she sleeps at night in her Cot by the fire and Ellen on a Burdett [a kind of cotton fabric, possibly named after an English manufacturer, *OED*] by her side, she brings her to me generally twice in the night, she is a good child upon the whole. I wish you could see her papa nursing her, she loves to hear him talk and sing to her, and he will be very glad when she is old enough to romp with him.

17th – Mr & Mrs Henry called here on their way to Bellevedere, she is a very pleasing woman with a beautiful pair of dark eyes full of kindly expression, she admired my baby, as indeed every one must, she improves every day in beauty and strength. I told Mrs Henry what power she has, and how she lifts her head from my shoulder by herself and looks me in the face, she said that it was peculiar to the children of this country, most of them having extraordinary strength of body. Celia has quite the figure of a woman, as round and plump as possible, and her frocks sit beautifully, not all in a lump as you see babys in England. Edmund is the best nurse you ever saw, and I never feel so happy and proud as when I sit by the fire in an evening watching him with his dear little girl.

Yesterday Fanny and Matilda came to take me a drive, I went to Bellvedere, had lunch there, and then returned home, they were much disappointed that I had not the baby, particularly Narbon, who wanted, he said, to show Celia Peel his new horse, he would return home with me to see her. Mr and Mrs Henry are coming the first fine day for me and baby, she says it will do her good to go out, and told me when her eldest child was a month old, Mr Henry took him across the river at Sherbrooke in a Canoe and almost frightened her to death. Yesterday was as cold I believe as we shall have it, the Sun was out, the sky a clear blue, no wind but the air so sharp dear Mamma, it was just like drawing a knife across your face, yet the girls kept their veils up and looked clear and rosy whilst I was quite blue, they tell me I shall not feel it next winter.

Mrs Felton and her daughters are enjoying themselves at Quebec. Mr & Mrs Edmund Peel are there also, they are very popular in the neighbourhood. Mr Henry tells us that our cousin means to start as Member for Sorel, and that he thinks he has a good chance of succeeding. To day it is so warm we can scarcely bear a fire, it rains and there is a rapid thaw. Edmund has made me a Chiffonere [chiffonier, a high bureau or chest of drawers, *GCD*] and painted it black, it is very useful, you see we trouble the carpenter very little.

18th – Edmund had a letter from his cousin saying that he and Mrs Peel set off to come and spend a few days with us but he was taken so unwell at Yamaska he was obliged to return home, he wants us to go and see them and offers us the inducement of a ball at Sorel, I need scarcely say we shall decline the invitation, I would rather nurse my darling Baby than go to the gayest ball in the world. Talking of balls, there were three the same night at Sherbrooke last week, one young Lady was fashionable enough to attend two of them, this does not appear like being in the bush does it?

22nd – On Sunday last Mr Charles Felton called, Mrs Colclough & three of her children she is an agreeable woman. We are now come to the coldest weather, and certainly I never felt any thing like it, the windows in this room, though we have a very large fire are so frozen we cannot see through them, and though we have a great stove close to our bedroom door which is kept open, the water was frozen in the Jugs and the Jugs to the basins this morning. The meat freezes in the kitchen, and all the cloths which were washed this morning & were drying by a dumb stove and two pipes are likewise frozen, how should you like to be here Mamma? I think I could keep you warm notwithstanding this account. The Sun is shining as brightly as possible and Edmund is out in the Woods, he came in a short time since looking nearly petrified. Sturges if you will come you shall have excellent ice creams. I made some the other day and they were frozen in ten minutes.

Celia is quite blooming in spite of the cold, she will soon be as fair as alabaster. I think I never told you a very modest request which was made to us two days before I was confined, we were sitting at dinner about half past five when we heard a knocking at the hall door, upon its being opened a Man, his wife and eight children walked into the passage and said they wanted a lodging here, their Sleigh was broken down and they could go no further; I sent Mrs Salt to say there was a Lady ill in the house and that they must go away, at first they positively refused, but they were persuaded to change our house for Mrs M'Ready's, and she could not get rid of them for three days.

Edmund has bought a beautiful grey mare with a long tail four years old and this is the first winter it has been used, he gives sixty dollars for it. It is a capital goer and will do all kinds of work from drawing Logs from the woods to carrying a Lady, we were obliged to buy a horse, for our Oxen being done for, we should soon pay double the price of a horse in hire for we give two dollars a day for a man and one yoke and *train* or *Sled*, and we are constantly wanting wood drawn to keep up four large fires. I assure you we indulge in no luxury and though all our friends are visiting, we remain quietly at home without either Sleigh or waggon, we are determined that should our plan of living here not answer, our friends in England shall not have to say extravagance is the cause; we have neither of us spent a farthing upon ourselves since we came into the country.

24th – Yesterday was dreadfully cold, Edmund was up stairs and had a nail in his hand which froze to it before he could hammer it in, he was obliged to tear the skin from his hand in taking it away, and what is still a stronger proof of the intensity of the cold is, that the Bistre which drops up stairs from the stove pipe when there is a fire in it froze before it could drop and hung in small icicles from the pipe. To day it is warmer and very fine. Edmund is just gone to try the Mare, she set off as gayly as possible with him.

28th – On Saturday Mr & Mrs Henry called, Mrs Henry is to come and spend a day soon. I like her better every time I see her. After they left Mrs Witcher called, then Edmund drove me in a borrowed Sleigh to Sherbrooke, the Mare went very well but rather gay, too gay for you Mamma. Celia never cried during my absence. I am certain she knows her papa and me, last night she was delighted, Edmund carried her about for more than an hour and I played the Harp. I have made her a cloak and bonnet out of my silk cloak which was spoiled on the passage, they are much admired by the Miss Feltons, the bonnet is wadded & quilted blue lining and ribbons, Baby looks very pretty in them. I am making some pinnafores from the pattern you sent.

29th – Fanny & Matilda came this morning to take baby and me to Bellvedere. Celia behaved like a dear good child and they were all delighted with her; Edmund rode over on horseback, we returned home to dinner. The Chateau at Quebec, Lord Aylmers house is burnt down to the ground, it has not however stopped the gaiety for Lady Aylmer is giving a pic-nic, does not this sound strange in a land of frost and snow? But this pic-nic, as she calls it, consists of good eating and a dance at some house near Quebec. Edmund is now very busy manufacturing a rug with canvas and round pieces of cloth, I think it will look quite the thing for our cottage. Give my love to the Wrays, tell Susan she shall hear from me in the spring, that at present my ideas are all buried in the snow, and my time taken up with the most beautiful baby in the old or new world. Edmund writes with me in love to you all at the Cottage and Church Bank, Celia sends kisses, believe me

yr affect. child
Lucy Peel.

My next letter will be to Rosa.

No 11

Feby 1st 1834 –
To Mrs William Birch

My dear Rosa –

I continue my journal to you. Mrs Henry came to spend yesterday with me and her husband joined us at a five oclock dinner; Mrs Henry is lively, amusing and Lady like, she told me some of her adventures when she first came into this Country. She and her two brothers came to prepare for Mrs Felton and her family. The house they had taken contained one table, two chairs, two knives and forks, and two broken plates, for months they had nothing to eat but salt pork, without either bread or potatos. When some of their goods arrived from Quebec, Miss Charlotte Felton, as Mrs Henry then was, had constantly notes from the different petty farmer's wives asking her to lend them things, one wanted a *drawing* of tea, meaning enough to put into the tea-pot for once, another sent an invitation to a dance, and a third hoped Miss *Charlotty* would lend her a bonnet to go to meeting in. Mrs Henry kept herself as free of them as possible to avoid future annoyances.

I wish you could see Celia there certainly never was a prettier baby, Mrs Henry thinks so too, and says she is beautifully made, such a fair skin, such falling shoulders I cannot keep her frocks on them. I have had a Sleigh full of little Feltons to call this morning, it is a splendid day, quite warm and the sun shining full into our comfortable and English looking drawing room.

2nd – Capt & Mrs Colclough called this morning to take Celia and me a ride, they came in their pretty double Sleigh drawn by a pair of nice Canadian Ponies, with seven dollars worth of very musical bells round their necks, we went to Bellevedere and I enjoyed my drive exceedingly. I wish William could see the pretty grey Mare Edmund has bought, she is just such a one as he would like to drive, she is so sprightly, I hope to have many agreeable rides upon her next summer. Mr Hamilton of Stanstead is dead, his Death occasioned by a too free indulgence in that destructive and seducing beverage eau-de-vie. He has left a wife & four children without any provision. The Chateau or Castle of St Lewis, which was Lord Aylmer's residence at Quebec, is to be rebuilt, the estimate £30,000.

5th – On Monday Fanny and Maria Felton brought the Sleigh to take Celia and me to Bellevedere, we remained the day and Edmund joined us at dinner. We have had several lovely days quite like spring over head, the snow alone reminding us of winter. Edmund is very busy cutting down trees to make a path up our beautiful Rock, he has nearly accomplished it, and he took me yesterday to see what he had done, I enjoyed my ramble exceedingly and waded through the snow which in many places came up to my knees, and once I sunk up to my waist. I wish Sturges had been with us, we afterwards walked to our Sugary, and I then returned home to my dear baby, and had not to change a single thing the snow being so dry it all shook off.

If, my dear Rosa, you wish to retain your health, strength, and beauty come here without delay. I never felt so young, so well, or so happy in my life, and when I see all the comforts I possess, the kindest of husbands, the prettiest of children, a house and land, all my *very own*, I fancy some Magician's wand has been used in my behalf. As to Edmund I never saw him look so well, he works like a *Neger* and still gets fat. He is an excellent nurse too, and Celia loves to be with him and hear him sing, the dear child is as fair as a winter rose and her eyes dark blue, and as bright as a silver dollar, as the Yankee's would say, I would give anything if you could see her.

9th – Yesterday Fanny Felton called and took baby and me to Sherbrooke, we called upon Mrs Hale who admired my little girl exceedingly, and would nurse her all the time we remained. I went to see Mrs Fletcher, the Judges Lady, and she was quite delighted with baby, when I returned home I had our Clergyman and his Wife, Mr & Mrs *Doolittle* to call, he is a pleasing gentlemanly man, she rather pretty but not Ladylike.

Edmund has completed the path up the Rock and a place at the top for a summer house. I have been with him to see it to day and was quite pleased with my husband's work, the view from the top is grand, too grand for my pen to describe or for you to imagine dear Rosa. We sat on the rock this morning looking on a hot Sun scarcely a breath of wind, not a cloud to be seen, not a sound to be heard save at distant intervals the cracking of the trees in the woods below from the frost.

14 – On Monday we went again up the rock, Edmund armed with an old Coffee pot full of fire, without a handle and balanced upon a shovel, I, with a large saucepan containing the like material, we did not rest until we reached the top, I arrived there breathless. Edmund had previously heaped a great number of trees upon each other, he now made a fire underneath and we soon had a large bonfire, the next morning this immense pile was a mass of Ashes and the next summer I shall begin to prepare a small garden. I have composed many new pieces for the Harp which I am writing in a book to be ready for Celia when she be old enough to learn them, I call them Canadian airs.

16th – Again I have been to the Rock and made a great fire dragging small trees and placing them on myself, concluding all by setting fire to my dress. Edmund fortunately came in time to put it out and I escaped with only a hole in my sleeve. I have just had a large batch of hard & soft soap made it has not cost me a penny, it is manufactured out of the ashes from our own fires, the skimmings of the pots that we boil our meat in, candle ends and old bones, the person who made it was content with some of the soap for her trouble.

18th – Two pigs that we bought lately, jumped upon our canadian oven yesterday, took the peg out of the door, opened it, and walked in, there were seven beautiful loaves about half baked and these gentlemen positively remained in their hot birth until they had eaten one loaf. I wish I had been behind them with a good stick and a pin at the end of it.

21st – Received Mamma's journal No 7. I had expected a letter some time. Mr & Mrs Henry have just called to say adieu, they are off to Montreal, their youngest boy is ill there, Maria Felton is gone with them. It is beautiful weather, the snow gradually disappearing and every hope of an early spring, it is so warm I can scarcely bear a fire, and yesterday I had the window open, I believe such a winter was never known.

26th – On Monday Mrs Felton sent for me and baby to spend the day with her, I heard all her proceedings at Quebec, they were very gay indeed and Charlotte finds Bellvedere stupid after Quebec. I had lunch at their early dinner and returned home to dine with my dear husband at five. Yesterday we had snow, nevertheless Charlotte and Miss Nelson, who arrived with the Judges after I left the evening before, walked to see me, they asked us in Mrs Felton's name to go to dinner to meet the Judges, Fanny called for us and we went baby too, she behaved like a little Lady and Judge *Valier* [Vallières] thought her a very fine forward child, we had a pleasant day. Mrs Felton looked very pretty, I am sure you would admire her, she is such a perfect Lady and her spanish accent so interesting, she always shows great attention to me and expresses much affection, she says how sorry she is that difference in religion will prevent her being Celia's second mother.

March 1st – The Judge and his Lady, Mrs Fletcher called to day, they sat a long time and were very agreeable, I played to them two of my own pieces, one which I have just composed and call the Dunstall Opera, the Judge admired and begged I would repeat it that he might keep it in his mind, he seems to have a great knowledge of music, indeed all sciences seem familiar to him, he has a wonderful memory, he never forgets anything that he hears or reads, he tells me that he measures forty two inches round the chest. He made us promise to dine with him tomorrow, he will send his carriage for us at twelve.

3d – We had snow all day yesterday, but we went to Sherbrooke, we had a pleasant day, met Mr & Mrs Hale, I like her better every time I see her, Celia behaved very well, laughing & talking all the time, Mrs Hale nursed her most of the day, she is only twenty and has two children, she appears to be quite a domestic woman.

5th – Miss Nelson, Fanny & Mr John Felton called on Monday, Mr & Mrs Hale yesterday, she brought Celia a pretty pair of boots made by herself of fine white flannel bound and tied with white ribbon. This morning I have had Mrs Witcher, she is gone on to Bellevedere. Edmund is gone out with his Axe to chop.

6th – Edmund has been to Sherbrooke to day to buy wheat, he is just returned in time to save a soaking it is raining fast. He brought me a letter from Mrs Peel of Sorel to congratulate me on the birth of Celia, she says she is tired of the long winter, that their place, Richelieu Cottage is very pretty and warm in winter but that they are miserably off for society, there being only Steam boat Cap^{ts}, Pursers, etc etc. in the neighbourhood, so they decline all invitations, she writes in a friendly and quite *girlish* style.

Thank Mamma for the Calico, I cannot get any here under a shilling a y^d that is fit to use. Cambric, [a fine white linen fabric, *OED*]. what you would give ten shillings for in England is 25 here. Celia made her first attempt to take anything yesterday. She tried to pull the bows off her cap. And tries to take hold of the flowers on my dress, she gets more interesting every day, sleeps all night, and is very good in the day time. We doat upon her but shall not spoil her I hope, and believe.

12th – Yesterday I received Mamma's letter No 8. Tell her we get very good wheat, Lower Canada Wheat which makes brown bread at 7/6 a bushel, Oats from 1/8 to 2/ a *Stoop*. The Upper country Flour 30/ per barrel at Montreal & then the carriage brings it to more than 40/. The sap is now running fast from the Maple trees, we had some yesterday after dinner, it is as clear as Spring water, scarcely coloured and very sweet, I always fancied it had been a thicker liquid. Since my baby was born I have had nothing to drink but water, the beer not agreeing with her, she is quite fat, I would give anything for you to see her, for though I think with her handsome features she will grow up pretty, yet as a baby she is at times, beautiful, such a delicate colour and transparent skin.

14th – Mrs Felton has been very unwell, Doctor Wilson attended her and she liked him, she came to see me yesterday with Mr John Felton, she always appears to be really attached to me and speaks so openly to me, you would have been amused to see Mr John nurse Celia, he is an officer & married Mrs Felton's sister, he is doatingly fond of children and unfortunately has none of his own, Mrs Felton says little Narbon calls her his wife, he said the other day, you know Mamma I must marry Celia Peel. I went a ramble with Edmund yesterday, the snow is quite gone in many places, where it still remains it is crisp and like walking upon comfits. I hope we shall now soon have venison, I have just read to Edmund Mamma's delightful No 9. So you have really given a Quadrille party and christened your baby. Thank dear Papa for his few and first lines, it did me good to read them. You all praise us too much, indeed you do Rosa. Tell Sturges I like his writing very much and I will some day send him a letter all to himself so he must continue the correspondence, he sent us a long *ship indeed*, I think he had better come out here, the new land company will find him employment. Tell Mamma I waited for her receipt to cure bacon before I killed my pig and that it is very good. The sheep, notwithstanding Papa's doubts, were fat and tender. Edmund has put a Gate & a rail up at one end of the Veranda, he means to rail it all along to prevent Celia from falling down the bank when she begins to walk. Celia joins her Papa & me in best love to all at Barton Lichfield, Tetlow Fold and Church Bank, we constantly talk of you all. How kind of Miss Winter to make that handsome present to Sarajane, I wish her purse were as full as her heart is affectionate and generous. My kind love and Edmund's regards to her, tell her she must love Celia though she has not seen her.

17th – It is as warm and clear as spring, the snow quite gone near Sherbrooke. I will write to Kate when the St Lawrence is open again, Celia will soon know one Grandpapa, I shall teach her all your names and make her love you as soon as possible. Kind love to William and the Children, ever your

attached Sister

Lucy Peel

No 12

March 18th,   Dunstall Villa –

My dearest Mamma.

The good accounts we hear from you delight us, and we are much pleased that our letters give such general satisfaction, I shall be quite vain if you praise me so frequently. It is now snowing fast and a dismal day, we have however just had a visit from a Madman, he rode up on a jaded horse, went into the kitchen and wanted to see the Man, what Man, said Margaret. The Man he replied, well he is outside chopping, pointing to Parkes, Oh, I want to see the Man of the house, if you mean Mr Peel I will see if he is in the parlour and ask him to come and speak to you, the Madman said he would go to him, my servant would not allow him so he walked out of the house and came round to the varanda where Edmund happened to be with his cap on making some rails. How do you do my fine fellow, said the man, putting out his hand, how is your family? Busy working I see, I sometimes do so, do you ever wear a hat? fine day! Sun shines! Bloody wars across the water, go and meet them half way; in this incoherent way he went on for some time and then set off to pay other visits. His name is Kendle. One morning to the great surprise of Mrs Felton, he walked into her bedroom.

19th – Celia is three months old to day and is a dear good child, I walked with Edmund to Sherbrooke, it was fine over head, but the road in a dreadful state, the snow nearly gone, we called at Captn Colcloughs, the Major and his wife had just returned from Quebec, she is a pleasing old Lady, the Major was very talkative and told me he never saw so many young Ladies in Quebec as there were this winter but that their mammas had to trot them all back again, not one being either married or engaged. There is a gay and dashing Tandum Club, and the beaus drove the belles every where but to church.

After we left the Colcloughs we called upon the Judge, he came to us in his dressing gown which I have described in Edith's letter, Mrs Fletcher was in bed, the Judge began a *long yarn* to Edmund about politics which appeared to me to be endless, so seeing my good husband rather tired I put a stop to the learned discourse by getting up to take some bread and butter, the Judge would have me taste some of his Anchovies and he scraped them for me, in the midst of all this Mrs Fletcher made her appearance, she rose on purpose to see me, she looked ill. We then went to the Store where I bought some pretty blue and white jean to make Celia some frocks, we then walked home and I did not feel much tired.

22nd – I have finished one of Celia's frocks, her papa admires it which is every thing. I have not seen our Bellvedere friends lately, our roads have been so bad, to my great surprise Mrs Felton & Mr John came this morning, she looks very well, and said she did not like being so long away from me, oh Mamma I wish you could see her, she is a most *lovable* woman, then though so small, her figure, hands, feet are so Aristocratic looking, every motion, every act like a Lady. I deliver all your messages to her and she said with her pretty spanish accent, I hope you do think of me to your Mother when you write. They have began to make sugar, in the good years they have about eleven hundred pounds but this year Mrs Felton says they will only have six hundred. I am sorry we cannot do anything in that way this year, we are not rich enough to buy all the necessaries we must have, a hundred buckets, two boilers, and other things, we can buy sugar cheaper than we can make it at present.

26th – I mounted our pretty Grey yesterday, Edmund walked by my side to Bellevedere, they were glad to see us, we there learned that there was letter and paper for us at the Post Office, I cantered home and sent Parkes off for them, we had the pleasure of receiving Mrs Peel's letter, I am glad to hear our accounts of Celia's birth reached England, it appears that Edmund's second letter arrived first. Celia begins to be very amusing and Edmund daily improves in nursing, I believe he is quite surprised to find himself so fond of a baby, as he could scarcely bear to look at one before he was married, I am sure you would be delighted to see him with his little girl, he puts me in mind of Charles and his children, he is not able to work to day having cut his hand with one of his chisels at the first finger joint, it was much inflamed yesterday, and this morning I have been applying poultices all day, he is very good and does as I wish him, you know some men are troublesome to nurse. The sticking plaister you sent is excellent and often comes into use. I am sorry to say my cotton and tape is fast disappearing and these articles are bad here & very dear.

28th – This morning dearest Mama we received No 10, if you could see Edmund and me seat ourselves comfortably by the fire, and watch our faces when one of your amusing letters arrives, you would I am sure feel rewarded for your kindness and trouble in writing so fully. I read slowly to make it as long as possible, and as we proceed we quite fancy ourselves with you, were we rich I should entreat of you to favor us more frequently, but postage costing so much we must for the present content ourselves with your monthly journal; as I said before in this letter you praise me too much.

Edmund is beyond praise. I could, had I the delight of now sitting by your side, inform you of some simple but affecting facts which would prove to every thinking mind that he is a man of high principle; and warm feeling. I told Celia about your letter and what Uncle Sturges says, she stood straight upright on my knee the whole time laughing, and when I was silent talking in her way. Oh Mamma, as you say, there is no feeling to be compared to a mothers when she clasps her first child in her arms.

Give our kindest regards to Miss Atherton, tell her I am proud of her approbation and that I love her for what she says of my valuable husband; when I have the pleasure of introducing my pretty Celia to her, I hope she will accord to the little Canadian a share of the friendship she has so kindly expressed for the parents. Dear Papa your bad pen did not make you write unintelligably, and when I say it does my heart good to see a few lines from you, I trust you will often indulge me. Sturges you are beginning early in life to flatter, you must love your little niece, she shall love you I promise you; and shall play on the harp to you à la Mama if you will wait patiently a few years. I am afraid you are disappointed about the Oldershaws. I want to hear more of Mr Mayne's plans.

31st – We had an encrease in our family last Thursday in the shape of a fine Lamb, an important event to us young farmers, we have had no milk for two months which is inconvenient, as the men servants expect tea or Coffee and sugar when they have not milk. The frost going so much sooner than usual has obliged us to salt our fresh meat so we shall be badly off if we cannot get milk for puddings, Edmund had enough of salt meat at Sea, I hope our cow will have a calf soon, at Bellevedere they have eight cows and have been without milk some time, Mr Felton is seldom at home to look after these things and his head man Dodds is a Goose not fit for anything, Mr Felton is aware of this, yet keeps him and gives him fifteen dollars a month and his board.

I think the Mr B — — are right to go to Upper Canada if they go out with the intention of making anything by farming, and can put up with eating at the same table with their *helps*. This is not a country for grain, and supposing it were, there is no one to buy it, each petty farmer growing enough for his own consumption, and we are too far from the market towns to make it answer to send it there; at present this is only a country for a Gentleman who wishes to live quietly and cheaply, without an idea of accumulating money. Land is low enough but the expense of clearing is very great for a gentleman; a labouring man with a family of Sons might soon clear a number of acres. The lowest charge is 12 dollars an acre for clearing.

1st April – Many happy returns of the day to Uncle Lyon. Edmund, yesterday, purchased a yoke of Oxen, the Owner of them was going to the States, so we got them very cheap, they are a heavy yoke six years old worth 60 dollars, we gave 42 dollars, the man could not resist when he saw the money ready for him, and another thing, the Oxen would have been seized in a day or two by his Creditors, his money they cannot touch. We shall work the oxen the spring and summer, fatten them in the fall, and kill them for our winter stock, putting them into the snow. They will also provide me with a hundred pounds of candles, and their skins are worth ten dollars each, so I think dear Mamma we shall have more than the value of our 42 dollars, independant of their work, we cannot hire Oxen under two dollars a day in the summer.

Mr Barnard has been over from Stanstead to collect his debts, the Gossips say he played high at Sherbrooke, indeed this little Town in the Wilds of America is a sad place for vice, and I would not advise any young man to live there who has not the greatest command over himself, for every vicious pleasure may be there obtained at a cheap rate. Edmund paid Mr Barnard seven pounds for attending me, a large sum for us to pay.

4th – A lovely day, Celia is gone to take a walk, one of our sheep brought us two Lambs this morning. Edmund and I are going to make some fires on the Hill, he has been several days preparing the dead wood, he has cleared a quarter of an acre himself. I am not surprised that Tom Tylecote found out the puzzle.

5th – This is really spring in earnest, Oh Mamma! you would be delighted with this beautiful climate in the Spring, We now get up very early, having, generally, finished breakfasted by eight, and in a short time we shall be earlier still as Edmund means to work before breakfast, and I, you may be sure, have full occupation with my house and baby. I will tell you how we generally pass our time. After breakfast Edmund goes out of doors clearing, chopping etc etc. till between one and two, in the mean time I wash and dress Celia, make my arrangements for the day in my house and work, sometimes practice the Harp; when Edmund returns we sit and chat a short time then he takes me out for an hour or two, we then come home and prepare for dinner between four and five.

In the summer we intend dining at three, after dinner we play with our child and talk, knit and have music till ten, and as the weather gets fine stroll on the Verandah, we then prepare for bed, cheerful, happy, and contented with our simple fare and way of living, the only variety to this even tenure of our way, occasional calls from our friends and sometimes dining at Bellevedere, our only beverage drawn from the clear spring close by, and a cup of excellent tea night & morning. Our Wine, though cheap, we have put on one side to be used only in case of illness, and our beer given up for the present because sugar is dear and bad. Do you not admire Edmund, Mamma, for having such command over himself. I am sure, yes more sure every day, that he has sufficient strength of mind to do any thing he considers right. Parkes is gone to Lenoxville [Lennoxville] to day to the Mill, about five miles from here, Dolly does not much like drawing the Cart, the noise frightens her. We gave eight dollars for our Cart.

8th – Edmund and I walked to see Mrs M'cready, my first visit, she soon spread a beautiful damask cloth and regaled us with her maple sugar, Oat cake, bread & butter and new milk, at half past six we went to see the Sun set at the top of the rock. Yesterday, we had finished breakfast soon after seven, we had five grand fires on the Hill, dined at half past three and after dinner began to lay out the garden and form the beds, I picked off the Stones and raked, I expect to be very fond of it and Edmund is so good assisting me and always taking an interest in what pleases me, should you not like to see us at work? Little Celia was out most of the day, she loves to look about her, her cloak and bonnet are now too warm, besides she will have her arms at liberty, I am making her a silk pelisse [a long mantle worn by women, *OED*] out of another dress that was spoiled on the blue ocean & I have half finished a pretty little bonnet made of the nice piece of Nankeen [a cotton fabric, originally made in Nanking, *OED*] you sent me, every thing comes in, I never till now knew the use of odds and ends, you often told me I should if I were married.

9th – Many happy returns of the day to you dear Sturges, and may you be as good a man as your brother Edmund then you will indeed be a great comfort and blessing to Papa and Mamma. The beds in my garden are laid out, I shall describe it in my next letter, Edmund and I wished for you dearest Mamma to plan it for us, and I think you would have liked the employment.

11th – Piping hot day, Celia is glad of her thin cloak and bonnet. Oh I fancy if I could see you kiss her round fat soft fair cheek, see papa smile upon her and say God bless her, I should be perfectly happy. We have just been into the woods to see Old M'cready boil sugar, we had some hot and Mrs M'cready sent over a basket of Oat cake and cheese for me.

12th – Yesterday afternoon Mrs Felton and Mr John called. I had not seen her for nearly three weeks, the roads being so bad, she expresses great sorrow at this, and much affection for Celia, called her a little pet, a dear little blessing, and said how much they all wanted to see her again. Our lamb, whose mother refused to nurse her is dead, and another of our sheep has brought two into the world.

15th – Mr John Felton, Charlotte and Edward walked to see me on Sunday evening. Yesterday so hot we had no fires, and our pretty french windows open, Edmund busy in the garden soon after six in the morning and all day long, he has put in some of his seeds; we have two men fencing with posts and rails, à la Francoise. I bought two quarters of nice veal at 2^d _ a pound. Celia out most of the day. She gets prettier every day, her eyes, eyebrows & eyelashes are beautiful. I think the most discontented person would feel happy [with] such weather as this. I received your letter No 11 – this morning. Sturges my blood ran cold as I read of your narrow escape. Caroline Loaden writes like a dear sensible girl. I am sure you must have written a delightful letter to her. Edmund has planted Currant, Gooseberry, Apple, and butter nut trees this morning, our garden already begins to make a show. Our best love to all friends and kisses from Celia.

From your affectionate children,
Lucy and Edmund.

16th – Love to Miss Winter she must not forget us, our Orchard is being fenced this morning.

No 13

Dunstall Villa   April 17th 1834

My dearest Mamma.

No 12 took its departure this morning and I hope it will have a quick passage. The night before last, just before our fencing was finished, our new yoke of Oxen and our Cow took it into their heads, seeing I suppose, that it was their last chance to leave us, Parkes was out till after eleven at night making a useless search for them. This morning he has walked twenty miles on a similar errand but alas! in vain, if they do not return it will indeed be a most serious loss, just at the time when most wanted to prepare the land for seed.

18th – This morning Capt Colclough, his Mother, Wife and little girl Annabella came to call, I played to them on the Harp, they were surprised to see Celia so much grown, thought her a beauty and said they were sure she would walk at eight months old if she had her teeth easy. When I put her in her tub she holds each side and stands erect whilst I sponge her, she will be four months old tomorrow. Parkes found our Oxen near the Magog, we were very glad to see them again.

20th – Yesterday Parkes went with Dolly and the Cart to Capt Colcloughs to bring us some hop cuttings & black currant trees, also two Plain Trees, Edmund set them in the garden and Parkes put in the hops all round the fence, at each Pole of the veranda, and a row to divide the kitchen garden from my flower garden, they will look very pretty when they run up the Poles. Charlotte, Matilda, Louisa & Octavia Felton walked to see me, I took them to the top of the rock, they were delighted with the view. We go off the Veranda down a sloping bank to my flower garden, which is to be covered with moss, a wide walk in the centre, on each side a large bed not any decided shape, narrow walk round each, after this two long narrow beds on each side, walks round and a butter nut tree in each of them, the butter nuts are beautiful. I have sown some seeds, and Edmund has made for me three nice boxes for mignionette. Mrs Colclough has sent me lillies and has some geraniums preparing for me, I shall ornament the Veranda with these.

23d – We have had two wet days, it is now raining hard. Margaret is making me 8 lbs of candles from what we have saved during the winter from the running of the candles, skimmings from meat pots, and such. Celia is more engaging every day, how you would love her dear Mamma! She is so good, she will sit in her cot, on the bed, or on the sofa for a long time, with a pillow for her table, and I give her different things to play with, her favorites are a newspaper and a large jug with fine blue flowers, she will talk to the flowers sometimes for half an hour. When her Papa begins to talk to me about anything, whatever she may be doing she leaves off and looks at him till he has finished, really seeming to understand all he says. I am afraid I shall tire you with writing about my darling. You know how very fond I always was of children, therefore you may imagine how I must doat upon one of my own, and one I should be so proud to show to you.

27th – We have had some very disagreeable weather since I last wrote, rain, frost, and snow. Mr Felton and Eliza came home on friday, and this morning, they, with Mrs Felton, Isabella, and Charlotte called. Mr Felton gave Edmund some hints about gardening. Little Celia was almost annihilated amongst them, she let any of them nurse her, I played on the Harp, Mr Felton said he was dying for some music, there being little & that little worse than none, at Quebec.

We have bought 200 lbs of Salt Beef, it would just suit Papa, we gave 2 1/4 a pound, it is very tender. We have six pretty Lambs, they have a famous play ground, having the run of the hill and rock to the left of the house; we are told by every one that ours is the best farm in the country for sheep, we intend keeping a large flock. Papa will you send us word what is the average price of wheat per bushel, we give 7/6. I have bought fifty pounds of well made Maple Sugar at 5^d per lb, this is cheap considering it is a bad season. The Canadians make the best and mine is chiefly Canadian.

29th – Edmund and I were busy last night getting Moss and placing it on the slope into my flower garden.

May 1st – a most important day. Celia went into short petticoats, as she sat smiling on my knee looking the picture of health, good temper and beauty. I longed for you and papa to see her and admire your grandchild. Eliza and Charlotte Felton came over in the Gig, Eliza has forgotten all her tunes, she is expecting her Harp soon, and is determined to remain at home all summer to practise it – I do not think she will ever play well, she is a bad tunest. I believe she has made a conquest at Quebec of a Mr Davidson.[6] Margaret brought Celia an Indian rattle, a present from Mrs Hale, and an Indian basket from Caroline Felton, Mr Charles Felton's daughter. Celia is quite pleased with this rattle, she is afraid of the one you sent her. Mrs Colclough sent me some lillies and sweet brier. I must tell you Celia's dress to day, a net cap and border worked by mamma, pink ribbons, sleeves tied with pink, green and pink boots, Eliza's present, and Kate's handsome frock, you may guess what a large child she is when I tell you it just fits her.

3d – yesterday Mr Felton, Eliza, and Charlotte called, they brought us lilac and rose trees, Mr Henry is expected every day, his mother is dead. The expense of the hotels in this country is great, Mr Felton paid at the Albion, at Quebec for two months lodging and board for five of them, and they were scarcely ever at home to dinner, one hundred and twenty pounds, every public amusement was 5/ each, so I think his daughter's introductions were no trifle to him. Why are Doctors and Lawyers Women?

5th – Yesterday Mr Felton sent the Waggon and Edmund, Celia and I went to spend the day at Bellvedere, poor Celia did not enjoy it at all, every thing was strange and she would not let me leave her, I was obliged to stay with her during dinner and could not join the party in the Hall, Celia sat on the Sofa playing with a newspaper whilst I eat my dinner beside her, contented with looking at me. I am going to wean her, I need scarcely say it will be a great trial to me.

9th – a beautiful day Celia, Ellen and I have been gathering flowers & shrubs in the woods, and I have sugar plum, a flowering shrub pale green leaves & pale yellow bell flowers, in the fall it bears red berries good to eat, another called Adders Tongue, deep crimson and a yellow centre, how delighted you and Mrs Garnett would be could you be here to gather them, they will only flourish in the shade.

12th – Eliza & Charlotte came on Saturday they think Celia prettier every time they see her. Yesterday Capt Colclough called, he took our cart to send to three rivers for his summer stores & left us a cart to ride in, but we cannot use our mare just now.

13th – To day I received your letter No 12. and Mrs Mayne's packet from Montreal, best love and thanks to Mr Mayne, Sarajane, Rosa and Edith Bourne for their letters. Mr Maynes is a beautiful note so much that is pleasing and affectionate expressed in few words, I wish he *were* in strong health if that would bring him to Canada. Celia stood upon her Papa's knee whilst I read Mini's letter to her, she looked as if she understood it all, and I shall keep it till she is able to read it. I am very glad Mr Mayne is so much better, the peace and quiet he will now be able to live in will surely bring strength and ease to body. Dear Rosa writes as if she loved me. I hope my little Celia will grow up good, for I know dearest Mamma, beauty without good conduct has no charms in your eyes.

Mrs C. Bourne wants to know what a person should bring out to Canada, I answer, all kinds of cloathing, lots of Calico, it is very dear here, plenty of shoes, the leather here shocking. If they mean to keep house blankets, double rose blankets, the light ones are nearly useless in this cold country, what we gave ten dollars a pair for at Montreal, the wind really blows through. No wood furniture it shrinks so with the Stoves and the servants will not keep it in order.

14th – We had a good deal of snow yesterday, this is a strange climate.

15th – Snow half a foot deep this morning, a most extraordinary thing we are told. The old snow sometimes remains as long, but a second edition in May is scarcely known. Edmund begins to despair of seeing summer.

17th – Edmund walked to the Town to see the Honorable Peter M'Gill who came from Montreal with a Mr Moffet [Moffatt][7] about the land belonging to the Company and to survey roads. I see by the Papers that one of our English Noblemen is coming to settle in Canada, Lord Powerscourt, he is already in the Country. Mr Felton is gone this morning to Sorel to Lord Aylmers, I have written to Mrs Peel by him, I dare say she and her husband will be asked to meet him at the Governors. Tell Sarajane there is no fear of the duties of a wife and Mother making me forget those of a daughter, indeed I never loved you so much as I do now I have a child of my own.

18th – Last night I was awakened by a loud noise, I fancied carriages were passing at first, then from the roaring that the nursery was on fire. Edmund said it was thunder, it continued some time shaking the house and windows at last dying away, after a little thought we said it was the shock of an earthquake, and this morning we hear that it went towards Sherbrooke, near which place a thick mist rose from the earth. I do not know when I was more alarmed, it was a long time before I recovered myself, I felt such a strange sensation.

19th – Celia five months old to day, Mrs Felton, Eliza, and Narbon dined here. Edmund walked to Sherbrooke in the morning, all the people there in the highest spirits, the Company[8] having fixed their head quarters at that Town, which will doubtless in a few years become a place of great importance, it, till this week belonged to Mr Felton who has parted with it to the Company for £4000 and has sold land to them & to the amount of £6000. The Company has bought Mr Goodhires [Goodhue's] Factory and Land for £5000. I wish we had more land, it will of course rise greatly every year. What we took for an Earthquake was the burning of a Meteor; at Bellvedere it lighted up the house as if it were on fire, which appearance took place before the roaring noise. I send this to New York by Mr John Felton and have only time to add affectionate love to relations and friends, I shall write next to Sarajane – ever yours

L. Peel.

[No 14 missing]

No 15

Dunstall Villa, June 18th

My dearest Mama,

On Sunday evening Mrs Felton, Charlotte, Fanny & Mr John came over & took Mr Mayne's letter; Edmund was very unwell all day and did not see them.

Monday morning – Edmund better but I persuaded him to have his breakfast in bed; after breakfast I took Celia out on the Belvidere Road & met Mr Felton and Charlotte on their way to Quebec, we got into the waggon and rode to our gate with them; yesterday Eliza & Matilda came in the waggon and took Celia and me to Sherbrooke. Celia went to see her Godmama and had a cup of milk there; she was very good and was very much admired. Mrs Fletcher had a Bride staying with her, her nephews wife, Mrs Wickstead; he is Sir John Colvilles[9] right hand a very clever man but a strange looking being; she appears remarkably shy and not much of a lady. We went to call upon Mrs Hale she played for us her piano in a back room, all out of tune and she not the least idea how to play.

Edmund much better today, he had not eat meat for two days and I bought a fowl for his dinner which he enjoyed exceedingly. This morning it is raining fast and is cold but it will do good so we must not complain, we have a carpenter at work making the doors tight, they had all shrunk so much owing to the wood not being seasoned. Edmund looks himself again today and dear little Celia quite blooming, she is now sitting on my knee watching me write; she cries if I leave her a minute, I shall not be sorry when Ellen can nurse her again, for it makes me rather too busy to attend entirely to her with the other things I have to do.

22nd – Celia is certainly the best Child in the world, I have been her nurse day and night a fortnight to day so I am able to judge. On Thursday she was six months old, she gets stronger every day, she can get up in her cot, I now put her in before she is asleep and it is quite curious to see her raise her little head several times before she settles to look if I am there, being satisfied I shall not leave her she falls to sleep: on Friday, Mr and Mrs Wickstead called, I played to them and they were much pleased. After dinner Edmund and I took Celia a walk, returning when we were about half a mile from home it began to rain torrents, we stood under some trees in the wood which afforded us a short[?] shelter; the rain being so heavy we thought it best to brave the storm and we all got a complete wetting.

Yesterday Celia behaved beautifully, I never nursed her all morning, she sat in her chair talking whilst I ironed and afterwards worked. Edmund carries her out after dinner. We have had disagreeable weather, rain and cold, we have had a fire all the week, so you see this climate is as changeable as England.

The Bishop[10] is now at Sherbrooke and Mr Henry called this morning to ask if I would like to ride down with him and hear him preach, I could not leave Celia so was obliged to decline his offer. In the evening Mrs Felton, Fanny, and Isabella came, they brought us a basket of strawberries and Mrs Felton asked us to dine at Belvedere tomorrow to meet the Bishop, she pressed us very much but we declined for two reasons, in the first place Edmund has been suffering with Rheumatism in his shoulder, and in the second we have no carriage of our own at present and we do not like to be so troublesome as to be sent for.

24th – We killed our calf yesterday, only three weeks old, but we could not spare the milk longer, it weighed 62 lbs. This morning I had a call from the Catholic Bishop,[11] Mr Robinson, and another older person I forget his name, he is come to live at Sherbrooke, I played to them, Mr Robinson asked me saying at the same time to his companion "If Madame Peel will play you will hear the first musician in the province," how do you know, said I, for you have never heard me. Ah Madame but your fame has spread in Canada and I hear of you wherever I go. He then asked for God save the King. Edmund did not return home till after they were gone, he was busy weeding his Indian Corn. Celia was quite amused with the Gentlemen, smiling, & looking first at one then at the other, they had their robes on bound with white silk.

I am suffering from a Musquito bite on my foot and cannot bear to walk. Celia sends a kiss to dear Grandpapa and begs to inform him she knows his picture quite well, it hangs over the sofa and every day I let her stand on my knee and say where is Grandpapa and the dear child turns up her beautiful blue eyes to the picture and gives it a smile, I shall be delighted when I have yours to show her.

26th – We have very hot weather, I should like it if it were not for the flies. Mrs Felton & Fanny called yesterday, they wanted us to dine at Belvedere to day, I declined and told Mrs Felton the reason, she appeared quite hurt, so we at last consented, we are to meet Major Colclough and a young man just come to settle at Sherbrooke, a Surgeon out of Devonshire, he means to purchase land from Mr Felton. Mrs Felton seems to be much taken with him, she says he is handsome, gentlemanly, and quite English, she is sure he has been either in the Army or Navy. I hope he will be steady and clever and I am glad he is English, but I wish he were older and married.

We can get half a dollar a pound for our wool, we have between twenty and thirty pounds. I wish Charles Meek could see the Indian corn in our Garden, I never saw any thing so beautiful, Edmund pits it up and is well rewarded for his trouble. Mrs Felton told me the Bishop was sorry we did not go to dine at Belvedere the day he was there, he said he should like to see Mr and Mrs Peel for he understood they were very different to the Mr and Mrs Peel of Sorel whom he had met at Lord Aylmers, they were very fond of gaiety and he understood we liked retirement and he admires those who live quietly. I am told he is an excellent old man, very plain in his manners.

27th – We had a very pleasant day at Belvedere, Mr & Mrs Hale were there, Mr Henry brought the Waggon for us, and as we were driving down our road we met Major Coclough [Colclough] and the doctor, Mr Buchan on horseback coming to call at Dunstall on their way to Belvedere, they turned back with us. Mr Buchan is Gentlemanly has good eyes, but I think him rather plain, he is tall and has a nice hand, he said he did not come out with the intention of settling, but merely for a cruise, yet he thinks he shall remain at Sherbrooke; he has studied in London, was four years in Edinburgh and afterwards at Paris, he says a man at Sherbrooke told him yesterday by way of compliment, he thought he was a chap to get on he was so blunt. He has been to several Tea Parties in Sherbrooke, and Mrs Hale said he appeared highly amused with the people.[12] Mr & Mrs Hale took him to call upon Doctor Wilson.

We had a tremendous thunder storm when we were at Belvedere, and returning home we found many trees blown down. I found my darling Celia asleep, I left her for the first time. Ellen said "Oh Ma'am you never *seed* such a good child as she has been, she told me the storm shook the house and blew some boards, on which our wool was put to dry all round the shed, up to the oven. Margaret was returning from Sherbrooke at the time and said she expected to be killed every minute, the trees crashed and kept falling so near to her. Edmund asked Mr Buchan to come to Dunstall to day and he would take him to see the two farms near us, but he is going nine miles beyond Sherbrooke to cut off a man's leg.

29th – Mrs Felton left Eliza here to practice whilst she went on to Sherbrooke, I was very anxious for her return for I saw in our Albion that several packets had arrived from Liverpool and I felt almost certain I should have a letter, and I was not disappointed, she brought me your journal 11 written by you and dear Sarajane, what good accounts of you all, and how happy you must be together, I wish Edmund and I could pop in and have a chat with you, Sarajane was kind to write so much, and Mr Mayne's few lines gave us great pleasure, it is delightful to know you approve so much of our proceedings and that our letters continue to amuse and gratify you, dear little Mini! Celia would love to play with you, and I am sure you would think her own dear self as pretty as her name. I hope you will continue your accounts of our relations at Church Bank. I am glad to hear Hart & Bessy are happy and prudent. My love to Miss Winter, tell her so kind a friend can never be forgotten by me.

On Friday the New Hotel at Sherbrooke, the whole range of buildings belonging to it, the barn belonging to the other Inn containing Hay worth 50 dollars, were burned to the ground, not a vestige of them left, fortunately the river was at hand or most likely the whole town would have been destroyed, these wooden houses are most dangerous, I am told it was an awful sight, barrels of Gun Powder rolled into the river, all degrees giving assistance, and some much burned in saving others. Mr Marriott, who keeps the old Inn, lost a great deal of furniture that was carried out into the square, 14 Mirrors were destroyed, it will be a long time before Sherbrooke recovers from this disaster. Now to go from the dismal to the ridiculous, at Church two Sundays ago the School *Mam,* as she is called, appeared in a white gauze hat, a book muslin dress low in the neck nothing over her shoulders, and a wreath of artificial flowers all round the body of the dress.

July 1st – We have began to make butter, we have only one cow and we shall have more than five pounds this week. It is so good that I am not using it, but buy the little we want from Mrs M'cready and put ours down for our winter consumption, we do not pot it Irish fashion, but preserve it in the following manner, I make brine as long as the salt will dissolve in the water, let it stand to cool, strain it into a nice tub I have with a cover, and as we make the butter up in two pound pieces putting to it rather more salt than if we were going to use it, we put it in the brine, it is very superior to potted butter and has never a strong taste or disagreeable smell.

Edmund is beautifying our house a little, in the way of painting, he does it all himself, and by degrees as he can afford, he is about our bed room now, it is pink, and looks very pretty, the window frames black. I wish you could see your Grandchild at tea with a large piece of dry toast sucking it for an hour quite pleased. She is a good child for she does not cry if I take anything from her, but quickly allows me to replace it with what is suitable, and if I give her nothing she plays with her pretty little fingers.

4th – Yesterday Edmund and I rode on horseback, Dolly was so gay that Edmund changed the saddles, I have seen the time when I should have laughed at giving up the management of any horse, but I feel now that I have no right to run such risks [Lucy is once again pregnant]. We went to Belvedere and returned home loaded with the useful and ornamental in the shape of a beautiful quarter of a Leicestershire Sheep and a large bunch of roses. Dolly went quietly with Edmund, how Papa & Sturges would like to ride her.

Edmund has had a letter from his Agent in London who has obtained him leave of absence for another year so we are safe till next January which I am glad of. Edmund is painting the Drawing room. Eliza & Isabella Felton have been here most of the morning, we have also had Mr Henry, Capt Colclough and the two Mrs Colcloughs. Capt Colclough has a brother living at Berkley Hall in Notinghamshire, and he believes that some of his family are now in Staffordshire. All admired Celia greatly & thought her like her Papa.

6th – We have had a week of beautiful weather, every thing growing fast, but it is very hot, Celia sits most of the day without either Frock, stockings, shoes, or Cap, she would be constantly on her feet if I would let her, I never saw so strong a child. Send Sydney Peel word we have ten acres cleared and lugged ready for a bonfire, and if he make haste he will be in time to lend a hand. Edmund has finished painting the drawing room, the walls are a french grey, the window frames, skirting board and chimney piece doors and chimney piece Salmon colour, the room looks very cool and pretty. I have made Celia light clothing, it is impossible to be cool such weather.

8th – Sturges you should have been here yesterday, Mr Henry came to breakfast, he, Edmund and five Men went to draw the lines of our large Estate, it is rather an expensive affair for we pay and feed them all and they will be several days at work, it is very hot weather, and they are almost roasted in the Woods, Celia is dressed and out walking by seven, it is cool and pleasant at that early hour.

11th – Still beautiful weather, Oh! if Charles could see the Barley he gave us, it is in full ear, and set in drills, something quite new here, and the Yankees don't know what to make of it, I should think there cannot be finer. We have had a dish of peas out of our garden from those you gave us, and we are having some young potatos to day. Eliza & Matilda came yesterday, Mr Henry is completely tired with three days work, he found that our next neighbour had twenty acres of our land so you see it was high time we had the lines drawn. Celia is to be vaccinated by Mr Henry.[13]

13th – Yesterday Mr Henry came, Celia behaved very well. Edmund and I went to Lenoxville to call upon Mr and Mrs Doolittle, they live in a small house, they gave us excellent bread and butter & cake. Mrs Doolittle has three little girls, pupils; we went home by Sherbrooke, called at Capt. Colcloughs and at the Judges. Old Mrs Colclough said, I made her think of her younger days seeing me in a Habit and Hat. Oh! said the Major that is my favorite dress, Mr Henry rode home with us and remained dinner. Mr John Felton called afterwards, and they returned together to Belvedere.

Mr Felton is still at Quebec and will be some time, he sent for Mrs Felton to join him, but she is daily expecting a young Spaniard, her Sister's Son and she cannot leave home, she has not seen any of her family excepting a niece, since she came into this Country. Edmund has finished painting the house. I am sure you would admire it. We had a great fire on one side the rock yesterday, it lighted our bedroom most of the night, it is sublime to see a fire in Canada. Give our best love to all friends, our dear love to Papa yourself and Sturges – yr much attached child –

Lucy Peel.

No 16

July 16 –

My dearest Mamma

Edmund rode to Sherbrooke on Monday to take my last letter to the Post office, we have had fine weather for ten days and the garden wanted rain sadly, last evening we had a thunder storm which refreshed every thing greatly, when we were sitting in the veranda yesterday morning playing with Celia, to our great surprise Mr Felton called, he arrived at Belvedere the night before, quite unexpectedly, he said he was so much disappointed Mrs Felton did not join him at Three Rivers, he came on determined to take her back with him, and I believe they set off tomorrow. I have been bottling Green Currants. We have Venison in the house for the first time, an English farmer, living near sent me a quarter, I gave him 4^{d} a pound for it.

17th – We had a thunder storm yesterday, it cleared up in the afternoon and Mr & Mrs Felton called, he leaves to day, but his nice little wife notwithstanding all his trouble to have her company does not return with him, she is disarranged with her servants & does not like to leave her house. Mr Felton is sadly disappointed. Edmund has began to mow to day and we have a heavy crop, Mr Felton has some hundred acres to get.

19 – Yesterday Mr Henry, Fanny, Matilda, Mr John Felton and Mrs Feltons Nephew called. I played to them on the Harp, Mr Quartin is eighteen, and when he entered the room I thought it was Sturges, he has just his style of figure, manner, & dark eyes, he has been educated in England, has a good fortune, and is now travelling for pleasure. We dined at three upon our Venison, and just as we were finishing, a dashing Tandam with two beautiful Greys drove up to the Veranda, out jumped two young Men, and to our great surprise, in came Edmund Peel of Sorel, and Mr Buchannan,[14] fortunately we had plenty of Venison and I assure you they enjoyed it exceedingly, he left Mrs Peel at Sorel, she is near her confinement.

Mr Buchannan is quite pleased with the country and prefers our place to Sorel, he seems to have a great desire to be married; he had a parcel for me, but coming up they had all their luggage stolen out of the carriage, they have offered twenty pounds reward. Edmund Peel says our Villa is quite a Mansion compared with his cottage. This morning, the gentlemen in their gig, Edmund and I on horseback went to call at Belvedere, Mrs Felton is always pleased to see Englishmen. When we returned home, we found Mr Henry, Eliza and Louisa at Dunstall, Mr Henry came to see the baby's arm, she looks very pale.

The Hales have had a sad overturn, the Horses took fright & the carriage was upset, Mrs Hale was hurt on the head besides having a hole cut in her ancle. Dr Wilson was sent for when they arrived at Sherbrooke and last night Mrs Hale was not expected to live, she is, however, better to day.

21st – Yesterday morning the two Edmunds walked to see the horses, in the mean time Mr Buchannan and I gathered some Peas and shelled them on the veranda for dinner. At half past two the Gentlemen left us Mr Peel having promised to be at home on Tuesday, he wants us to visit them before his wife is confined but it is impossible for us to leave home this summer, his place is small but I hear it is beautiful finished off, he has spared no expense, he has given it three coats of oil paint, and his veranda, though smaller then ours, took two men six weeks to complete it, he gave them a dollar a day, fed them & gave them rum, he first painted his drawing room a pale pink but was obliged to change it for a slate colour as Lady Aylmer told him it looked like Adam and Eve, she is continually calling upon them and expects to find every thing in order. Lady Aylmer often gets up at four oclock to ride through the woods, Mr Peel tells me his wife takes snuff, he takes a great deal himself. He keeps four Cows, 15 Sheep and 17 Pigs, that he & Mrs Peel were at first quite ignorant of house keeping & were sadly cheated by their servants, the first winter they consumed 18 quarters of beef and seven pigs.

Edmund has bought a very nice horse for me, a dark chestnut, four years olds [*sic*], Captain Hillard wanted money so we got him cheap. Sturges would like him for the Wilton Races, we gave only 12 pounds ten, we have now some delightful rides and are set up for the summer, if we can afford to buy a Sleigh in the Winter I shall be content. It would be dismal to be shut up in the house seven months, and I am sure Celia would feel the confinement. We cannot get Sleigh under ten pounds and harness will be five more, I am almost afraid we shall not manage it this year, for Edmund's barn, an indispensable thing will cost him sixty pounds and he will pay for it the moment it is finished, it is 30 by 40 and contains Stable, places for Cattle and Sheep, for Hay & Grain and a thrashing floor.

23d – We had sixteen men here yesterday raising our barn, the four sides were fixed together on the ground and then raised by hand, just as one end was partly up, down it fell, four men were hurt but not dangerously, and the barn was raised by evening – We went a ride, called at the Hales, Mrs Hale much better, then we called at the Fletchers and upon Mrs Witcher who told us that Eliza Felton & Mr Quartin, who set off last Monday to attend the races at Three Rivers were returned, that the Cholera was very bad at Quebec and that Charlotte, Maria, Mr Felton, his Son William and Miss Loyd were all coming up on friday. Miss Celia was glad to see us at home again, she can now walk with holding two fingers.

25th – Yesterday I sent the women into the Hay Field, and we carried some of our hay into the new barn, in the evening I gathered some Raspberries, and we had a large bowl of them with sugar & cream to our tea, we regale ourselves most evenings in the same manner, I have made fourteen large Jars of Jam for the winter. Celia has a cold and is fretful, I was up with her from one till five this morning when Ellen relieved me and I went to bed.

26th – Yesterday Mr & Mrs Felton called, Edmund was helping to carry his hay, the party from Quebec arrived on Tuesday and Mr Felton says seventeen sit down in the dining room, we are invited to join them whenever we feel inclined & Mr Felton says we have now no excuse, having two horses, he called upon Mrs Peel of Sorel as he came up and thinks her a pretty, chatty, agreeable little woman, Edmund Peel and Mr

Buchanan had just arrived and expressed themselves much pleased with their visit here. Mr Peel found his English farmer dead of the Cholera, on Sunday last sixty died at Quebec and thirty on Monday, however it is abating. The Gents did not hear anything of their baggage, so I fear I shall never see my parcel. Mrs Peel of Sorel told Mr Felton she quite longed to see Celia, for Mr Peel told her he never saw so beautiful a child.

27th – Mr Henry was here to day to finish his surveying, we are busy with our hay again, Edmund and Parkes are mowing.

29th – I have had eight of them from Belvedere. Celia is ill with a bowel complaint.

August 1st – Yesterday I walked down to the Judges for medicine for Celia, he told me he had every kind, and hoped I would let him know whenever I wanted any, he wanted me to stay dinner, and offered to drive me home in his carriage but I refused, he said God bless you, good bye, he was in the midst of his books and papers, a sad dirty figure, he said he had seven hundred volumes to dust and arrange, and twenty thousand papers to look over.

I called upon Mrs Hale, she gave me some arrow root for Celia and a pair of red morocco shoes, on my return Mrs Witcher called, and in the evening Mrs Felton and Eliza in the Gig, & Mr Felton and Mr John on foot, called, they were uneasy about Celia and wanted to see her; Mr Henry goes to Montreal on Monday & I am preparing my parcel, perhaps you may receive it before this. It will be directed to Charles Lyon, it will contain your lace border, a Cap and strings, I have worked for you a little present from Celia to Mini, to Williamson, and to Maria, letters to Papa, Sturges, Miss Winter, Mrs Lyon, a note & Music for Mrs Reiss, I have not written to Rosa because my next journal will be addressed to her.

I was so tired yesterday with my walk, Edmund made me go to bed directly after tea I was asleep as soon as my head was upon the Pillow & did not awake till twelve, Edmund was not come to bed so I got up, and in the dining room I found him feeding Celia, he would not leave her and he did not like to have her cot into our room for fear of disturbing me they both looked as happy as possible. This morning Maria Felton brought me your letter 15 to which Mrs Mayne has so largely contributed, and dear Sturges too, I hope you will send Edmund & me how fortunate you were. Mamma you will soon be younger than any of us, how I should love to see you.

3d – Celia is much better to day; The Cholera is now so dreadful at Montreal that Mr Henry is not going, so I know not when you will have your parcel.

4th – Yesterday afternoon when we were on the rock gathering Raspberries for tea, Mr Henry and Mr Buchannan came, the latter is just returned from Upper Canada, he looked so fat and brown I scarcely knew him, they remained tea. Edmund asked Mr Buchannan how he liked Upper Canada, his simple answer was, you see Mr Peel I am returned to day. Mr & Mrs Witcher called, I played on the Harp, Mrs Witcher cried most of the time, she has a fine ear for music and can detect the slightest error, she said, hearing me made her think of England and former days. Tell Sarajane, with my love that I do mention all the bad of this country that I hear of or meet with. The insects I have told you of and how terribly they annoy us. There is not one venomous reptile in the Country.

7th – We have had two dreadfully hot days, I think such weather would half kill you, our Hay is all finished, and I am not sorry, Edmund worked so hard at it. I wish you could have dined with us to day to partake of some of our own lamb and young potatos, they were excellent and I remember how fond you are of them. Mr & Mrs Doolittle called this afternoon. Mrs Doolittle remained with me whilst her husband proceeded to marry two old people who were asked in Church last Spring, the wedding had been put off because Mr Doolittle had heard that her former husband was living. They marry any hour of the day here, at the Brides house or at the Clergymans, Mr Doolittle returned without having married them, he heard such an account of them, the old woman is nearly blind.

9th – Yesterday Edmund & I went to the Post Office for letters, Sherbrooke was full of gay people, a Waggon full from Belvedere and several others. Edmund had a letter from the Admiralty giving him leave of absence for two more years from the last of May. The Belvedere party called on their return. – My next to Rosa, best love to dear Papa & Sturges, ever yr affect. child

L. Peel.

No 17

Sept 10th

Dearest Mamma

Last Sunday going to Church we called at Mrs Hales and put up our carriage. There I had a long chat with Mrs Hale about gardening, she understands it, and is going to teach me to graft and to bud, she will have grafts from Quebec of all kinds, & has promised me some when my young trees are ready. Mr Doolittle gave us a long sermon, it is difficult at times to understand him. After dinner Mr Henry and Mr Buchan called, they were going to Belvedere, we were asked, but declined. Yesterday Mr Henry called for your box I sent it to Mr Buchanan.

Mrs Hale tells me the wild flowers will grow out of doors in England and are larger than in this country, her Aunt, Lady Amhurst [Amherst], has a garden of American wild flowers in England sent by Mrs Hale, and I believe they are the admiration of every one who sees them, I shall collect all I can and let you have them the first opportunity. Mr William Felton and Miss Loyd are to go to Quebec to day. I have began a bed quilt, it is to be wadded and lined with flannel for the winter, blankets are very dear here, I am glad to find a good and cheap substitute.

11th – On Wednesday we went to our Sadlers at Lenoxville and took Celia, returning we called upon Mrs Kimball in Sherbrooke, she is in her new house close to the river, it is three stories high, and has a veranda to each story, it is pretty from the house, but the building itself is ugly; Celia admired the fine red carpet in the drawing room and was delighted to crawl upon it. Mr Kimball has a large garden full of fruit. The girls from Belvedere were there. Yesterday was a very wet day, nevertheless Mr Quartin and three of the girls called after dinner. The Gentlemen came to say farewell, they left to day. This morning Edmund drove Celia and me to call upon Mrs Witcher, she lives on the other side of Sherbrooke, she gave me apples to bring home, it is a cold day and at six this morning the ground was white with frost. We killed a beautiful lamb last night, it weighs 42 pounds, we have sent a quarter to Belvedere, Parkes is a capital butcher.

16th – Last Sunday Mrs Felton & two of the girls called to ask me to lend them some candles. I gave them two green Melons to pickle. To day we have been down to Sherbrooke. Fanny Felton, dear Mamma says she could look at your picture a whole day it is so beautiful and kind looking, indeed it is universally admired. Miss Celia begins to show great spirit, she seems to understand every thing and is very sensitive, her Papa is the favorite when she wants to play, and I when she wants to sleep or be caded [a cade is a spoiled or petted child, *OED*]. I wish you could see Edmund carrying her about and singing, it is quite a picture, her little hands in motion all the time, sometimes over her head, and in every graceful posture you can imagine, the elbow & wrist rounded as though she had been years under the hands of a dancing Master.

19th – On Wednesday just as dinner was ready, Mr & Mrs Hale called, Fanny came with them, Celia kissed her all the time. Yesterday I had Mrs Felton & four of the girls; Charlotte drove a pair of horses, all the Girls are excellent whips. Mrs Felton said she never sees me unless she comes to our Villa. This morning Edmund and I went to see Mr Hales house, it will be completed this evening. It is beautifully finished, the work as good as you see in England, but the arrangements not half so good as ours none of the rooms so large, except the drawing room which is the same width and two feet longer.

22nd – I had a large party from Belvedere to call they went to Mrs M'Creadys for apples. When Parkes went to catch the horses to take us to church they were not to be found, he had left a bar down on Saturday, he was all day after them, making a fruitless search, this morning he went again at day break and about eleven oclock I had the pleasure to see him return with the runaways, he found them on a farm beyond Belvedere. Edmund has just finished building a shed for Carriages and Sleighs, he superintended & assisted Parkes, the Shed we had before for wood cost more than twenty dollars done by a regular hand; this, nearly as large, cost six, so you see to what good account my husband turns his tastes for carpentering, he has also built a porch to the back door which will keep us much warmer in the winter. We have had a ladder made out of a spruce tree, not one joining, it is 32 feet long.

24th – Yesterday we went to Sherbrooke, returning we saw Mr Buchan, he had that morning arrived from Montreal and brought Mrs Henry with him. Celia is becoming quite a chatterbox, she can say, there pretty little girl, Papa, she calls me mammon, she tries to do every thing we do, and when we want her to do what she does not like, she shakes her little head and laughs.

26th – Eliza & Maria spent yesterday with me, I taught them to knit purses. Celia can now say baby, and cousin Billy. I am beginning to quilt my bedquilt. The Girls at Belvedere say they are sure they should love you & they think if ever they go to England, however great the distance may be from you, that they should go to see you.

Oct 1st – Mr & Mrs Felton & Mrs Henry dined here on Sunday. I played several pieces. Mr Felton as usual, quite delighted, he said it was a shame my talent should be buried in the woods. Yesterday we went to Sherbrooke, took Celia, we met the Belvedere Carriage & Gig part going to Montreal, they said how dashing we looked coming along, and I must say ours is the prettiest set out in this neighbourhood. We are now doing all our washing at home, one of my servants is an excellent washer & the other irons very well, I paid four dollars a Month for Edmund and myself & part of Celias, the washing can be done at home for one dollar. Edmund is now busy ploughing, we have bought a *Creature* for twelve dollars, and are making it fat to kill for beef and candles. On Monday we had a good deal of snow, but it passed quickly away, it however begins to be cold, and we have fires all day, it freezes at night, our tubs had ice an inch thick. Edmund has began his knitting again these long evenings. Give our love to Papa, Sturges & all friends, & believe in the continued industry and love of your children in Canada –

Lucy Peel.

From Mr Edmund Peel Sept 7th
1834
to Mr Meek

Dear Father

I have just washed my throat with a cup of Bohea,[15] which was much obstructed by Ashes, smoke etc etc and now I will tell you of the glorious burn I have made on my lower farm of several acres which are to be ploughed this fall, ready for wheat and Oats in the Spring with some Grass seed. It is fine rich land and will give twenty Tons of Hay. I send you a specimen of Canada spring Wheat and Oats, the former is very good, I sowed some Wheat Charles Meek gave me, it is not yet ripe but bids fair, I have picked out a small piece of rich new land for the remainder, it will be a most desirable object to make the winter Wheat succeed, it divides the labour, all the work of a Farmer comes at once.

Every production this season is good & plentiful, the other day, my help told me a man would wish to trade some wheat of this year for 8 s/ a bushel. I told him I would sooner send to England for it, however he sold to the Inn keeper for 6^d and it will come down to 5/. Hay will be £1-5 a Ton, Oats from 1/6 to 1/8 a bushel. This is not a good Country for Grain, but well calculated for Cattle, Sheep especially, to the breeding of which I shall turn my attention. My gutter snipes[16] will not cut such capers as the last, they have good stout wooden *Cravats* on which have pretty considerably impeded their motions. I wish you could just step in and see how very comfortable we are. My best love to all at the Cottage

y^{rs} affec^t E. Peel.

From the same to Sturges Meek –
Sept –

Dear Sturges

My dear friend Mr Box, before his departure from England, offered to
convey a letter or parcel to any of my friends, knowing your chaste taste
for slippers, I send you a pair made by the Indians made of the Moose
Deer's skin, I shall picture you to myself sitting with your feet thus
encased in that comfortable chair supping your glass of port wine by the
dining room fire, blazing right cheerfully under the skilful hands of your
father, you should see what roaring fires we keep up to prevent being
frozen. When Balloons become more manageable let me entreat you to
make an aerial excursion over here, but have a care and don't get entan-
gled in the trees.

I have just purchased a farm for my brother Tom, of 100 Acres with a
small house and barn for 800 dollars. The man *guessed* he could not sell it
for less than 900, but in a few days finding I remained firm, came to my
terms. It is requisite to bargain hard with these republicans, they always
take less than they ask, if you hold out and appear indifferent they call it
trading with you and say, well now I guess I should like to trade this horse
with you, I presume he is an excellent goer, perhaps a Cow, a yoke of Oxen,
a Cart or Waggon, any thing, though they may want it the next minute,
provided they can make something by it, trading suits them better than
hard work. Your little niece sends you all lots of kisses – yʳˢ affect. –
E Peel.

From Mrs Peel to Mr Meek –

My dearest Papa

I am not going to trouble you with a long letter. I shall only tell you how
much we think of you, talk about you, and wish we could have you with
us, to show you our land and all we have done and are doing towards
improving it, if you had seen the rough state we found it in I think you
would say we have accomplished wonders considering the short time we
have been in the Country. We are proud of the praise you accord us for
our industry – we are determined to work, work, work, and should we
succeed we are amply rewarded, should our undertaking fail, we shall at
least have the consolation to know we have done our best, I have not the
least doubt but that if we have health and ordinary good fortune, we shall

prosper, of course it must be up hill work for the first year or two. We are considered a most quiet domestic couple, and Mrs Felton tells me she wishes her daughters may have as good a husband as I have. Edmund is a great favorite at Belvedere. Indeed he is a striking contrast to the dissipated Men they meet with. Edmund often talks of the comfortable chat you and he used to have after dinner over your wine when the extra piece of coal was ordered and the fire began to Blaze. I am sure you would enjoy our large wood fires. Pray write some times in Mamma's letters to your affec^n. Child –

L. Peel.

From the same to Sturges –

My dear Sturges

Sometime ago I promised to write to you in return for your agreeable additions to some of Mamma's letters. I will now perform my promise. You seem to be very gay & are enjoying yourselves much in England, and quite gallant sitting by two Ladies a *whole* evening at a concert. It is a pity Miss F – is not younger, her fortune would be a nice help to you in a country where riches are so necessary and so difficult to obtain. I do not know what you would think of surveying in this Country, Mr Henry says an English Surveyor would soon be at a stand in Canada, the flies when he is taking a sight nearly blind him, sometimes driving him out of the woods in spite of his *Smug* [smudge].

You would be highly amused to hear Mr Henry tell his tales about the Indians. He was in the North West Country for four and twenty years in the Fur Trade, & saw no one but the traders & the Indians, and for eighteen years saw neither book nor paper, suffering dreadfully from hunger and cold. Nothing will grow in that Country, in the summer the ground is parched up & in the winter covered with snow. Mr Henry let his hair grow, and his beard reached down to his breast, he did this that he might look more formidable to the Indians.

He and three men were once out ten days, and during that time had only one partridge amongst them, they were reduced to such a state that they could not stand & crawled upon their hands and feet, in this terrible condition, he one night heard the Men plotting to shoot him for food, he said nothing but quietly took possession of the only piece of arms they had, an old Gun and threatened to shoot the first who approached him, he made them lie down till morning, when they had three miles to go before they could find food and assistance; about half way they reached a Mountain at the base of which they found the head legs and bones of a sheep that had been killed a few days previous, they eagerly seized the prize one man took the head dashed it open with a stone & devoured the brains raw, two more took possession of the legs and Mr Henry took the bones, cracked them and eat the marrow. He told us several stories of Men being eaten in the woods & of one Man who eat eleven of his companions, he was afterwards taken to Montreal and stood his trial, but he was not hanged, he was a Canadian. Mr Henry made his fortune in the Fur trade.

I wish you were here now to shoot me some pigeons, there are thousands near to us. I am sure we could amuse you, there would be farming, shooting, Fishing, riding, and in the house, nursing your beautiful niece, Music & your favorite game backgammon, then there is *calling & doing* as old John says, which beats all, as the Yankees say, how you would laugh to hear some of these people talk. Anything that gives them trouble they call *laboursome*, looking sideways they call looking *Slanticularly*. Edmund sends love – & believe in the everlasting affection of your absent but loving Sister

L. Peel.

No 18

Oct 5th

My dearest Mamma

We have to day been a year in our house, it seems only the other day that we left our kind friends at Belvedere. It has rained all morning so we did not venture to church. Celia has made an excellent attempt to walk alone, she gets up without the least assistance and stands quite steadily & yesterday walked two yards by herself to get to her papa. Friday the horses could not be caught so Edmund walked to Sherbrooke. My bed quilt is finished it is very large and heavy and will be a warm comfortable covering in the winter. Mr & Mrs Hale are in their new house.

7th – This evening we went to Sherbrooke in the hope of getting our box, alas it came not, Mr Atkinson says he sent it to Three Rivers some time ago. The next box you send to Montreal, I wish Mr Atkinson might be directed to send it to Mr Henry, who would forward it immediately to us. I see by to day's paper that Tom Peel has arrived safely at New York.

In one paper he is styled the *Honn* Thomas G. Peel and in another *Sir* Thomas Peel.

You will see by the Paper that this country is not in a very settled state. Lord Aylmer, an excellent Man, is very unpopular with the Canadians who hate the English, these Canadians wish to have all the power in their own hands and Lord Aylmer, to show his superior power, has just appointed a Montreal judge they do not approve of.[17] When his Lordship went to that Town the papers were put in mourning, and they contained most abusive language about our Governor. Many Gentlemen, holding public offices, have been suffering greatly owing to the house refusing to vote the usual supplies, in consequence of which no salaries have been paid of two years; there are eight hundred pounds in arrears due to Judge Fletcher.

A Man came here with 300 lbs of honey to sell, he was much disappointed because I took only 25 pounds, being told by some person at Sherbrooke I should be certain to take all. I gave 7_ a pound, canadian money. Mr & Mrs Hale and children are gone to Quebec. We have had some new bread at ten this evening made from our own wheat, it is beautiful & quite a treat after the bad french flour we have lately been using ful [*sic*] of the black pea, which gives it a most disagreeable taste, should you not like a piece of our own, dearest Mamma.

11th – Yesterday Celia walked alone several times, her papa & I looking at her as proudly as two fond parents possibly could. I never told you that she has a light brown mark on one arm, about two inches long and one broad. The knowing ones tell me it is a slice of fresh meat, I wished so much for some when I first went to Belvedere, where for some time we had Salt Beef and smoked ham & bacon. We wish very much to have my Ottoman sent, but in its present state that is impossible, I wish you to have the work & trimmings taken from the frame and sent the first opportunity, Edmund can easily make a frame for it.

14th – No Tom yet, we wish him to come on two accounts, one that we may have the pleasure of seeing so near a relative, and another that I may get your August journal, for I conclude he is the bearer of it. I do not like being so long without hearing from you & we cannot think what keeps Tom at New York. Yesterday we had snow several inches deep, & there it is this morning & great icicles hanging from the veranda, we have not half our potatos in, however, we are told this is nothing, that the snow will soon disappear and warm weather come afterwards. We are getting our pretty Grey Mare, Dolly, in condition for sale, we cannot afford to buy a double Sleigh this winter and hay and corn are too dear to allow us to think of keeping an idle horse, I wish papa were near enough to purchase her, I *guess* he cannot in England get such a one for sixty dollars.

17th – On Wednesday we went to Sherbrooke, took Celia to see her Godmamma, who, with the Judge admired her very much, he said she was a most lovely child & had beautiful intelligent eyes, he was sure she understood as much as children of 18 Months old; indeed both Edmund and I have frequently been astonished at her quickness of intellect. Mamma, you would doat upon her, she would make you laugh at her antics. Mrs Henry says she never saw such a young child. Mrs Fletcher gave us excellent chocolate and Celia some bread & milk, they wanted us to stay dinner, but Edmund brought me a journal from you & I wished to get home to read it. How ill you have all been dearest Mamma, however I hope the sea air will set you up again.

We have had a letter from Edmund Peel of Sorel, his wife has a son, and is doing well. He has had the Cholera dreadfully, his medical attendant told him that nothing but the breaking of a blood vessel saved his life. He has advertised his farm for sale, he is tired of Sorel. Mr Farmer, who I mentioned in my last, has bought 2000 acres of land in Upper Canada, he has fifty men, women and children with him, another English Gentleman with a family who bought a farm in Stanstead has been very unfortunate, he brought out from England furniture of every kind, two pianos, an Organ, one of his careless helps put some hot ashes into a tub and they set fire to the house & every thing was burned but a few sovereigns, & more of these destroyed than saved, these wooden houses disappear so quickly in the flames that you are fortunate if you escape yourself, and it is next to impossible to save your property.

When I ask Celia where her Grandpapa is she is not satisfied till she touches the face. She says *pretty* to your picture. The snow being nearly gone, yesterday Edmund and Parkes went to the lower farm to get in some potatos, they were scarcely gone when when [*sic*] old Salt, the Judges servant, drove up and brought Tom with him, I sent for Edmund and he was soon with us.

20th – We think Tom much improved in appearance and something like Johnathan, he is certainly a fine young man and very gentlemanly, I am sure he will be a great acquisition to us, he seems so determined to make himself useful, ready to put his hand to anything, he is helping Edmund to day with our potatos, he is pleased with his farm, he thinks his niece very pretty, he calls her old Lady and Mrs Peel-y. I suppose the girls at Belvedere admire our brother for they said it was a shame he should live in the woods. Eliza is not at home, and Tom does not think either Charlotte or

Fanny pretty. I am surprised for I think Fanny sometimes, almost beautiful. Celia sends you a kiss & many thanks for the pretty letters. The tin you sent is most useful to me, it looks like an old friend.

Mr & Mrs Felton called, they brought me some immense apples and two pieces of Cheese, she asked us all to Dine at Belvedere tomorrow, we mean to go. I wish you could see how merry we three are together, Tom makes us laugh exceedingly at his adventures in Swan River, he thinks my good husband in excellent spirits and asked me if he were always the same. Yesterday we killed a two year old *creature*, it weighs 428 pounds, we have lots of candle fat, and shall make five & twenty pounds tomorrow, we have kept some of the meat fresh and salted all the rest, you would have been amused last night to see me Superintending the cutting up of the *creature*. This morning I have cut out a case for a straw bed for Tom and am going to make it for him.

27th – We had a pleasant day at Belvedere on Thursday, the Priest[18] was there, Mrs Felton looked very pretty, and Tom, as most Gentlemen do, thought her nicer looker [*sic*] than any of her daughters, on friday we went to Sherbrooke & had the delight to bring up the long expected box, how shall I thank you for the handsome & useful presents it contained, the first thing I saw was the chap [edible lower half of the cheek of a pig or other animal, as in pickled Bath chaps, *OED*], which we began upon the next day, it is most excellent, and a great treat, how thoughtful dearest Mamma to send it, and the preserves.

Dear Papa, Edmund and I think my dress lovely, I never saw such beautiful shades, it was very kind to have it made up. Edmund's waistcoat is very handsome Sturges. Every thing for Celia just what I wanted. Rosa's frock is very neat, it just fits Celia. Mr & Mrs Mayne's presents very nice indeed. Your presents dearest Mamma were too numerous to mention, they are all invaluable, particularly the Calico. Edmund is delighted you have written to Mrs Felton, he has been wishing you to do so some time, I shall give her your present to day, I am sure she will be delighted with it. I should love to see Rosa's baby, she must be almost as beautiful as Celia. Edmund made some cheap purchases, 4 Chairs for one shilling; a smart table 3/9- two candlesticks one shilling – quantity of Wheat at 4/ a bushel, Potatos 7_ bushel. You will be surprised I dare say to hear that the tin inside of the lid of the box proves a very valuable article, we have sent to every neighbouring Town and even as far as Three Rivers for some to mend the boiler of our cooking stove and could not get any, what you sent is just the thing for it. Mrs Felton has just been in, she is delighted with your note, she said Oh, Mrs Peel, what is it I have done to deserve such a note as this. She thinks her scarf very pretty. Edmund & Celia send with me best love to all – ever your much attached child.

Lucy Peel.

No 19

To Mrs William Birch   Nov^{re} 2nd

My dearest Rosa –

We have had snow a foot deed [*sic*] and I do not think it will disappear this winter, we have sharp frosts every night, and feels fires quite necessary. On Friday last Edmund drove me to Sherbrooke, to make some purchases for our brother, we took the things on our return to his house, he is anxious to begin house keeping, and fortunately for him, knows enough about it to prevent being imposed upon. I think he is sure *to get along* well, as the Yankees say. His house will be comfortable for a single man, his sitting room 16 by 12, it has, according to the fashion of the country, four windows and two doors.

To day we have been to Church, we put up our carriage at the Judges, Mrs Fletcher was in bed, but sent for me to see her and gave me a nice cup of hot Coffee. Celia had on the frock you sent her, it fits beautifully, I wish you could see her walk, it is such a pretty sight, she is quite firm upon her feet, and can stoop to pick any thing up without losing her balance, she follows me from room to room like a little lap dog, she almost runs some times; her uncle is very fond of her & thinks her exceedingly pretty, she begins to play with him in a most gracious manner. I have been making long sleeves to Celia's frocks and wadding her bonnet, on Tuesday Mr John Felton called to make me a present of a fine Goose, we were not dressed, he told me there was a bag of apples for me at Sherbrooke which he bought in the States.

On Wednesday we went for the apples and found Mamma's welcome journal, she seems to think there is no place like home and I am sure all sensible persons will agree with her, I am delighted to hear they are all well again. I always think of my darling Celia and your little Frances together, they are so nearly the same age, every thing Celia does, I wonder whether her cousin is equally forward, she is very fond of her Doll which she calls *dooly*, herself, she calls baby.

12 – Edmund drove Celia & me to call upon Mrs Hale, she did not enjoy her visit at Quebec for the children were ill all the time, she

brought Celia a beautiful pair of shoes lined with white wool and sable fur on the outside, we had lunch and very good beer. Miss Boen [Bowen] is a very agreeable girl but plain; we broke the waggon, going over Mr Hales bad road. Sherbrooke was full of people Electioneering, our Town sends two members to the house & there are four candidates, Mr Moore a Lieut. in the Navy,[19] Mr Gregg [Gugy] a Lawyer,[20] a Tory, Mr Toldford [Tolford], a radical,[21] and Mr Gilbert a radical, Capt Colclough wanted Edmund to stay and give his vote, he said he did not mean to vote unless he were wanted to decide the day when he would support Mr Moor [*sic*].

Mr Felton is gone to Three Rivers to bring home Eliza, her friend Miss Nelson was married on Monday. We had a good deal of snow last night. Mr Bartholomew Roland Augustus Gregg [Gugy] & Liet. Moore are elected to represent Sherbrooke. I have a squib now before me about Mr Tolford, it gives his history & ends thus. Independent, honest & enlightened Electors of Sherbrooke are you willing to submit to the disgrace of being represented by this man in the next provincial parliament? Will you confide your rights, your liberty to the keeping of a man with whom you will not trust a copper of your property, are you willing to be represented by an insolvent in principles, character honesty and Talent? If so vote for Calvin Wilson Tolford.

17th – We have now very cold weather, every thing freezes, all the snow is gone, we have our stove in the hall lighted and it keeps us very warm, our bedroom close to it is very comfortable, warmer than any bed room in England with a fire in, for every corner is warm & in England if you move from the fire you are cold. Saturday Edmund drove Celia & me to call at Belvedere, the air was cutting, Mrs Felton and the children came running to meet me. We had a hot lunch, I enjoyed it exceedingly, they never seem to think they can make too much of me, we sat a long time, the Priest was there.

On Sunday Edmund, Tom and I walked to church, it was so cold and the roads so rough we preferred it to riding. Parkes took down the carriage to be ready for evening, we dined at the Judges, Mr & Mrs Hale, Miss Boen & Mr Hallowell the Lawyer[22] were there. In the evening I drove home & my two gentlemen ran by the side, when half way I got out and walked, it was too cold to bear. Edmund led the horse, we wore holes in our shoes the roads were so rough and sharp. Tom could not help laughing at the high key in which Mrs Fletcher gave her orders at dinner, orders which should be private, but every one heard; we had for dinner boiled beef, Fowls and ham, & when the servant was taking away Mrs Fletcher said, do not touch the ham, but I don't care if you eat all the fowls. Celia has been very fretful the two last days, she is getting more teeth.

23d – Thursday I made eleven pork pies very good. Isabella Felton came to play with Celia, it is beautiful to see them together. Celia kept screaming with delight, she is a most sensitive child and a grave look is sufficient to bring tears, she never takes up anything without first touching it & looking at her Papa or me to see if we approve. Edmund is busy chopping to day & has two large fires on the rock, I have been to help him.

27th – I forgot to say we drank Jaspers health on the 13th, and I hope & believe mine was drank last tuesday by many friends in England. The Snow has now set in and Sleighing has began, we are daily expecting our new Sleigh. Our brother has been confined to the house this week with cold & rheumatism. Tell Mamma the Damson cheese [a thick conserve of damson plums and sugar, *OED*] was delicious, there are no damsons in this country, I hope she will never send a box without putting in a little.

Celia quite amused Mrs Felton yesterday, she went from one person to another shaking hands every time and talking in her way, altering her voice just as if she were holding a conversation. Her Uncle admires her more every day, he says to her you are a pretty creature. Her Papa is now the grand favorite, & no wonder, for there never was a more doating parent, he is constantly playing with her & she always cries when he leaves her.

Edmund was chopping wood yesterday and cording it, he means to cord all he can this winter to be ready for next, we are obliged to have it cut a year in advance as green wood will not burn in the stoves, it gives no heat and makes the Pipes run, the black hot bistre spoiling every thing, we use nearly a hundred cords a year, so if we can chop even a few it will be a saving as we pay two shillings a cord, the cords are eight feet long, four broad, four high. In the winter when both stoves and two fires are used night and day we use a cord 1/4 daily.

30th – On Sunday our new Sleigh arrived, it is very commodious for a single one, the man promised it Parks [*sic*] for forty dollars, twenty he owed Parkes for work & he was to pay him down the other twenty, we sent him out money, but he said he must have ten dollars more or he would take back the Sleigh, we refused it and our carriage was really soon gone. I believe two people on the road had admired it and offered fifty dollars though I much doubt whether it would have been paid in cash.

On Friday morning we sent off Parkes to try to buy another, he could not meet with one, but found his cousin has not left Sherbrooke with the one he brought here, so after a long parley and a threatening from Parkes to sue him for his twenty dollars he gave up the Sleigh for the price first agreed upon. What will you say when I tell you the colour of our carriage and when I further say it looks very stylish and pretty though I fear we shall *melt* all the Snow as we go along, the body is bright *red* varnished, the inside fills, as the shafts are here called, and runners, bright yellow, the runners of a Sleigh are like the rockers of a chair, shod with steel and iron.

Yesterday Edmund took Celia & me to Sherbrooke, we went delightfully, so smooth after the shaking summer carriages, Celia talked nearly all the way, in the afternoon Eliza & Charlotte called. Toms [*sic*] thinks Eliza prettier than any of the Belvedere family, I do not think so, but I am sure she is the one any man would chuse for a wife. I love her very much, she is affectionate, and warm hearted and has a sweet good tempered expression.

I am the only one up this morning, my cook sent me word she was too ill to work, so Ellen has all to do. I am nursing baby, she is playing at my side as good as possible. Have you read The Pilgrims of the Rhine by Bulwer? I never expected to see such a work from his pen, some few pages are beautiful but the greater part of the work, mere trash[23] – Best love to all friends – ever your much attached Sister

Lucy Peel.

No 20

Dec[r] 3d

My dearest Mamma –

On Sunday my cook went home, I sent for Mrs M'ready, she came though far from well – I have not been well the last few days. Papa & Celia quite well. I have scarcely seen Edmund in the house all week, he goes into the Woods directly after breakfast to chop and remains till dark. Yesterday a large bough fell upon him and Parkes and knocked them both down, they were not much hurt. We have the comfort of knowing that we do not owe anything, we make a point of not buying unless we have money to pay at the time, I am sure you will approve of this plan. My cook is come back –

7th – Edmund has suffered with head ache & I with cold, nevertheless on Tuesday we went to Sherbrooke for I felt as if I should have one of your invaluable journals and I received No 19. But my dearest Mamma how ill you have been, and I fear far from well when you sent off the letter for I know you would make the best of yourself, pray take the greatest care all this winter. Celia coughs, I fear she is beginning of a cold. The snow is now pretty deep and we shall have good Sleighing, I am sure you would like a Sleigh, they are so warm and go so smoothly and near the ground, there is no fear of an upset hurting you.

13th – It is six days, my very dear Mama, since I wrote, and how much has happened since then, how quick the transition from bliss to misery; then I was the happiest and proudest of parents, and now I am – yes, the dreadful truth must be told, *childless*. Oh, Mama, I know you will deeply feel, and bitterly grieve for us when you know; our little darling upon whom we so doated, who was our all, our comfort and joy, so good, so affectionate, so very fond of us both, is taken from us, and now lies in her cold and last bed. I must collect my bewildered thoughts, and tell you every particular.

Last Monday, when Celia awoke, and I took her, as usual, into our bed, I found she was so hoarse she could not speak. Her head appeared quite free from cold, and I concluded her cold, like all ours, had affected her chest. I dressed her after breakfast, and she smiled and played with every thing on the table all morning, but would not go off my knee. She ate little, and liked some gruel I had made, better than any thing; she drank a great deal, nothing seemed to satisfy her, but this she had done some time. I supposed her gums felt hot from some teeth. Towards evening her breathing became much affected, and her pulse was quick, her hands and feet hot, but her face quite pale, and cool. Edmund carried her about the room, and she would go and touch Papa's picture, and then smiled. I fancy now as if she was bidding it farewell.

At night her eyes were heavy, her bowels quite loose. I put her into her tub, up to the neck in salt and water. She appeared better after this, and fell asleep on my knee. Not feeling at all happy about her, I had her brought into the drawing room, and sat up with her all night, Edmund remained with me till nearly two, when I prevailed upon him to go to bed, as he was far from well. Celia kept dosing all night, sometimes in her Cot, sometimes on my knee. Towards morning her breathing became much worse. She had a rattling in her throat, which appeared to come quite from her stomach. Her face was much altered. Ellen was up and took her, whilst I called Edmund. We sent off immediately for Mrs Felton, she came, and said, she thought Celia had a very bad cold and looked ill, and though she apprehended no danger, yet, as every thing with children was so sudden, she begged I would send for Dr Wilson directly. He lived six miles off. Parkes went that moment, and Edmund set off to Belvidere on foot, tho' the roads were scarcely beaten and knee deep in snow, for medicine, thinking the Doctor might not bring any.

I had Celia across my knee, she kept drinking as much as I would give her, and was very sick, and fainted several times, being evidently in great pain, and putting her little head first on one of my shoulders, then on the other, and at times slightly convulsed. I had her again put into warm water and rubbed. The convulsions became stronger every moment, and in a short time she did not know me. She fixed her beautiful eyes on the ceiling. First a black spot came on her cheek, then several on her body, then one arm, then the other blackened, and her legs the same. Her head then was convulsed, and every feature distorted. I held her tight to me, but looking at her all the time. In an instant every feature became calm, and as she used to look when asleep. I kissed her, and whilst doing so, her little spirit fled, and her face became like marble. Oh, Mama! the horror of that moment I cannot describe. I did not cry; I sat like a stone, and felt as if my heart would burst.

Doctor Wilson came soon after she died. He said it might only be cold which caused her death, or it might be her teeth, but it was impossible to say. I fancy it must have been partly her teeth.[24] Mrs Mouney [spelled "Mousy" below] fancied the child had worms. Tom was in the room when Celia died. He was greatly affected, and wanted to go and meet Edmund to prepare him for the event; but I thought he had better get home first, and then be told before he came into the room. I never shall forget him when he heard. He came into the room flushed with running five miles, and covered with snow. He took no notice of any one, but threw himself upon the sofa, and wept like a child. When a little composed he had some conversation with Doctor Wilson, but without gaining any satisfactory intelligence.

All our friends have proved their sincere regard for us by the most kind attentions in our affliction. Tom has been invaluable. He took every thing off Edmund's hands, and saved his feelings in every possible way. Mr John Felton went to speak to Mr Doolittle to come to bury our darling up here, for the church yard at Sherbrooke is not consecrated, quite exposed, and it is shortly to be removed, or rather, changed. Tom fixed upon a quiet spot near the house, but out of sight, for the grave, and he and Parkes prepared it; they were from nine in the morning till five at night, about it, and it was hard work, for the snow was deep, and the ground hard. Four were dug before they could get one deep enough, owing to the solid rock a short way below the surface. Mrs Felton sent their own Carpenter to make the coffin, and when it came home I had striking and affecting proof of her care and attention to my feelings. It was painted white, lined with white, and stuffed with linen[?]. The pillow frilled all round, and a plaiting of gymped calico round the edge of the coffin.

The good old Judge came up to see us, and brought Mrs Salt to stay if she could be of use. I did not keep her. Mrs Hale came to offer to stay, or to take home any work I might have to do. I had not occasion for her services, for Mrs Mousy made my bonnet, and the body of my dress, and Mrs Felton had the shirt made. Yesterday we had the funeral; only Mrs Felton, Mr John Felton and Mr Doolittle here. Our clergyman told us it was astonishing the number of children that have died lately from cold, and very suddenly. One little boy, who had a cold, and whom the doctor attended, was getting pretty well, and sat up in his cradle; he asked for his play things, and begged his Papa would sing to him. In an instant he gave one start, his mother flew to him, and he was dead.

If you could see Edmund I am sure you would all grieve. He is very quiet, seldom cries except when alone with me; but he sits like a statue, talks of nothing but Celia, and, when any one but I, am present, never speaks from morning till night. He looks as pale as death, and ten years older since Celia died. The first morning I thought he never would leave his room, for she always met him peeping at the door, and wanting to go to him. He always played with her till breakfast was ready, and vain would be any attempt of mine to make her come willingly to me; when I offered to take her she shook her head, and clung to his shoulder for fear of losing him. I do not think any father would miss a child half so much, for he saw Celia constantly night and day. He was wrapped up in her, was so proud of her, often saying what a perfect form and face she had, and what a beautiful woman she would make.

I now fancy we made too much of her, we almost idolized her, still she was not spoiled, for she never took a single thing if we said no. She might have known she was going to leave us, for all the last week she would not go to sleep till ten or after, and scarcely ever in the day time, but would sit laughing and talking; and the night before she died we were both sitting on the sofa with her, and she first kissed one, and then the other, for a number of times, putting her lips to ours, and looking so pleased, and then taking her Papa's handkerchief, and blowing her nose, like any grown up person. But alas! you will never see her now to be certain that all we have said of her is true. Every one said she looked almost too perfect in face and figure; such a brilliant complexion, and an expression never the same two minutes together. She really was, as a lady said, more like a little angel, than a mortal. Our only consolation now is in talking of Celia, and thinking of all her endearing ways.

We have a long dreary winter before us. Edmund is kinder than ever, if possible, to me. We have only each other to love. We mean to employ ourselves as much as possible. I shall send away my Cook, I have engaged Ellen to remain, and I shall have to assist in the house a good deal. I must remember, though in sorrow, it is a difficult task, that I have still the duty of a wife to perform, and I may still say, that of a mother, for I know if I neglect my own health, I may injure that of my infant yet unborn, whose birth I look forward to with joy, yet fear and trembling.

I often fancy if William Birch had been near, Celia would have been saved; he is so clever, particularly with children. Oh! if he will in the Spring send us a medicine chest, for we cannot get good drugs here; also scales, and weights, and directions what doses to give to children and adults; also write and tell me the different complaints children so young, generally have, the symtoms and remedies. He will lay us both under very great obligations. I should like to hear whether he can form any opinion of the cause of Celia's death from what I have said. Was it not remarkable that her hands, feet, and body should be so hot, her pulse high, and yet her face quite cold and pale, and her lips, and under the eyes rather black? I shall enclose a small piece of hair. Part I wish Mary Lyons to have, she expressed a wish to that effect. I know she, and, indeed, all my friends, will feel for my distress. Every Mother must, I am sure.

Oh! may I never see such another scene. I fancy I can never love another like Celia. You may imagine how thankful I am now that I have done so much for her. I was not only her Mother, but her constant nurse, and Tom called me her Slave. I always felt I could never do too much for her, she loved me so. I miss her so when I ought to be washing and dressing her. Every thing I look at reminds me of her. She knew every thing, her shoe, necklace, ball, rattle, in short, all things. Edmund will thank you to write to Church Bank. He is not equal to it, and I know they will excuse me writing a second letter upon such a heart rending subject. Adieu my dearest Mama. Write and comfort your affectionate child. Indeed, I greatly need comfort. Kiss dear Papa and Sturges for me, and believe me Your attached

Lucy Peel.

No 21

My dearest Mamma

My last melancholy journal sent off last Monday, Edmund went down that day to Sherbrooke, Tom accompanied him, it was the first time my dear husband had left the house since our darling was taken from us, he is now more composed, and so am I, but we have many bitter moments & talk of every thing Celia did. I miss her most in a morning when I am at work, she was then always in the room and used to run off with my sewing to a corner of the room, when a game at play generally followed. Her death appears a dream, and her short existence a bright speck in our lives which can never be forgotten, we can have no regret on her account, for she is supremely happy, all our sorrow is selfish, still it cannot be conquered at once, time alone can soften our affliction.

Mrs Felton has not been here since the funeral, she said if I wanted her she would come, otherwise not, as she saw Edmund would be better with only me for a time. On Monday my kind friend Mrs Fletcher came and sat a long time, she said she could not be happy till she had seen me. She pressed us to go & spend a quiet day with her next week, I felt I could not leave home at present. Edmund prevailed on me to take a ride, we went on the Belvedere road, but not to the house. Yesterday Tom took possession of his house, he appeared sorry to leave us, and we miss him exceedingly he was always cheerful and talked amusingly, he will often come to see us. Mr John Felton sent us three fine Codfish.

19th – Celia's birth day, you will all to day drink my darlings health, little thinking she is no longer an inhabitant of this world. On Wednesday Mrs Felton came and staid several hours. Edmund went to see Tom, he had been almost dead the night before with cold though he had a large fire in his bed room, every thing in the morning was frozen, even the sheet where he breathed, we had several days dreadfully cold, the glass 18 below Zero.

Yesterday it snowed and looked dismal. Mrs Hale came up, she remained a long time whilst her husband and Sister went on to Belvedere, she appears to be fond of me & is exceedingly kind and attentive, offering to come any time to see me, or nurse me when indisposed, we talked a great deal about Celia. Mrs Hale, notwithstanding her own children are very pretty, thinks Celia was the most beautiful child she ever saw, she said, she & Mr Hale often talk about her heavenly expression and lovely soft blue eyes, she has not the least doubt that Celia died of Inflammation on the lungs, many children died of that complaint when she was at

Quebec. The medicine men at Quebec always gave emetics the first thing, perhaps if Celia had had earlier advice she might have been saved, but this is a dreadful thought for a mother and I endeavour to think it impossible.

Whilst Mrs Hale was here Mr & Mrs Doolittle called, he is a very good man, he entered upon the subject of our affliction, and talked long upon the comforts of religion, he said we must grieve under such a loss, he would not wish it otherwise, but we must not mourn without hope, he considered it a beautiful & holy sign of God's great love when he called to himself beings of a tender age, thereby making them certain of heaven and partakers of ever lasting glory. He asked if Mr Peel were more calm, for he saw how full his heart was, and how deeply he felt the blow. He certainly is more composed, every day but he feels as if his heart had been seared and he shall never feel at all as he used to do till he has another child, he had promised himself such pleasure all this winter in Celia. Mr Witcher came up to inquire after us. Mrs Hale gave me a beautiful little book containing Gems of sacred Poetry. This morning Edmund went to Sherbrooke and returned immediately to take me a ride, it did me good.

23 – Mrs Kimbal has just been to call, she is a very kind woman and feels for me having had a similar loss. We wished Louisa & Rosa many happy years yesterday & the day before.

26 – Mr Felton called and was, as usual, very agreeable. Tom came to see us. On Christmas day we thought and talked of you all and said how merry you would be at Oak Hill, perhaps performing a play, we were very quiet and comfortable, we went in the morning to church and received the sacrament, we put up our Sleigh at the Judges, & I paid Mrs F. a visit in her bed room. Tom dined here, we had excellent Peas Soup, a Leg of Mutton which had been hanging three weeks and a hunting pudding, after dinner we indulged ourselves with a little wine to drink health and prosperity to all our friends in old England. This is a lovely morning, Edmund is gone out to chop, but said he should return at twelve to take me a walk, he certainly is the most attentive of husbands.

31st – Mr & Mrs Felton called & brought Miss Felton a Sister of Mr Feltons, she is a Lady like good looking person, very animated, whilst they were here Mr Hale and Miss Boen called, Mrs Hale was in bed with a cold which had settled on her chest. Mrs Felton brought me a nice plum pudding, half of which I took to Tom, he had just received his long expected box, I helped him unpack it & hung his cloathes to air, he brought out two pieces of blue and black furniture [hanging and ornamental drapery, *OED*], very neat, he gave me one piece, as soon as I got home I set to work, it was two oclock, and by dinner time, five, I had made and nailed up the dining room curtains. Edmund was quite surprised at my expedition, in the evening I made the valence and trimmings and Edmund fastened them up. I mean to make Tom's curtains for him, I find I am better, and less sad when fully occupied, I cannot then so frequently revert to the one dreadful subject.

Jany 1 1835 – Many happy new years to you all dearest Mamma, and many happy returns of the day to our father at Church Bank, pray send him word we remembered him. Last Tuesday we went down to Sherbrooke and afterwards to Belvedere, they made us stay dinner, Miss Boen was there. Miss Felton from Montreal admired Edmund exceedingly, she said she expected to see a much older Man, and can scarcely fancy so young a Man & a Naval officer settling so steadily in the woods. Edmund is now I am happy to say, recovering his good looks, it was quite distressing to see him a short time back. We brought home with us a Turkey and a Goose.

My servant Margaret has this week done all the washing & Ironing herself besides the usual work of the house, I never wish a better servant than she has been during Ellens absence. Yesterday Miss Goodhue called and her brother Charles. This morning Capt & Mrs Colclough, Annabella, Beacham the eldest Son, and Mr Bare called, he is a young Lawyer, a genteel looking young man.

Saturday we spent the day at Mr Hales, Mr Hale and Edmund went over the farm together up to the knees in snow, we came home by moon light. Yesterday Edmund walked to church, he would not let me go it was so cold. This evening Charlotte, Fanny and Maria came. My bed quilt gets on famously, I think I told you it is all in squares of about half a nail, I hope to finish it this winter, I have to tack every piece on paper before I sew it. I am reading a very interesting work "Henri Quatre" or the League, the Author not known.[25] Tomorrow is post day, surely I shall have a letter to tell me you are quite well.

Judge Fletcher is gone [on] one of his Circuits, Mrs Fletcher wishes me to go & spend a few days with her during his absence, I need scarcely say that I have declined. Tom tells me he begins to be more a convert to a married life, he often feels dull & says how he should like to have a nice wife to talk to when he is tired of chopping wood, I am sure I would not be unmarried in such a country as this for all the riches in the world. I send a piece of Celia's hair which I wish to have put into a ring the same as yours. Edmund sends his best love with mine to Papa you & Sturges,

Bessy, Hart, & all friends at Barton & Elswhere – Mr Felton went to Quebec on Saturday, the house meets on the 27th when much important matter is expected to be settled, I should not like to be Governor of Lower Canada, it is said Lord Aylmer is to leave. Your attached child

L. Peel.

22nd

My dearest Mamma

Edmund and I went to Sherbrooke this morning, I called upon Mrs Colclough, we afterwards drove to Belvedere, we have not yet heard anything of the box. I think Eliza Jane is a sensible girl to like a Man past thirty, as men of that age generally make the best husbands. So you hope Sir Robert Peel will remember Edmund, I hope not, and that he will have so much to do in his responsive Situation that he will not be likely to think of his humble Cousin in Canada unless reminded of him, and I think no one will do this except it be our Uncle Bolton who appears so fond of Edmund, but I trust he will be silent, for I am convinced it would not be a good thing for us, if you look to the future instead of the present, and if they will let my husband keep his half pay and remain quietly here our children, if we have any, will be the gainers, it would take a hundred pounds to convey us to England, and at least a hundred more to fit Edmund out for Sea. As for my own feelings I should not allow them to interfere with what would be right, but I should be miserable to part from my husband, his attentions hourly experienced are become necessary to my happiness, we have been dependant on each other for every comfort since our marriage, and you may imagine that we cannot look forward to parting for some years, without much grief.

19th – On Saturday Mrs Henry called, she had a very disagreeable journey from Montreal, Capt Colclough came with her, the first night they stopped at an Inn kept by a Yankee, and to give you further proofs of the delicacy of these people, who think it a shame to have their husbands take any notice of them. When going to bed a woman said to Mrs Henry, we have only one spare room, I suppose you will not mind sleeping with the Gentleman, there are two beds, I guess. Mrs Henry said she must have a room to herself, the woman said, well I calculate the gentleman must sleep in the loft but he'd do you no harm here I guess, now you must know the Yankee beds, are minus curtains, Capt Colclough accordingly slept in the loft amidst peas, beans, and various kinds of grain, & had companions all night in the shape of mice.

The next night when Mrs Henry was taken up stairs at another inn, she found there was another small bed room through hers & no entrance to it but through her room, she said she shd prefer the small room, the woman said, well now I guess thats my room and I shall come to bed late but no one else will come so you need not be afraid. Mrs Henry had not been in bed very long when the door opened and in walked a tall Yankee and the woman with him, Mrs Henry said, who's there, only the boy going to bed said the woman, I have given up my bed to him but he's very quiet and will not hurt you, so saying the man walked to the bed and Mrs Henry knowing it would be useless to remonstrate composed herself to sleep, a man came in the morning to light her fire and she asked if she or the boy was to get up first, I guess the boy will lie quite quiet so you may get up, Mrs Henry said she would never go to the place again and the man said, well now I guess you may just do as you like, we urges none. The more I hear of travelling in this country the more I am inclined to remain at home.

22nd – We drove to Sherbrooke & there received your journal full of interesting matter, it has not been more than a month coming, I was exceedingly surprised to hear of the Oldershaws. What a dreadful trying sacrifice to make, and what strong minds it must require to execute such a plan, now dearest mamma you will be happy in the society of Louisa and her children, how I should like to have them here for a short time. I am not surprised to hear of Mr Peels death as all your late letters have contained bad accounts of his health. So you remembered my birthday and kept it as usual inviting the old party. I suppose I may now consider the picture I have of you my own, what a treasure it will be to me. We dined at Belvedere yesterday. Mrs Felton sends kind regards to you, she would like to see you very much.

How little you think when you mention Celia so affectionately that you are distressing your absent child, but you will soon know all and then I shall be spared having her named. When I am alone, or only Edmund talks to me about her I cry and feel better afterwards, but if any one else alludes to her I feel as if I were on fire and as if my heart would burst, I cannot speak for some time & feel very faint. The poor Priest at Belvedere the other day began to talk to me about her and I had one of these attacks, Mrs Felton saw my agony and got me out of the room, I did not recover all day, and returned home the minute Edmund came for me, I dread seeing any one least they should talk about Celia, I am quite a different being since she died. Poor Mary Backley [Buckley?]! how I pity her, what trouble there is dearest Mamma in this world.

Great hopes are entertained here that this Country, now in a very unsettled state, will be benefitted by the change of Ministry in England.[26] There have been several duels lately in Montreal, all occasioned by Politics, if one man look rather savagely at another he is thus addressed. Is that look intended for me Sir? Yes – a card is then presented and they meet the next morning. The Feltons can none of them bear to think it possible we shall leave them, though Mrs Felton seems to consider it certain that Sir Robert Peel, without being asked, will forward Edmund in his profession. Give our affectionate love to dearest Papa & Sturges & all our friends, ever your attached child.

Lucy Peel.

No 23

Jan^{ry} 25th 1835

My dearest Mamma

Edmund set off to walk to Sherbrook but the snow was so drifted he could not get on. On friday we drove to Sherbrooke, the snow very deep and the roads heavy, we were obliged to go on the walk nearly all the way. Mrs Felton, Eliza, Isabella & brother Tom dined here, the Belvedere party go to Quebec tomorrow, Mr Felton said the road was dreadful from their house here, they were obliged to send a horse Sledge first to open it and two men held up their Sleigh most of the way, they returned home early. It is very cold this morning, I persuaded Edmund not to go to church.

31st – On Wednesday Mr & Mrs Peck called to bring me the list of things they can part with, all their furniture is very handsome and they are selling it at a great loss, Mr Peck gave a flaming account of the place he is going to *Chicorgo* [Chicago], it is on the Illinois and has three thousand inhabitants the winter only six weeks, the land all Prairie and a dollar and a half an acre, but the summer very hot. Mr Peck asks four hundred pounds for his pretty house and other buildings in Sherbrooke built on an acre of land, this will be a great bargain for any new settler.

On Thursday we went to Lenoxville to call at the Doolittles, he was just going to a funeral, we saw it, there were twenty Sleighs, it was a beautiful sight though a most painful one to us just now. This morning we went to the Pecks to buy a few things we want, we got blankets at three dollars a pair as good as the pairs we had at Montreal at seven

Dollars, Good strong kitchen chairs at a shilling each. Mr Peck wanted Edmund to buy his handsome carriage, he will part with it for fifty pounds, his Sleigh also very handsome, dark Green varnished all new this winter, double seats and lined with Cloth and stuffed, either for one or two horses, it is a great temptation, it cost sixty dollars, it has two robes, there are skins lined with green baise, they cost seven pounds, Mr Peck would sell altogether to us, for fifty dollars, only ten more than we gave for our single one, we mean to try to part with ours, in which case we shall buy Mr Pecks, we shall never have such another chance. Tom has cut through the tendon of his great toe with his axe. He will take our Sleigh, so we are able to purchase Mr Pecks, I wish you could see it, the hair on the Robes is five inches long, the skin of a Muscock [muskox], a very large animal.

Mr Charles Buchannan sent us the English papers full of Politics. Edmund has finished his Rug made of round pieces of cloth sewed on Canvass, we are busy putting on it a black & red fringe, it looks very pretty & will be down tomorrow. My bedquilt is more than half done, I have put in 13 hundred squares, every one admires it, and wonders at my patience. We have been to the Post to day, no letters, we saw Mr Hale, his wife has been dangerously ill with inflammation in the bowels which I am sure you will not much wonder at when I tell you that the day before yesterday, the Glass, being at Sherbrooke, 36 below Zero, she was running out of doors without any thing on, she was scarcely seventeen when she married & is very young in manner.

12th – On Sunday it was dreadfully cold, we did not go to church, the drift was so deep we were obliged to send Parkes with the ox Sled on Tuesday to beat the road before we could go down to Sherbrooke. On Wednesday we called at Belvedere, the children were delighted to see me, we brought Octavia home with us. We find our new Carriage called a Burline, very comfortable and much warmer than our Sleigh was, it will hold four. On Tuesday last dear Celia had been dead two months, I constantly think of her, there are some things that can never be got over, and one, is, the death of a child, you may become calm and resigned to the loss, but there must ever be moments when your grief will return. Do you not agree with me dearest mamma? You have lost three darling children and are able to judge.

17th – Friday last was a very warm day, we went to call upon the Hales & found Mrs Hale quite well, she wanted me to spend the day there but I declined, she promised to dine with me to day, but I have just had a note from Mr Hale telling me his wife is again in bed with another attack of inflammation. On Saturday I spent the day at Belvedere, Edmund came to dinner. Yesterday we bought a Pig weighing 210 lbs we gave £2 – 12 – for it, we also bought 50 lbs of fine Beef for 12/6. I expect it will take nearly a week to thaw the Pig, it lies in the kitchen as stiff as a post.

20th – On Tuesday we called at the Judges, Mrs Fletcher wanted us to remain dinner, but we refused. When I was making pork pies and brawn, [pork, boiled, then pickled or potted, *OED*], as I never saw any in England as Mrs Felton makes it, I shall tell you how it is done. The snow is very deep this winter, generally speaking four feet, and more than six in the drift.

25th – On friday I went to call upon Mrs Goodhue, she has been four months in bed, I much fear she will not recover, Mr Goodhue has proved himself an exception to the generality of cold American husbands, he has been his wifes only attendant every night since she was first taken ill. On Sunday it rained all day, the second time we have had rain this winter. I don't know which is the most anxious for May to arrive, Edmund or I, we do not expect such another child as Celia, two such would hardly fall to the lot of one woman, but it will be very dear to us boy, or girl, pretty or plain, and that I may keep it when it does come, I morning and evening pray God in his great mercy may grant. Mrs Hale is pretty well again.

27th – Fanny Felton spent yesterday here, she is a nice girl, we dine with her tomorrow to meet Judge Valeure [Vallières]; we went to Sherbrooke this morning and I received your journal, many thanks dearest Mamma for it, I knew you would feel deeply for us in our affliction, and I wish with you, I had you near to comfort me. I shall be delighted to have Papa's picture, the Engraving I have does not do him justice. I think Mr Freeman is very generous. We are expecting Mr Buchan soon, he has been heard of in the shape of money to pay for his land. Edmund will write in my next, ever your attached child

L. Peel.

No 24

March 2nd

My dearest Mamma

I will answer your questions about candle making, I had not room in my last letter. I make both dips and Moulds, I buy the cotton wick in balls.

1/6 a pound, and one pound will make 50lbs of Candles. We make rods of wood each holding six wicks which are twisted round and hang down, we melt the fat, pour it into a large tub and fill it with boiling water, this must be added to as it cools to keep the tallow warm which all rises to the top. We dip the rods into the tub one after another, and then begin over again and so on till the candle is thick enough. The Moulds are less trouble as you have only to put the wick through the tube, fasten it to sticks at the bottom, melt the tallow and pour it into the moulds; all these things are very simple and it makes us very independant to be able to do them.

On friday Fanny sent to ask us to dine at Belvedere on Sunday to meet Judge Valliere and Mr M Man, I declined as we do not pratonise [*sic*] visiting on a Sunday, my young friend was determined to have us for she changed the day to Saturday, we went and spent an agreeable day. The Judge is a sensible and amusing man and I like to converse with him, Fanny gave us an excellent dinner, the best arranged one I have seen at Belvedere, she does the honors remarkably well. Narbon & Isabella kept close to Edmund all afternoon, they are very fond of him. I engaged Mrs Salt, who is staying at Belvedere, to come and nurse me during my confinement, she is a kind cheerful woman.[27]

This is the time, Sturges, for deer hunting, there have been several killed on our farm, I bought a quarter yesterday, 21 lbs at 4 Cents a pound altogether 4 – 2 1/2. Ten Cents are six pence, should you not like to be here? But I think you would at first have many falls walking in the snow shoes which are sometimes more than three feet long, and require a particular kind of walking. Old hands go at a great rate in them.

You cannot think Mamma how well my Servant Ellen manages for me. When she first came she knew nothing, not even how to clean a room or wash a floor, she did not know when water boiled, now she does everything. I only go and order dinner, she makes beautiful bread and pastry. She does all the washing and ironing without any assistance, and some times finds time to sew for me. She is always clean and civil, & is only sixteen. She has four dollars a month & well deserves it. I wonder what girl in England is receiving or deserves such high wages. Yesterday we went to Sherbrook and received Mrs Peel's & Ann's letters dated 16th of December, it was sent by Halifax.

16 – Edmund drove me to Lenoxville yesterday – I have been unwell, & am much better in the air, Parkes has been obliged to kill one of our sheep which was to lamb this month, one of the others had hurt its bag & it was in a dreadful state. To day we have been at Sherbrooke and

called at Capt Colcloughs, Mrs C. was ill in bed with a cold, we received two Liverpool papers from our kind friend Mr Buchannan, he gave me the agreeable intelligence that my box sent for you, has arrived safe in Liverpool, I expect you would have it a day or two after you sent off your last letter. When we came home we found we had two lambs born from one sheep, Edmund is gone to attend to them. Sturges have you read Japhet in search of a father by Capt Marriott [Marryat], if not, pray do, it will amuse you greatly, we are now reading it.[28]

10th – Parkes found 15 bushels of our potatos rotten with the frost, a considerable loss and most provoking when we consider the trouble & expense we have been at to make the Cellar frost proof; the wall is two feet thick, built of stone and mortar and banked up outside, it cost us twenty pounds. Tom will do no good in the housekeeping way until he have a wife.

11th – We dined yesterday at the Hale's, their wedding day, Mr Hales brother was there, he is a Lawyer & lives in London, he brought his Sister to Quebec last fall, she had been visiting her great relations in England, he does not like Canada and is now on his way to London but I have no letter ready to send as he leaves tomorrow. He is very ugly, a great Coxcomb, but Gentlemanly. Mrs Hale was very kind & attentive to me, she gave me oranges & several other good things, we remained tea and had a delightful drive home, not a breath of wind & a rapid thaw.

14th – Thursday was a beautiful day, Edmund took me a drive, I went to see the children at Belvedere. We went to the Store to provide, Sugar, tea, etc. – we pay for every thing as we purchase it, I don't think the Store keepers like this, they would rather come upon us for a large sum at the time they go up to Quebec to purchase goods. I wish Sturges could read a book we now have, it is the Life & adventures of Mr Henry's Father amongst the Indians, he has a great many narrow escapes, he was amongst them at a very unfortunate time for his own safety just after Canada had been taken by Genl Amherst 1760.[29]

19 – We remembered Charles's birth day on the 12th, & tomorrow we shall not fail to wish dear Papa many many happy returns of his. I have the last few days been unwell with a cold & Rheumatism. I am better to day. The snow which had gradually began to disappear is coming down again in grand style, making us fear Winter is recommencing, Edmund tells it is two feet deep already. I am very anxious for an early Spring that the kitchen may be finished before my confinement, the Men will come as soon as the snow is off. Drummond the Carpenter was here yesterday, the kitchen will be 24 feet by 16, a large one in this country is

indispensible for comfort, there is so much to be done in it. Washing, Ironing, making Candles & Soap. I shall have an open fire place besides the cooking stove, and oven and a boiler. We have three Lambs & have lost five, they are rather too early, we must manage better another year.

25th – A beautiful day but very cold, we have had so much snow since I last wrote we are almost blocked, I believe there has not been such a winter in Canada. Mrs Felton and the Girls returned home last week, I have not been able to call upon them the roads are so bad. Yesterday we ventured to Sherbrooke and in returning there was such a drift we were upset as neatly as possible, the horse lay very quietly, Edmund was at first frightened least I was hurt, I soon relieved him from all alarm but I lay unable to assist myself. Edmund raised me up & I went on to a farm house to send him assistance to help him up with the horse and Burlin, the worst is I have lost my bag containing my keys and purse with six dollars in. This morning Parkes & another Man tried to find it, but no bag made its appearance. I had it in my hand a short time before I fell out, only one Man past, and we suspect him of finding it, for he changed countenance when questioned about it. Parkes is gone to Sherbrooke & has taken a paper on which I have written what is lost & offered a reward, but I fear I shall never see it again.

27th – I have had a letter from Mrs Peel of Sorel, they are well & she says her baby is a fat little fellow, they mean to visit us this summer, she is anxious to be personally acquainted with Edmund and me & also to see the Townships which she expects to like better than Sorel. She says there is a very pretty girl on the look out for a husband near to them, and begs I will tell Tom he had better go and see her unless he already be in love with one of the Miss Feltons. Tom says he will never marry a girl who is on the look out. I shall tell Mrs Peel we shall be very happy to see her any time after June. In this country you must do much yourself to make visitors comfortable & I should like to be strong before their arrival.

We have been to call at Belvidere, Charlotte gave me a long frock, very handsome. They wanted us to remain dinner. Mrs Felton said the Hales of Quebec wished much to see us, & fancied they knew me, my friend Mrs Hale had written such flattering accounts of me, this proves, at all events, that she is sincere in all she says to me, or she would not write in my praise to Quebec. Mr Bell[30] has taken possession of his situation at Sherbrooke, the Pecks leave to day and Mrs Hale's brother, Mr Frederic Boen,[31] is come to take Mr Pecks place, he is a Lawyer, so we have now plenty of Beaux for the young Ladies. Edmund begins to talk of moving to get quiet, there is such *calling & doing*, as Old John says.

I shall have my bed quilt ready for quilting this morn^g and every one admires it, Edmund says I must keep it to show my children that they may have a visible proof of their Mamma's patience & industry to induce them to follow her example, there are 7151 squares in it.

29th – On Friday the girls from Belvedere called, & to day Mrs Felton & Eliza came after Church, Mrs Felton said she had a nice dinner, and my favourite pudding, she came to pursuade me to deviate from our rule of not visiting on a Sunday, we were proof against all her kind entreaties, for had we once given way, we should often have had similar requests, Mrs Felton left us saying, that as I would not go to eat the pudding she should send me some in the evening. If you could, dear Mamma see these excellent puddings you would never forget them, all the children like it, and being so large a family you may imagine that a small one would not go far. I am certain those at Belvedere are as thick as my waist, and they are brought in uncut.

30 – Mr & Mrs Hale & Mr Boen called, he is a very plain young Man but Gentlemanly in his manners and apparently good tempered. Mrs Hale remained with me whilst the Gentlemen went on to call upon Tom, they admired his farm.

31st – This morning we went to Sherbrooke & I received Mr & Mrs Maynes letter, it has had a long passage. How affectionately they both write, & how much they seem to enter into & participate in our sorrow, give my best love to them both, tell Sarajane I will write to her next Month, her praises are quite a reproach to me for not better deserving them. I certainly do my best to keep in good health and spirits, but human nature is weak, and often I fret dreadfully, it is nearly four months since I lost my darling, and I cannot even yet bear to hear her named with composure. Oh! how trifling the every day disappointments and annoyances of life appear to me and I feel how, almost, wicked I have been to make so much of them as I used to do. I am now schooled by affliction, of which my present situation every instant reminds me, for each motion of the little treasure I bear carries my thoughts to Celia, & then I wonder whether my next will be like her.

Edmund sends his best love to you all. He does not wish any of his Relations to make an application to Sir Robert Peel on his account, his wish & mine is to remain as we are. Of course if Sir Robert should offer to promote him, Edmund will as a point of duty once more brave the deep, but his inclination is to remain quiet. This kind husband, dearest Mamma has quite spoiled me, even last night when he went for an hour or two to see Tom I felt quite restless, I could neither work not read, and only regained my comfort when I heard his welcome step on the Veranda. My Harp still remains untouched, I cannot make up my mind to uncover it, but this is a weakness I must endeavour to get over.

I expect your journal in a few days, you are the only person we can depend upon hearing from. I fear Mr Mayne is far from well. Dear Mini, how I love her for showing such a warm heart, thought it could scarcely be otherwise having such parents. Parkes is gone to a gay wedding, our beef came in 70lbs & Edmund has cut it up famously, by this time you must, from all I have written be convinced that my husband can do most things. Our best love to all friends, ever your attached child –

Lucy Peel.

No 25

Dunstall Villa   April 3d

My dearest Mamma

We have had two beautifully warm days, and the snow is gowing fast, Tom drank tea here last night & said it was lightening when he came. We have been to Sherbrooke this morning, the snow is all off in the Town, it was heavy pulling for the horse and we cannot go down again in the Sleigh, but I dare say up here we shall have Sleighing for more than a week. I have put my quilt in the frame and quilted a little.

5th – Yesterday, though far from a fine day, two of the girls came in the morning to take me to Belvedere, Edmund was to follow me to dinner, but it rained so fast he dined alone and came for me afterwards, I was quite annoyed, he did not come to dinner & wished myself at home with him. Mrs Felton sent me a quarter of Veal. Edmund has walked to Church.

10th – On Monday the girls came to help me quilt, they stayed dinner. Mrs Felton brought them and sat some time. Mr & Mrs Kimbal called, our room was full. Tom has been here the two last days. It is now quite warm, and we can see the ground in several places. Edmund is covering up the Sleigh till next winter, and getting our summer carriage ready. A week such weather as this will take off all the snow, the sun has now great power. We have a Man coming next Monday for a month to make Slash fences[32] and clear some land for potatos. What had potatos last year, we take this year for wheat, and I hope we shall grow nearly as much as we shall want, we give this man twelve dollars a month and his keep, he stood out a long time for fifteen, but ready money tempted him. We wished Sturges many happy returns of his birth day.

14th – The three girls came on Saturday and finished quilting for me, and the Quilt is on our bed, for complete children like we wanted to use it as soon as it was ready. Edmund went to Church. I cannot move about much.

18th – Snow & Frost since I last wrote. Thursday was warm and fine, Edmund took me to Sherbrooke in the Waggon, we walked the horse but it tired me very much. I was very unwell at night, Edmund is certainly the best, kindest, and most tender nurse in the world. On Friday they sent me some buns from Belvedere, it was a miserable day so they did not venture out themselves. I received your journal containing so much to surprise me. I am glad you are pleased with the box, the Cap is my work, how I should like to see you in it. So Robert Garnett is really engaged, he & his Bride will be young house keepers. The accounts from Ceylon are delightful, Louisa & Charles are rewarded for their good intentions and their sorrow is turned into joy.

I feel deeply indebted to William Birch for being so prompt in preparing a Medicine chest for me, I am sure he & Rosa have felt for us, & it was kind and considerate of you dearest Mamma not to enlarge upon the subject of our affliction, the wound is still far from being healed, I never now mention my darling's name even to Edmund, for I find I cannot with composure, but my thoughts are constantly with her, and vain, at present, are all my attempts to banish such melancholy and overpowering regrets which daily assail me; surely when I have another child to caress & love I shall think with less agony of the one I have lost.

Now you are leaving your Cottage, how I wish you dared to cross the Atlantic, then you might perhaps be able to make this a comfortable home till a more eligible one offered itself, how proud I should be to have you at a house of our own and for you to see how happy and comfortable I am, and how much reason I have to be so, I am sure you would love and admire Edmund if you could see all he does, never saving his own trouble if he can at the same time save his pocket. How very uncertain is all pleasure & comfort, it was only the evening before your letter arrived Edmund & I were talking about you, and I was envying Bessy the delight of having you with her during her confinement, and now she cannot have your cheering presence, she must be greatly disappointed.

20 – The Carpenters are here & our Kitchen is began. Edmund went to Church yesterday and stayed the Sacrament.

27th – I have this morning received Rosa's and William's kind letter, pray give our love and say we are much obliged to them for it, and particularly indebted to William for the trouble he so willingly takes in our behalf, his advice I shall strictly follow especially as to warm clothing. I shall be a most anxious mother for a long time, for the impression left upon my mind by Celia's death can never be erased, I am most thankful my dear husband did not see her as I did when in convulsions, I shudder whenever I think of it.

28th – The alternate Snow and Thaw since I last wrote which makes it hard work digging the foundation for our kitchen chimney, the men went down two feet through chips and ice and still found frost in the ground, they must dig away till there is no frost or our chimney will be upset. Yesterday very fine and warm, to day fine, the sky quite clear. Tom has ploughed his Garden & fenced it and Edmund will begin directly, there is only snow now to be seen in small patches in the clearings, but plenty yet in the woods. We are having a railing put round our dear baby's grave to day, it is near the house so I hope I shall be able to pay it one visit before I am ill. I mean to plant some rose trees inside this summer, it is a mournful but I think a very great pleasure, and also conveys a useful lesson to visit the place which contains the earthly remains of one so very dear.

30th – I had your journal last Tuesday. I shall not comment on the first page, you must all have felt deeply upon such an occasion, and most sincerely we both enter into your feelings, and again we wish we were near enough to offer you our house as your home for as long a time as you would be happy and comfortable with us. Thanks dear Mamma for the nice presents in the box, Kate too is remembering me, how very generous you all are.

May 2 – The Carpenters will finish to night, I am heartily tired of them, they will leave me an empty house, they have eaten more than two hundred pounds of Beef in a fortnight, besides several pieces of Pork & Peas Soup & Generally six loaves of bread a day, & I cannot say how much tea and sugar. Our Kitchen is really a very nice one, it has two windows nearly to the ground on one side, and a small one on the other, a famous dresser to iron on, and a large cupboard. It is 27 by 16.

I was busy last Thursday putting my store room in order. I often flatter myself dear Mamma, I am getting like you in tidiness. Ships are expected at Quebec every day, so I may get my box in time. I shall send this off tomorrow and begin another directly which Edmund I hope will finish to say you have again a Canadian Grandchild. We received Johnathan's letter yesterday, he seems to make sure of seeing us soon in England, I hope he will be wrong. Best love to you all from us both, ever yours affectionately

Lucy Peel

No 27 [33]

May 14th

My dearest Mamma –

I am now sitting by a nice large fire in the drawing room and feel wonderfully well and as strong as I can possibly expect. My dear baby grows daily, and is very pretty, all her features are good, but she is not strikingly like either of us, as was dear Celia. Her nurse says she is one in a thousand for goodness. Now all is over I think little of past suffering, and in the delight of nursing my child, I almost forget every thing disagreeable connected with it, and I daily pray that this darling may be spared us. Tom is to be Godpapa to his little niece, he likes the name of Flora, which we shall give to her. Eliza Felton called this morning before I was up, she was going on to Sherbrooke. Edmund is busy with several large fires, and Parkes is sowing Wheat. My husband has finished painting the spare room and passage, they look very well and our house is now quite complete, every one admires our new kitchen, indeed there is not such an one in Canada. We hear Sir Robert Peel is out of office, I suppose our paper tomorrow will give us all particulars.

16th – Oh my dearest Mamma what a dreadful fright I have had since I last wrote. All Thursday the dear baby was very unwell, my medicine operated upon her instead of me & she was in great pain and lay moaning all day, & looked black under the eyes, and round her mouth. Edmund sat up till one and I lay awake full of dismal thoughts. Mrs Salt said she should sit up all night, she gave her a drop of Laudanum[34] & the child was easier, Edmund went to bed & I was just falling asleep when I heard Mrs Salt go and call Edmund and then hurry up stairs to the Servants, she then returned to the nursery & I called to her, she said the baby was ill, I at last got from her that she was in a fit and quite black all over. Edmund came to comfort me, it was all I could do to remain in bed. I felt in such a state. Mrs Salt said she might live, but she did not think she would, she kept rubbing her and put her into warm water, at last she moved and swallowed a drop of milk, she gradually recovered, Mrs Salt telling me to hope for the best for the child was getting warm and had never been quite cold. I cannot express my delight when Mrs Salt brought the baby to me to try if she would suck and I found she would, she then went to sleep and seemed quite easy, in the morning, Mrs Salt said all danger was over.

This morning she has been awake a long time taking notice of every thing. Mrs Salt tells me she never was more alarmed, and that she had made up her mind if the child died she never would attend any one again. I dare say if she had not been here I should have lost my child. As for myself I feel quite strong and well. I am dressed as usual to day and feel able to go about, but fear of taking cold keeps me quiet. We have snow this morning, I almost dispair of seeing settled warm weather. We heard yesterday that Mr Hale is very ill with his leg which he hurt with a Sap bucket, and it is feared he will lose it, he is going to consult the Quebec Doctors, I feel much for poor Mrs Hale.

21st – Mr Hale is better & does not go to Quebec. On Monday Mr Doolittle came to Christen Miss Flora. Tom and he dined here. On Tuesday I went out on the Veranda, it was a very warm day and I enjoyed the fresh air. Tom came to Tea and brought me a large tin of Milk, he & Edmund walked to Sherbrooke in the morning. Flora keeps pretty well upon the whole, but suffers occasionally with pain in her stomach, Mrs Salt says she never saw so patient a child.

27th – Last Friday was Edmund's birth day. I dare say you did not know but you must remember it another year. Mr & Mrs Felton have been so kind as to ask Tom to go and stay with them whilst his house is being altered, I think he will accept such an agreeable invitation. Flora went out of doors on Sunday and had a long sleep afterwards, I don't think she will ever be so pretty as Celia, I fear she will have my nose & Celia had her Papas, Oh when shall I think less about that dear child! I am putting basket work of Osiers [willow branches] round my beds in the garden they look very pretty.

June 1st – Tom is staying with us, his Servant being ill in bed. Our box has arrived safely at Quebec & we shall have it soon, the one at New York I have given up. Flora grows strong & fat. Edmund is painting the Veranda Posts this morning, they are white and when the Hops twine round them they will look very pretty, the front of the house is to be painted a pale pink. I did not tell you that my Harp was uncovered at the Christening, not one string was broken, both Edmund and I felt melancholy on again hearing sounds which so forcibly reminded us of happier days.

4th – Last Tuesday Edmund drove me to Sherbrooke, to make calls. Mrs Colclough gave me some pretty plants and amongst the rest a beautiful fine Geranium. I have it on the Stove in the Passage and the scent is delicious. I received your Journal, I am glad to find you are all well. How mistaken Louisa is about the Climate in Lower Canada, it is proverbial for being healthy & it is remarked that women wear exceedingly well here, and if you could see the Ladies here you would be of the same opinion. The tiresome Mosquitos have began to attack me, I have both feet stiff and swelled with bites, yesterday I had an attack of Erysipelas,[35] my face, neck, hands & all over my body were as red as scarlet, Mrs Salt rubbed me with vinegar, I was better in an hour or two, this morning I feel quite well.

16th – It is some time since I wrote dear Mamma, all last week I was too unwell to do anything, I had a dreadful cold with pain in all my limbs, sore throach [*sic*], cough, & sick head ache, I am still unwell though better, Edmund too has had a bad cold, now baby has began, she is better to day. Edmund drove me to Sherbrooke this morning, no box yet.

We have a new Doctor a handsome Gentlemanly Englishman, I only wish he were older, his name is Watson, from London, his father a Clergyman with twelve children. Mr Watson has been to the East Indias, as Surgeon to some Ship, & last year was wrecked, himself and two others only being saved, he has nothing to depend upon but his profession. Every family here is allowing him so much a year according to their means and the number of their children. Mr Boen introduced Mr Watson to us this morning, he says he likes the Country very much and wishes his friends were here. I hope he will prove steady and clever, his appearance and manners are greatly in his favor. I must though it is time to send off this letter keep it back a little to see if we have the box. I am surprised to find how patiently I wait for it, such disappointments after my one great and never to be forgotten sorrow have little effect upon me.

20th – I must send this off tomorrow or you will be uneasy. The box is not come, but we shall have it & the parcel next tuesday. Baby improves every day and gets more like Celia, her Papa now thinks her very pretty & I am sure you would pronounce her a beauty. I grieve to say Mrs Salt leaves me tomorrow. Mr Watson was here last night to give me something for my cough, I think we shall like him, he says he has been in practise twelve years, he must be older than he appears to be – he is rather grave & a sort of person you can talk to.

The weather is so changeable we have fires to day and the wind is high. I shall write soon to Sarajane & Rosa. Edmund desires his best love with mine to all friends. I long for your next letter, I conclude it will contain accounts of the arrival of the Oldershaws. Tom begins to build his new house next Monday. We had Mr Boen here the other evening, he is excessively fond of music, I played to him, he said he never heard the Harp played so before, he did not believe it could be made so much of. Kiss dear Papa and Sturges for me, also Kate, Charles & my sweet little nieces, I should dearly love to see you all, but it is a thousand to one that all our family never meet together again. I will not dwell on this subject, adieu dearest Mamma, surely I shall embrace you again some time or other, till then believe in the great affection of your absent child

Lucy Peel.

No 28

June 26th Dunstall Villa

My dearest Mamma

On Sunday last Mr Watson called and drank tea here. On Tuesday he came to see Flora who suffers with her stomach, she quite alarms me, Mr Watson thought her very poorly we were up most of the night with her, Mrs Salt is gone so we sleep in the nursery on account of its being warmer for baby. Mr Watson says she has a delicate stomach but tells me there is no danger at present. He appears to know what he is about, and has made women & children his particular study. Edmund and Tom went in our Carriage to Sherbrooke yesterday Tom dined here. My cold and cough much better. Mr & Mrs Doolittle called yesterday. I have my parcel, thanks dear Kate for the book, I have read part of it & am delighted with the good sense it contains. Edmund is much pleased with the little he has read, thank you also dear Sturges for your letters they are very amusing.

28th – On Friday Edmund drove me to Sherbrooke, no box, but our nursery carpet had arrived, we set to work as soon as we got home, it is now down and the room looks quite smart. Flora much better, Mr Watson says she will do now, he was here last night, he dined with Tom & they came here to tea and to hear some music. Flora was asleep, Mr Watson went to look at her to see if she breathed freely, she looked beautiful, she is a small likeness of Celia, I could almost fancy her Celia some times. Edmund is gone to Church this morning, he began yesterday to paint the Gable ends of the house straw colour, it looks exceedingly pretty. I shall be glad when it is finished for I do not like to see him mounted so high upon the ladders.

July 2nd – Very cold, we have large fires in the drawing room & nursery. My cold defies the skill of Mr Watson. We went to Sherbrooke on Tuesday, no box, but we heard of it, I hope we shall have it tomorrow. Flora gets fat and does not suffer so much with her stomach. My cook asked me if I did not think the baby very pretty, I said yes, very pretty indeed, she said So do I Ma'am, I think she has a most genteel face. I could not help laughing, but the woman is right for she looks a perfect little Lady; she begins to be very lively, and will be well nursed. She knows me, she generally wakes once in the night, her Papa gets up and lights a candle, she sucks & then Edmund puts her in her Crib & puts out the light and she goes to sleep with a little rocking, I hope she will continue as good.

6th – On Saturday night about ten oclock to my great surprise Mr & Mrs Peel of Sorel arrived. I did not expect them quite so soon, we were all in confusion having no room ready for them, fortunately I had bought a feather bed that morning. I soon had every thing comfortable, and I am sure you would have admired the room had you seen it. The floor is painted a pale pink, a handsome Carpet round the bed. I gave them our handsome Glass, Mrs Peel appeared quite delighted with her accommodation. They both admire our place and the plan of the house, and envy us the possession of so large a one, they exclaim how nice every thing is! Mrs Peel is a little plain woman, but very pleasing looking and appears to be good tempered, remarkably lively & quite a french woman. She suits me very well, I can get on with her, and she does not want amusing, she this morning got Flora to sleep for me, and is ready to oblige in anything, she is delighted with the country about here, and Mr Peel will buy a farm in this neighbourhood if he can meet with one to his mind.

Yesterday Mr & Mrs Felton called and asked us all to dine at Belvedere to day. Mr Peel's horse was unwell this morning and could not be used so Edmund has taken our Cousins in our Waggon to Belvedere and I am at home for I would not leave baby and there was not room for me and Ellen. I have dined alone for the first time since I was married and I felt quite dull, not that I cared about going to Belvedere, for I like being at home best, but I wanted Edmund. I fear I am really childish about him for I do not like him to leave me only for a few hours.

The box is come at last, fortunately the day before the Peels, so I had all my nice things for my company. I am much pleased with the contents, the patch work pieces are really valuable, give my best love to Kate, her shawl is beautiful and her letter just like herself kind and affectionate. The mince meat and preserves are excellent, and the Hams superfine, we are now eating one, and Mr Peel of Sorel gives evident proofs of liking it he says he is much obliged to you for sending it. I have dispatched a letter to William and Rosa to thank them for their handsome presents. The ring is just the thing and I shall wear it as long as I live. Mrs Riess was very kind to remember me. The Gown is pretty & just fits. Papa's picture makes me almost think he is here, you may imagine how much I prize it. I like every thing and am exceedingly obliged to you for all the trouble you have taken.

18th – On Tuesday we took the Peels to call at Mr Hales, they were pleased with the place, Tom dined here. On Wednesday morning at 4 oclock our visitors left us. On Thursday Mrs Felton and Fanny called, yesterday Edmund and I rode on horseback to Sherbrooke, we saw all the Sherbrooke world, amongst others, Mr & Mrs Hale, they came up and dined with us, she was quite delighted with Flora, I like Mrs Hale better every time I see her.

I have received your Journal 27th. If it were not for the dreadful Voyage which I indeed fear would kill you, I should seriously advise you to come and live near us, or with us, a very small sum would build one large enough and your income would go three times as far here. Then Papa could help Edmund farm, & Sturges, Fish, shoot, survey and chop wood, but this is too nice a plan ever to be accomplished.

19th – It is some days since I wrote, we have had several calls from the Belvedere family, the girls have now permission to nurse Flora, but she must not visit Belvedere, she has been unwell again. Edmund is gone to Church. Mrs King of the Sherbrooke Hotel is dead. The Company has began the new road to Montreal, it is to be ready to travel upon next winter and to be only two day's journey, one Man working upon it has been killed by the Limb of a Tree falling upon him, he is a Canadian and has left a wife and five children.

Edmund was all last Thursday at Toms helping to raise his new house, he is quite busy with building and farming and finds the former sadly interferes with the latter. We shall begin to Mow tomorrow, we have some beautiful Grass and more of it this year than last. Edmund was working in my flower garden yesterday, he has made it look beautifully neat, I wish you could see it. Give my affectionate love to dear Papa, I shall begin a letter to Sarajane directly. I am sure she will think I am neglecting her, but not forgetting or ceasing to love her. I suppose the Oldershaws will be with you when this arrives, my best love to them,

Louisa will I hope write to me, how I should love to see her – my dear Mamma your attached child –

Lucy Peel

No 29

July 24th

My dearest Mamma.

Edmund is now very busy with his hay, he got a little in last night, I was nurse and sent Ellen to help. Flora is quite well again. We have been to Sherbrooke to day and received a nice long letter from Ann of Church Bank, we were delighted to hear from them. I was working in my garden a long time yesterday, and making all my little plants on the veranda clean and smart, can you fancy me so employed? Every thing looks well and I shall soon have plenty of flowers. Mrs Kimball called yesterday, she had been at Belvedere and told me the young Ladies were gone to dine at the Hotel at Lenoxville with Coln McDoogle[36] an elderly married Man who the winter before last took the lead in all Lady Aylmers parties, superintending the Tableaux,[37] and different amusements.

We have a new settler in the Shape of a Mr Austin,[38] he has a wife and family and has taken a house at Lenoxville, he is good looking and has the air of a gentleman, they were delighted with him at Belvedere, he is English. We have also a Mr Dampier who means, I believe, to begin brewing, and a Mr Twist,[39] a Lieutenant in the Navy, with a wife and family all his earthly store [illegible word], four hundred pounds and his half pay. A Mr Collard also, a young Lawyer, came up last week to live in Sherbrooke, he is English, plain, and I hear conceited. There were several strangers up to day by the Stage to look about them, so my dear Mamma there is less danger every day of our dying for want of society.

August 1st – Saturday Mr Henry arrived at Sherbrooke, he returned the same day, as Mrs Henry & Miss Felton were waiting for him at Montreal to take them a tour through part of Upper Canada. On Monday Eliza, Maria, and Miss David came here, Mr John Felton drove them, they almost pulled baby to pieces amongst them, Miss David said she was beautiful, Mr John Felton was as fond of her as any of them, nursing her far better than the Ladies, and when I sent Flora into the nursery he went on the Veranda and talked to her through the window.

On Wednesday Eliza and Miss David came again to try to persuade me to dine at Belvedere and take Baby, they said Mr Watson told them

Lake Massawhippy. The Peels passed by Lake Massawippi en route from Stanstead to Lennoxville, though they mistakenly felt they were in the St. Francis Valley. Bartlett's illustrations, which invariably include mountains and water, reflect the picturesque ideal that attracted the British gentry to the Eastern Townships. Source: W. H. Bartlett, *Canadian Scenery Illustrated* (London, 1842), Bishop's University Archives FC 72.W5.

there was no danger of infection now, I however declined till I had seen Mr Watson myself, so they went away disappointed. There is to be a grand Pic-Nic next Monday across the river to Westbury, the party is given by Coln McDoogle, he sent an invitation to us, but we declined, I cannot leave baby, and Edmund, besides being busy, has no inclination for such things. We have lent our carriage to the Feltons for the day, there are eight going from their house. I am afraid it will not be very pleasant for them, the weather is so uncertain, it is altogether a very wet summer, I hope we shall have a fine fall to make up for it.

6th – On Saturday last Mrs Felton and Fanny called to ask us to dine at Belvedere on Monday and take baby, I did not like to refuse as we had done so several times. Monday was wet, and I did not expect they would come for me as they promised to do in the morning and Edmund was to join us at dinner, however, to my great surprise Mr John Felton came about three oclock, I went, but did not take Flora, Edmund was too busy to go, he came in the evening for me, and Miss Flora behaved very well in my absence, she always feeds well when she does not see me.

The Belvedere girls had an overturn in Sherbrooke the day before, Eliza is quite lame, she hurt her knee, all the rest had sundry bruises and pains from stiffness, but I hope nothing serious, Mr Watson is attending Eliza, her leg is much inflamed. Of course he will use his utmost skill, I believe he greatly admires his patient, & I think the admiration is mutual, I don't know how it will end. I hope you have not made up your mind to Tom marrying one of the Miss Feltons for I think there is no chance of it, he has not entered the list with the beaux of Sherbrooke, he must go to England for a wife.

We have just put down a very pretty new carpet in our drawing room, it is a present from our kind mother at Church Bank. Edmund hopes to carry all his hay to day, we have had a great deal of wet, & every one began to be afraid for the hay and corn. Mrs M'Ready has been here a few days working for me, I have taken a lesson from her in *Tailoring* and we have made Edmund a beautiful dressing Gown, we took a coat to pieces & cut it out quite the thing, I am quite proud of it and shall attempt a cloth coat for Edmund next winter. Mrs M'Ready must give me another lesson, she makes the Collars exceedingly well.

8th – Dear little baby is a quarter of a year old to day and is as well as possible, and the best child in the world, it is a great pleasure to attend upon her. We went yesterday to call upon Mrs Witcher. Their place looks beautiful in the summer close by the river side, we were introduced to Mr Collard he is very gentlemanly. We were made much of, for, as we seldom make calls they are more thought of when we *honor* the Sherbrooke Gentry. Miss Boen is married to Mr William Bell, they are expected up next week, I hear it was a gay wedding. Miss Lucy Boen comes with her sister. Mr William Felton is married to Miss Lloyd. Tom was here last night, he brought a bucket of Raspberries and a bucket of Sugar for me to make into Jam for him.

11th – On Sunday Edmund and Tom walked to Church, last night we walked to Toms, I wanted to see how his new house got on, it is a very romantic walk. To day we spent at Mr Hales and took baby who behaved charmingly and was much admired. We were introduced to two new settlers who have bought a farm between them below Mr Hales a few Miles, they are delighted with the Country, they are really frightful men, one a Mr Campbell, an Officer, tall, thin, a florid complexion, very light hair, and has been wounded terribly in the face, he has a scar on his forehead and the centre of his upper lip, front teeth, & upper & lower Jaw all gone in front, and to hide this place he wears hair on his upper lip quite long just to the edge of the Gap. When he talks it appears a great exertion, &

he cannot speak plainly. His companion a Mr Hamilton. Tall, a thick set figure, great head, and large vulgar face, he had a large white Mustachio.

When we came home, Mrs Felton & Charlotte called, they brought the bottle for Edmund, a gentleman gave it to Mr Felton at Quebec, thanks dearest Mamma for your letter and the useful little presents, Ribbons and Gloves are always valuable being very dear & bad here. Thank dear Charles for his nice letter, it was very kind of him to favor me and I shall value it highly. Oh that you were indeed all out here, but why my brother should object to Canada on acc^t of the Government I cannot think. He would never be interfered with, and we have not a single tax, and there are a few in the States. The great objection to our part of Canada is there is no market for the Farmer nearer than Quebec or Montreal, the latter place two days journey from Sherbrooke by the new road, then I fear Charles would not like all the stumps in this country, no English farmers do, you cannot make money here but you may save it, for your wheat & Fat cows & sheep they will take at the Store and give you goods to the amount of their value. A Store here combines every kind of English Shop.

15th – On Wednesday I had quite a large evening party, I have had nothing in the shape of one for many months, I wished to have one whilst Maria Felton was at home. It was a lovely day and every thing looked smiling, our pretty drawing room nicely set out with flowers, the windows open and chairs on the veranda, the little garden in front full of gay flowers; I had Mr & Mrs Felton, Mr John Felton, Maria, Charlotte, Fanny, Matilda, two Miss Davids, who are staying at Belvedere, *Jewesses* and orphans, their brother, a Gentlemanly good looking Man, Captain Hayne, a little good tempered looking Englishman, who has some official situation in this Country,[40] and Mr Boen. Tom could not leave his Hay Field.

As soon as my company arrived, they all, save Mrs Felton and I, went up the Rock, Edmund leading the way, it looked very pretty from the Veranda to watch them ascending. On their return I played upon the Harp, we then had tea, I had a long table set out in the dining room, and the handsome large blue cloth you sent me upon it, I gave them three large dishes of Raspberries and cream, lots of Cakes and bread & butter. Charlotte made the green tea, I the black, they all enjoyed their repast and when we had finished, Mr Boen sang, "Rest Warrior Rest," he has a sweet voice and great taste, we then returned to the drawing room and had more music. Mr Boen and Miss Fanny David sang duetts and I accompanied them, the evening passed quickly and they all seemed sorry to leave and said what a delightful visit they had had, the Miss Davids thanked me over and over again for giving the party before they left, they went the next morning. Flora was very good and much admired, Mr John Felton nursed her a long time, and Captain Hayne took great notice of her, Mr David wanted to nurse her, but I would not let him, for I was sure he did not know how.

We were to have dined at Belvedere yesterday but it rained, we are going to day and take baby. Oh if dear Charles and Kate would come and live near us, how delightful it would be, but I fear such a pleasure is not in store for us. Captain Hayne says there is to be a market in Sherbrooke, so one objection to Charles coming here will be removed. He would be in a nest of Tories here, but he has too much sense to dislike persons because their politics are not the same as his own. I suppose you are all mourning the death of Cobbett.[41] Edmund has began to practice singing, you know he has a good voice, he has learned four songs, and I like to hear him sing them very much.

17th – We dined yesterday at Belvedere, it was Fanny's birth day, including the children there were 24 of us, we came away very early as we did not like baby to be out after Sun set. Tom came last night and returned home next morning, we shall have him here for, I dare say two Months, till his house is ready for him. No box from New York yet. Mr John Felton is doing all in his power to obtain it for us.

18th – We have been to Sherbrooke this morning and received your Journal, 28. So you have the Oldershaws at last, I think you showed great patience & I almost wonder they did not hurry to you when they found you were to part again so soon. You must indeed be disappointed, and as you say, this is truly a world of trials and vexations. Louisa, of course, must be delighted to remain with Charles, the separation of husband and wife must be dreadful, for the love between them is, or ought to be, "Strong as Death," and the longer they live together the harder it would be to part, at least I feel it would be so, for much as I loved Edmund when I married him I have treble the affection for him now, I did not know half his good qualities, he has never spoken one angry word to me and manages my hasty temper so well that I almost fancy at times I have become a most amiable person. You have not sent me word what we owe you, I am anxious to know that you may be paid.

22 – On Wednesday We had Mr Hale, Mr & Miss Bowen to call, they were going to dine at Belvedere, Miss Bowen is rather pretty, and very genteel looking, her name is Lucy, she is engaged to a Mr Montazambert [Montizambert] of Quebec, Mrs Hale remained at home, she finds the

shaking carriages of this country do not agree with her just now. I had Mr Doolittle to call, baby was much admired, Mr Doolittle looked at Flora till tears were in his eyes, he said to me he never saw such a striking likeness as she bore to Celia, whose face, he continued, "will for ever be engraven on my memory Mrs Peel, I have it now as perfectly before me as if she were living, it was a face, which, once seen could never be forgotten, indeed she was lovely." I often think, dearest Mamma, that Mrs Felton sees the likeness for she often seems affected when she looks at baby, but she says not a word to me for she knows I do not like to talk about our dear lost child. I shall send this off tomorrow & a letter to Mrs Mayne next week, I have nearly filled my sheet to her. Edmund sends his best love with mine to you all, not forgetting dear Charles and his family and all at Barton believe me your very affectionate child –

Lucy Peel.

No 30

August 28th 1835 –

My dearest Mamma –

On Tuesday we went to Sherbrooke, I called upon Mrs Bell. A Mrs O Brian who is her servant came to the door, and when I asked whether Mrs Bell were at home, she said no, and shut the door in my face. I knew she was at home, however as I turned to leave the house Miss Bowen & Mr Montezambert drove up, Miss Bowen knocked at the door, when Mrs O Brian again made her appearance and said, come in, but don't let that other one come, I was admitted notwithstanding, and we had all a good laugh. Mrs Bell had desired the woman to deny her to all but Mrs Peel, and she said she knew me very well, the result proved she was mistaken.

After we left Sherbrooke we went to dine at Belvedere, Mr Montezambert was there, he is a pleasing quiet young Man, not handsome. Mrs Felton was disappointed of her party, the Court sat so late they could not leave in time. After dinner we had Captain Hayne and a Mr Motram his brother in law, just arrived from England, a tall fine looking young Man but rather conceited, Mr Austin, Mr Watson, and Mr Collard, we think Mr Austin very like Mr Bolton Peel. It proved a wet evening and we had to drive home in the rain. The next morning, Mr John Felton, Eliza & Mr Montezambert called. Yesterday Mr & Mrs Felton & Eliza set off for Quebec, the Commissioners are arrived. To day it has rained all morning, Tom thinks he shall never get all his hay.

September 3d – Last Saturday we drove to Sherbrooke to see for some Meat, the butcher was killing at Lenoxville, we went on there, we met on the road Mr & Mrs Austin and Capt Hayne, we meant to have made our first call upon them, but of course could not after meeting them. On Sunday we went to Church and received the Sacrament. Mr Doolittle is indefatigable in his duties as a Clergyman, he calls on the families before the Sacrament requesting their attendance and last Sunday in his discourse, he hoped all would remain, even if they did not partake of the Holy communion, hoping that the solemnity of it would induce many to wish to prepare themselves to partake of it the next time. I am sorry to say many persons left notwithstanding all he said.

On Tuesday we went to call at Mr Hales, I took my little friend the bed quilt, she admired it greatly, she gave me a large bunch of flowers and some Corn, ours is not quite ready yet. I received your Journal 29 the contents are very pleasing. I am delighted you have determined to live at Barton, how happy you will be with dear Sarajane and Rosa so near and all your little Grandchildren to amuse you, Oh that Flora could sometimes be one of the number. I am also much pleased at the prospect for Sturges it would have been a pity for him not to have continued the profession he has made such progress in, and most sincerely I hope he will be steady, I feel sure that he will for he has an affectionate disposition, and I hope could not cause such parents as his one pang on his account. It must be a subject of thankfulness to all her friends that Mrs Birch is released from her sufferings.

Tom has again cut his foot very bad, it is cut through all the Sinews of the Instep, he keeps his bed and is not to move for a week. He was chopping down a dead tree with knots in it, the Axe glided off one of them, his Man, a stiff made little Englishman was fortunately with him and carried him to the house where the Carpenters made a frame, he was put upon it & carried to Dunstall. He was in great pain all Tuesday night, he is better & in good spirits. Edmund is reaping; our Indian Corn in the garden is ready to eat & we have had a large dish at tea, have you tried it yet? All the Corn set on the farm was eaten the other night by the bears.

I am obliged to Charles Oldershaw for what he writes, he means it kindly & so I take it, he need not fear I shall neglect my religious duties, I have opportunities, and a great inclination to attend to them, and this inclination has encreased manifold since the death of our dear Celia for I am constantly thinking of her, and endeavour so to act, that I may meet her again in a happier and better world, I sometimes think I would not recall her to this world of pain and trials if I could. I dwell, when sitting alone, even with pleasure upon the bliss she is enjoying, and consider her in the light of a guardian Angel. And perhaps, as Charles Oldershaw says, she may have been taken away in mercy to myself, for I did love her too dearly, and constantly found myself saying, I could not do without her, however I was to be taught otherwise. I hope, dearest Mamma, you will not pronounce me an enthusiast. I am no such thing. I know I am more serious and less fond of gaiety than I used to be, and, I hope, think more before I act, but I keep my opinions to myself. As long as I am happy and cheerful which is generally the case, I am sure that you will allow my religious opinions can have no bad effect upon me. Mrs Felton was not well enough to go to Quebec. Dear Flora is quite well and looks as blooming as possible, I wish you could see her and kiss her fat cheek.

8th – Flora is four months old, she has her short Frocks on, we are to have a plum pudding for dinner in honor of her. Tom is better but still keeps his bed, he is very patient. Edmund is ploughing, I fear it will be too much for him, it is a heavy Plough & there are two yokes of Oxen drawing it, I expect he will be greatly tired to night. Tom is obliged to hire another Man now, he cannot work so all his industry and economy is over thrown by one stroke of his Axe.

11th – Mr Watson came & Mr Bowen with him, he found Tom's foot not so well and had to open the wound again to take out the congealed blood, it was a painful operation and poor Tom was quite in low spirits and in great pain all day, his foot was tied to the bed post in a very uncomfortable position to close the wound, however he bore it with great patience and the next morning was much better. On Wednesday I wished you every happiness dearest Mamma, it was your birthday. Mrs Felton & Fanny called yesterday, they say Quebec is full of officers and very gay, there are three Frigates there.[42] Edmund has began upon the bottle Papa sent, I rubbed his side well last night, he has had wet feet the last three days ploughing and has in consequence taken cold, he is rather better this morning.

18th – The Sketch of Dunstall is finished. Mr Bowen spent a day here, we had music after dinner. I have made the drawing into a parcel, and it will go to Mr Cunningham of Montreal to forward to Charles Lyon, the inner parcel is directed to Charles Meek, so he can look out for it. Edmund and I have written a very long letter to Charles, I don't know whether he will have patience to read it, for it is crossed all over & is all about Canada & farming, I have also written to Kate, Edith Bourne and to Sturges to request him to copy the drawing and sent it to Mrs Hart Ethelstan asking her to forward it to Mr & Mrs Peel with our best love.

Tom is now up and hobbles about with a stick, Mr Watson says he will never recover the use of his foot entirely and will always walk a little lame, at present he cannot bend his foot, all the tendons were cut through. Charlotte, Fanny & Maria brought me some blackberries, they are now quite full at Belvedere, Mrs Felton has taken all Mr Charles Felton's eight children to her house, they were in a sad state for food & cloathing. Mr C Felton is in Prison & his wife has a room there & keeps her bed & will be confined in 5 Months. I believe she is not expected to live to give birth to her child. Mr C. Felton had a situation of four hundred a year & has been ruined by his wife.

22nd – Mr Watson has paid his last visit to Tom. Tom went a ride upon our quiet horse, Edmund walked by his side. On Saturday Edmund drove me to call at Belvedere, Mr Watson was there, he appears quite at home, and the young ladies seem to admire him greatly, Mrs Felton & Fanny came home with us, they admired my flower garden, I had two men at work all morning and I assisted them, it looks very neat & pretty and I shall have nothing to do next spring but put in my flowers. Mr Felton came home on Saturday, he left Eliza at Quebec, she having several pleasant engagements, he & Mrs Felton called on Sunday, he said the Ball in honor of Lord and Lady Aylmer was splendid, the theatre was used for the occasion; Lord Gosford appears an affable man, Mr & Mrs Peel of Sorel were at the Ball, and persons from all quarters.

We cannot hear anything of our New York Box. I have began another Bed quilt to use up all the small pieces left from my curtains which are nearly finished – Do send me word whether the Oldershaws went to Oak Hill. Mrs Wickstead whom I dare say you will remember me having mentioned as having had a dangerous mishap, is dead, she has only been married about a year. We have had some of our Hops gathered to day, they are very fine, and we have a large Crop, most of the crops have failed this year. Edmund has three men and two boys clearing some land, they do it for five & a half dollars an acre. The trees are down and a fire has been over, so they have only to log the trees for burning, we shall do no good in farming till we have more land cleared and it is very expensive work but would soon pay double what it cost, but then the ready money to begin with is the thing and all these men want paying immediately. We get things done cheaper than most people because we pay directly and in cash. Edmund joins me in best love to the whole *nest* at Barton, kiss dear Papa for me, I hope he keeps up his spirits and gets his rubber, believe me my dearest Mamma your very affect daughter

L. Peel.

We have had frost already and all the Potatos in the neighbourhood are touched but I hope not much injured, they have not got all their Hay yet at Belvedere. I never knew such bad management

23d – Mr Hale & his two Sisters have just called, they are nice lady like women. I played to them on the Harp, they are gone on to Belvedere and will call on their return. Mr Hale says our box is at Sorel. I hope we shall have it soon. The Miss Hales are quite charmed with the Country.

No 31

To Mrs Mayne- Sept 25th

My dear Sarajane as I think I shall soon have an opportunity of sending a letter to Quebec, I shall continue my journal from Mamma's last which went off on Thursday. Edmund is just gone to Sherbrooke on foot, our horse got out of the field last night and Parkes has spent three hours this morning in fruitless attempts to find him, I am therefore disappointed of my ride. We had eight beautiful fires on the Rock last night, a great part of it is now cleared, and when some of the young trees grow up it will be a great improvement. The Trees are now beginning to wear all their gay colours, I think the Fall, the finest and most agreeable part of the year in Canada, this is the time I should wish strangers to see the Country. Tom hobbles about famously, his house will soon be finished. Flora gets more interesting every day, and I think her Papa will be the favorite, she always wants to go to him, he is an excellent nurse and can toss her better than I can, she is very lively and notices every thing.

30th – Yesterday we went to Sherbrooke, and on to see Mrs Hale, she is always pleased when we call, I played upon her Piano and brought lots of music home. I dare say you remember I mentioned a Mr Campbell, the Man with *the Lip*. He told Mrs Hale he should like to see me again as he knew Papa. I believe he lived in Staffordshire, do ask Papa if he remember such a person. At the Post Office I received Mamma's first journal from Barton containing the hand writing of so many of our dear friends, how happy you are *all* together, I wish I could sometimes join your party. It seems your dear husband is to be continually a sufferer, life must, I should think, be almost a burden upon such terms. I am delighted to hear that Sturges has at last employment. Pray give my love to Rosa & thank both her and William for what they wrote in Mamma's journal, as they flatter me so much by being pleased with my letters, I can do no less than journalise to them occasionally.

What will you all say when I tell you I am again en famille, I hope Rosa manages to keep me in countenance. This morning to our dismay we found snow upon the ground several inches deep, it has snowed all morning, fortunately we have all our potatos in the Cellar, Tom has not one in. Little Flora can now sit in her chair, she is at my side as good as possible watching me write, & she likes to hear me play on the Harp. Edmund and Parkes are putting up the Stove pipe in the Passage.

Oct 2 – Snow nearly a foot deep, such a thing was never known here so early, it is melancholy to see it, but I am happy to say it has began to thaw, so it may soon all disappear. I am going to knit Edmund some stockings, the wool from our own sheep, a woman spun it for me and had hay for her trouble, it is a very dark brown, the natural colour, so it will wear better than if it were dyed.

Oct 7th – The snow all went the day after I last wrote. On Saturday we went to call at Belvedere. The Gentlemen were gone to attend a Sale at Three Rivers. Mrs Felton and Maria went on Monday to Montreal; we killed one of our Oxen; I was busy all morning seeing it cut up and salted. Tom had a quarter, Mr Bowen had some, and part went to Belvedere, so we keep only half. I have a bad cold. This changeable weather is trying, surely dear baby will escape, I take all possible care of her. Edmund is planing boards to line the kitchen which has been all rough this summer, it is Bass wood that he uses which is exceedingly white & nicely marked. I am curing some of my beef for hanging.

10th – Yesterday was wet, however we went to Sherbrooke. I called at the Judges, he and his Lady were both in bed; the Judge dressed and came down and I then went to see Mrs Fletcher. Oh my dear Mrs Peel, said the old Lady, I thought I should never see you again, I could not believe that your sentiments towards me had changed, but still I felt very anxious to have you. Poor old Lady, I had not seen her of two months. She gave us a nice luncheon & seemed as if she thought she could not make enough of me, her white bread, excellent Butter, Potted *Lunge*[43] (a Fish) some capital tea & lots of cream. When we got home Edmund went to Toms to help him get in his potatos, he is to have half what he gets for his trouble. He remained dinner. Tom's house is not finished yet, he is still here. Mr Bowen brought me up a Lunge, very kind of him, it was very good, some thing like Salmon in taste but in colour and shape like a Pike, I never saw such beautiful Roe –

12 – Mr Watson called to see baby, he says her two top teeth will soon be through & that he can feel the lower ones, he left medicine for me. Edmund is gone again with Tom this morning so baby and I shall be alone. It is a beautiful day.

17th – Thursday Charlotte Felton spent the day here, Flora let her nurse her if I sat by. Yesterday we went to Lenoxville to call at the Doolittles, Mr D. has bought an Organ. I find the Waggons are too rough for me now, I shall not go so far again till the Sleighing begins, I wish I could get over my faintness – I expect my confinement the end of next May, so if Charles and Kate come out before then we can have them all here till they have looked about them a little, I will do my best to make them comfortable, but she must not be too expectant.

We are now enjoying an Indian summer, we have had many fine days quite warm, we have the window open and the fires out in the middle of the day, I understand this weather continues some times a month, but this does not occur often. Our best love to Papa & Mama, Sturges, Rosa, William & Children, & to your dear husband & darling Mini, that you may all continue well and happy together is the daily wish of your affec^t Sister –

Lucy Peel.

Edmund is making fires to day on the Rock, his favorite employment. We have killed another Ox & sold it all but 128 lbs

No 32

Oct 19th 1835 –

My dearest Mamma

My letter to Sarajane went to Quebec this morning to Mr Felton. On Saturday evening Edmund and I took a walk, we met Mr Bowen and Mr Watson, they were going to Tom's to see if he could let them have some hay, I told them I thought we should want all he could spare, however they proceeded to his house as they wished to see his new buildings. Yesterday Edmund walked to Church. Mr Campbell told him he had brought our long expected box from Sorel, with some things of his own & that he would send it to Sherbrooke either to day or tomorrow, very kind of him I think. Edmund had not time to ask him where he had seen Papa and you, but we will the next time we see him.

My cook is an everlasting talker, and so loud she annoys every one in the house, I heard her this morning though both doors were shut and the passage is 38 feet before you get to the first door, I told her if she could not talk like other people she had better be silent, she replied, she talked no harm, I did not suppose she did, but I would not have such a noise, she said I had better leave the kitchen and that she should talk as much as she liked, so I told her she should only remain till her month is up, she is exceedingly hasty and I know will bitterly repent her impertinence tomorrow, however I am determined she shall go, for Edmund has long been tired of her; our house has such a good character I dare say I shall get another servant directly, indeed I know an honest industrious girl who has long wished to live with me and I think I shall try her.

The Judge wants Edmund to be one of the Magistrates for Sherbrooke but he has declined the honor, it would not suit him at all, he would frequently have to attend the Court twice a week, which would very much interfere with his farming, fortunately being an Officer, they cannot oblige him to take Office.

20 – We have had a bad night with Flora, I don't know what I should do if Edmund were not so kind, he was up walking about with her, feeding her, and at last got her to sleep. This morning she frightened us by having a hoarsness, with a slight difficulty of breathing just as our other darling baby's fatal cold began, but unaccompanied with her fever and languor – Mr Watson tells me I need be under no alarm at present, he has left me medicine to give her, surely our dear child will soon be well again.

21st – We were up all night with Flora, her cough is worse, Mr Watson was here this morning and left a stronger dose for baby, I never saw such stuff as came off her little stomach, she lay all the day quite exhausted, her eyes half open & her face as white as possible. Towards evening she appeared to revive, and again smiled upon us, and enjoyed one of her Papa's nice tossings. I had Mrs M'Cready to sit up with Ellen; Edmund and I had been keeping watch three nights and felt as you may suppose, much tired.

22nd – Baby slept very little all night, Mr Watson has ordered her into a warm bath & then to wrap her in flannel, she is now lying on Ellen's knee seemingly very comfortable. Edmund and Parkes are ploughing the garden, we have still beautiful weather, I am sitting without a fire.

24th – Edmund went to Sherbrooke yesterday. Mr Watson ordered Flora another warm bath, she slept much better last night but her cough is very bad. Mrs Felton and Charlotte came to see baby, Mrs Felton could not help crying, I knew what she was thinking of. Our long expected box is at last come, I am delighted with the contents, every thing is beautiful. The Ginghams, Holland, [a fine fabric, originally made in Holland]

Shoes, those pretty Jugs and baskets, the excellent preserves, neat pelisse and Bonnet. Mrs Felton is much pleased with your present to her little boy, and Ellen quite proud of the Ribbon, I admire the Plaid, the Miss Wray's presents are very pretty and Susan sent me a nice affectionate letter. Tell Rosa I think Frances' hair quite beautiful, I always think of that dear child with more affection than her other children, I fancy she must be like what Celia was.

We had a nice long letter yesterday from Mrs Peel and Ann, they have sent us out a box containing most valuable presents, four pairs of Blankets & a piece of Flannel, I believe Sydney Peel will join us next Spring, Tom will be very glad to have him, for Edmund being married is not much of a companion to him. Mrs Peel hopes I will not advise Tom to marry at present, and she pays me the compliment of saying, she does not think he could get such a good wife as I make; I assure you I feel quite proud of the approbation of such a particular and excellent woman, and I hope I shall always deserve her good opinion. We have Becket[44] here to day raising the kitchen chimney, and putting a *Whirlagig* at the top.

26 – On Saturday Eliza & Fanny spent the day here, Eliza will make up my Plush bonnet for me. Flora's cough as bad as ever, Mr Watson seems puzzled, he says I must try Rice and biscuit steeped in water. Charlotte Felton & I sat up with baby who suffered greatly for nearly two hours with her stomach, she is much pulled down. Edmund and I sat up last night, her stomach a great deal better, and she slept pretty well, she has a constant thirst upon her – Edmund remained at home most of the morning, I went to bed, I was tired and felt very unwell, he fed baby and does as well for her as any one can, I wish you could see him nurse. He is gone to Sherbrooke to day. Mr & Mrs Jones are arrived, they are gone to Montreal, he has taken out his licence there in order to practice, I have had a hundred and twenty eight pounds of butter brought me to day for my winter stock, by a Mr Hunter an Englishman, it is beautiful, prepared with very little saltpetre and white sugar, 7^d 1/2 a pound.

30th – I have been so engaged night and day with dear Flora I have not had time to write the last three days. On Sunday night Mrs M'Cready & Ellen sat up, Flora slept pretty well till about one, she appeared in great pain every five minutes making herself quite stiff, at five I sent for Mr Watson, he was gone off 40 Miles to see a Man who had been shot, Flora continued much the same all day. On Wednesday morning Mr Watson came, he thinks the baby is passing gall stones he has given her Taylors powders & they have done her much good, she is considerably better today, Eliza Felton sat up with me on Wednesday night, Flora was very good with her, she nursed her all the next morning, and is coming to sit up to night. Edmund was quite ill yesterday with a cold, hoarseness and sore throat, he kept his bed and eat nothing, this morning he is much better and at his carpenters work. We have still very warm weather.

November 1st – On friday evening Mr Watson did not think Flora so well, Mrs Salt came to sit up with me, I sent her back to Belvedere on Saturday morning and Eliza returned in the Waggon, she stayed all night, Flora was in a good deal of pain in the evening, I gave her Dover's powder,[45] she slept and appears much better this morning and more lively, she is taking chicken broth. Mr Hale & Mr Bell have just been to call. Eliza is gone home. We have had a letter from Quebec to tell us our box is arrived. Edmund and Tom are gone to Church.

3d – Mr Watson came yesterday he thinks the baby better, he says he did think her brain was affected, but not the seat of the disease, she certainly begins to look herself again, and is at times very cheerful. She is now asleep, her nights are very restless, we have sat up with her three weeks. My affectionate love to the Maynes and Birches, my next journal will be to Rosa, I am knitting some lamb's wool stockings for Flora, every day I wish I could have William's advice. We have still lovely weather. Edmund and Parkes are pulling out stumps, we shall soon have all up that are in sight. The Feltons have a new Piano just arrived from Quebec, I shall go and try it when I can leave baby with comfort. Tom left us this morning and we are enjoying our own society much. Edmund desires his best love to you all, kiss Papa for me & believe me your

very attached child

Lucy Peel.

4th – Baby very much better, Mr Watson says he generally looks on the dark side so I hope she will soon be well, he says he should not like to be a young man when she is seventeen for she will be a most dangerous young Lady, he never saw such beautifully soft blue eyes & such a fine forehead, I wish you could all see her. Edmund thinks her quite as lovely as Celia was. Mrs Felton & Fanny were here to day. I have received your journal this morning. Poor Mr Mayne! I shall answer it in my next to Rosa. How forward little Kate is with her teeth.

Book Three

No 33

My dear Rosa

My last journal to Mamma left here on Thursday, I have been much engaged since then, Flora takes up nearly all my time, I have besides a new servant to look after, she appears a quick good tempered girl, and very quiet, she has been well brought up and I hope she will suit me. Dear baby is six Months old to day, her cough is quite well, yet I cannot give a satisfactory account of her, Mr Watson thinks her bowels have been overstrained – he says she has a good constitution & there is no danger at present, he has ordered me to put her every day into a warm bath & to keep her as warm as possible. Poor Sarajane has her sorrows also, to see her husband in such a state of almost constant agony must be dreadful, dear little Mini will be a great comfort to her, and I trust she will grow up strong and hearty.

Mamma gives a delightful account of all your children, and says they are very well managed, I am glad to hear this, for I consider it a most difficult thing for children to escape being spoiled. I assure you I feel exceedingly proud that my talented sister Louisa should condescend to copy from her less gifted one, but I have heard that the wisest, if so inclined may learn even from the most foolish, so after all I must not feel over elated. Mr Watson has full practice, if he can get paid, I think he & Miss Eliza Felton are attached to each other. Flora has not one tooth yet, but she can say Papa very plainly, the Feltons were quite surprised to hear her. I hope Miss Kate is not to surpass her Canadian Cousin in every thing, but I am glad to hear she is so healthy.

11th – Flora has now been two days without pain, she has slept most of the time, she begins to like her warm bath which I am glad of, Mr Watsons last medicine has done her a great deal of good. Edmund drove me to Sherbrooke yesterday when we returned we found Mr Doolittle here, he came to see Flora, he is an excellent man, he is exceedingly fond of music. He paid Mrs Hale, Mrs Austin & myself a great compliment the other day at Belvedere, he told Mr Felton our husbands had no merit in being good ones to such wives. I don't quite agree with him, for I am sure I should be a very *rusty* wife to an indifferent husband, it is Edmund that makes me a good wife if I am one. Winter I think is now beginning, it has snowed all morning, I hope it will continue till there is enough to make good Sleighing.

14th – Yesterday we wished dear Sarajane many happy returns of the day, and thought you would all be dining together if Mr Mayne were well enough. We went to Sherbrooke in the Sleigh, I was at Mrs Fletchers more than two hours, whilst the horse had his winter shoes made and put on, she regaled me with ham, bread and butter, and some delicious English Porter, she said no one should taste it but me & herself, she was in a great hurry to put the bottle up before the Judge came from Court. Flora is certainly much better, she has the two last nights slept in her Cot in our room and only awakened once to take her food & went to sleep again directly, she has a little cold in her eyes, they look very red and she will rub them.

15th – Yesterday Eliza and Charlotte called to invite us to an evening party on Monday, I promised to go if Flora kept as well as she now is, Eliza said Mr Watson talked constantly about the baby and said he never was more anxious about the recovery of a patient, she told me she believed he daily prays that she might get well. He came to day and pronounced baby much better, he nursed her whilst I got him some Coffee. This morning Eliza sent my Plush bonnet, she has made it up very nicely.

20th – We could not go to Belvedere on Monday, we had two days rapid thaw which took off all the snow and we have had fine warm weather ever since, there was no moon, and the roads so bad Edmund did not think it proper for me to venture, Tom went, he & three more gentlemen composed the party, the Feltons having put off their other friends till the snow again makes its appearance. On Sunday we had Eliza, Fanny, Charlotte and Mr Watson, who drove them to call upon me, Mr Watson did not like the look of baby, she is miserably thin and does not gain flesh at all, yet in every other respect she seems quite well, perfectly free from pain, sleeps well and is cheerful. Mrs Felton was to go to Quebec to day. Edmund and Parkes have been getting out stumps, several days, they have nearly all disappeared that were in sight of the house.

26 – I have not written for some days, I have been working for Flora, she is now sitting by my side in her little chair, arrayed in her winter dress and looks very pretty, long worsted stockings and a frock up to the neck with long sleeves, you see William's kind advice is not thrown away, Mr Watson thinks baby would be quite well now if it were not for her teething, she has four nearly through, she is feverish and restless, the four last nights we have been up with her, it is fatiguing work. Mr & Mrs

Hale were here on Wednesday, my little friend looked very pretty, she expects to be confined in January.

Our Man Parkes has left us to live with the Judge that he may be in the same house with his wife, we have a new Man called Patrick Macarty, Edmund is in the woods to day chopping, it is a beautiful day and we have now good Sleighing. We had a great loss the other day, our handsome Colt 18 Months old hurt himself in the stable and died in a few hours, Edmund is much annoyed, it would have been such a nice creature in another year or two for me to ride. Tell Mamma I was exceedingly disappointed not to find in the box a book I sent for – Maynals questions, I hope she will send me a Copy the first opportunity.

December 2d – Flora looks quite herself again, she has often a nice colour and is at last getting fat, her food is arrow root. Mr Watson pronounces her well saving the teething, he has again lanced her Gums, he is gone to Quebec, baby has prevented his going until now. Edmund drove me to call upon Mrs Hale on Tuesday, Mr Hale was gone to Quebec, his Father is dying, and he feared he should not be in time to see him alive, he is the eldest Son, and will be rich for this country, he will have at least eight hundred a year. Tom went on Tuesday with his friend Mr Hallowell to Stanstead, he brought me some good black tea at 1/8 a pound, we give 2/9 in Sherbrook for what is not so good.

The servants and I have just finished knitting some large long stockings for Edmund, they are done the double stitch & are to be soled to wear when chopping wood or driving in the Sleigh, they are drawn over the trousers above the knee, every one wears them in this Country. Edmunds are black and made from the Wool of our own sheep, he is quite proud of them. My new Servant is a fast knitter, she is never idle, and generally knits whilst the dinner is cooking.

We have now such a number of new settlers I cease to mention them, we keep to ourselves, and only know of them from others, I have not yet called upon Mrs Austin, but I mean to do so very soon. One family at Brompton, eight miles from us came out this last Fall, the worst time Settlers can come, they have no time to prepare for the cold and long winter. The name of this family is Crispo, he is a Lieutenant in the Navy, he has a wife and eleven children, the two youngest twins and babies, they have bought a farm upon which is a common Log Hut with two rooms, very small, in this miserable place they are obliged to live the winter, they cannot find room for a Servant, two of the children are very ill, poor things I pity them.

Mr Watson says that Flora has a very good shaped head, her eyes have lost their unnatural appearance and are as bright as usual, she is very pretty, I wish you could see her. I hope you will all send long letters by Sydney Peel, tell Edith Bourne, with my love, that I shall expect one from her. Yesterday, though we had roaring fires, I never saw out of the windows, so you may imagine it was freezing a little. Edmund wishes Spring was here, & I should be glad to have warmer weather, I don't think any one can suffer more from cold than Edmund, he has been so much in warm climates, his hands and feet are seldom warm, it takes away my pleasure when Sleighing to see him so uncomfortable. Tom complains bitterly of the cold, he said it was dreadful coming from Stanstead yesterday, he bought a horse cloth & covered himself with it, only just leaving a peep hole for his eyes & made Mr Hallowell drive. We are going to Sherbrooke tomorrow.

Give our affectionate love to all our dear relatives. I am glad William is in good health and spirits, how could he be otherwise, with a nice affectionate wife and four darling children, it is indeed delightful to be a parent, not with-standing all the care and anxiety attendant, there is something so innocent, so lovely in a young child, all is nature with them, what a pity that increase of years should bring decrease of simplicity, that nature should give place to art, and all that is amiable be an affectation of good!! Good night my dear Rosa – your affect Sister –

Lucy Peel.

PS We are now eating every morning hung Beef done by your receipt it is delicious, I have cured more than fifty pounds. Baby gets quite a *wag*, she has now so many little tricks & looks so cunning.

No 34

December 8th 1835

My dearest Mamma.

I am not quite certain about the number of this journal. I mention this fearing I may have put too high a number, and there-by lead you to suppose the intervening one is lost. This is dear Flora's monthly birth day, she is seven Months old, and we, as usual on these important days, have a plum pudding for dinner. Edmund and I are now quite in good spirits and full of hope about our dear baby, she appears perfectly well, her limbs are fast regaining their roundness and plumpness, the Roses begin to predominate over the lillies on her soft cheek and she is always smiling and merry.

On Saturday evening some of the girls from Belvedere called, on Tuesday we went to Sherbrooke and I received your most pleasing and satisfactory letter. The accounts of Sturges are very good, and he appears in a fair way to get on if he be industrious, which I trust there is no doubt of. I am glad Mr Mayne is better. I find I have my selfish wish in regard to dear Rosa, I am quite annoyed to find she surpasses me in generosity; I shall highly value the shawl she is sending me, it is very kind of you all so often to remember us, and we are in a place where we can make little or no return for your presents, every thing here consists of the worst kind of English and French goods. Sarajane's presents will be very acceptable. I cannot bear to think that Charles will live amongst the Yankees, I fear he will repent it. I send you a few commissions – – –

Edmund and I feel the cold severely this winter, notwithstanding the fires we keep, we seldom are very warm, though I dare say you would call our house an oven. I am obliged to clothe like an old woman & sleep in flannel. I think if we were sure of not having a large family we should not continue very long here, at any rate I hope to spend my old age in my native country.

11th – We have been to Sherbrooke to day and I was delighted to get home again. We have a little black kitten which Edmund attends to as much as you did to Ann & Jane, he likes every thing that amuses Flora, and she is very fond of the kitten and pulls her ears, devoid of fear when she jumps to her upon the sofa, when we call puss, Flora looks for her on the carpet.

13th – Last night, Eliza, Charlotte, Fanny and their cousin Charles Witcher came, they stayed to tea, they were at a party the evening before at Mr Witchers and were dancing till one oclock. Our new Governor is taking the part of the Canadians and conceding much more to them than is thought prudent. His Lordship gave a Ball at which were Canadian persons who had never been heard of before in good society; how it will end I know not. Mr John Felton and the Judge appear quite alarmed; if the Canadians get the upper hand most likely, this will then be no place for the English. I am sure Edmund would be sorry to lay out more money than he can help in the present unsettled state of the Country.

There is a kind of Inquisition now at Quebec, people are impugned and not heard in their defence, Judge Bowen, and our friend Mr Felton are amongst the condemned, both, we feel certain to be innocent men, fortunately this committee can do nothing decisive without the consent of Lord Gosford and surely he will not be so unjust as to deprive the Countries best servants of their situation without positive proof of their unworthiness to hold them. Mrs Felton is at Quebec making herself very un-happy, but I hope her fears are groundless. Mr Felton's situation as Commissioner of the Crown Lands, brings him in seven hundred a year, it would be rather inconvenient to a man with eleven children to have this taken from him.

The Girls visit as usual though they are, of course very anxious. The Yankees are a spiteful set and delight in the over throw of the English. I am sure those about here ought to like the English for they are the only people from whom they get money, they never see the colour of each others dollars. Mr Bowen is impeached because in some case he gave a judgement which displeased the Canadians.[1] Edmund and Tom have walked to church, Flora is asleep on the sofa, I wish you could see her, she really looks beautiful. Mr John Felton has sent us a fine Cod fish.

19th – Last Monday though blowing and drifting, we went to drink tea at Belvedere, I played upon the new Piano, I think, when tuned it will prove a good one. Mrs Felton & Mr Watson arrived from Quebec about an hour after we left, Mr Watson called on Wednesday to see Flora, Mr Bowen was with him, they were both going to Belvedere, I think they drive out there most evenings. Yesterday we called upon the Austins, he is a most Gentlemanly man and very good looking, she, tall, very fat, pleasing but not handsome, she looks the picture of good humour. They gave us soup, wine, and cherry brandy. Tom came yesterday evening, I am making some flannel waistcoats for him, his servant is rather idle, and he, very cold, so I took pity on him, though I have plenty of work of my own to do. Mr Hale is come home, his father is better. To day is Celia's birth day, she would have been two years old.

27th – Our wedding day I dare say you have all thought of us; we, not liking Sunday company, keep it tomorrow very quietly, the Belvedere family and Tom are coming to spend the evening with us. I have been engaged the last week working for Flora, and superintending some bacon salting & pork pie making. Yesterday was so fine, the sun out, and so warm that we took Flora to Belvedere, she was much pleased with the younger children, we did not stay long.

Mrs Felton was in better spirits, she had heard from Mr Felton, who is allowed to defend himself before the house of Assembly, and has papers, and his correspondence with the different Governors and also with Lord Bathurst[2] which will clear him from the vile charges brought against him, every thing will be published; I shall be delighted to have these rascally malicious Yankees defeated in their scheme to ruin an innocent man, who has in fact been the making of all this neighbourhood. Mr Felton is accused, when Emigrants first came here, of selling land to them which was really a Grant from Government, and of pocketing the money.[3]

Poor Eliza Felton is in sad spirits, she and Mr Watson are attached and her friends do not approve her choice, I cannot help blaming Mrs Felton for the young Man for the young Man has had every encouragement to go to the house, and Eliza has been allowed to drive out with him, in short they have been constantly together. We dined with Tom yesterday, stuffed the back of his sofa for him and cut out the cover which I am making and Edmund is stitching at the cushions. I don't know what our brother would do without us – A few more commissions – – – – – – – – – – – – – – – –

We went to Church last Thursday evening, Sherbrooke was full of people, a great number of Canadians waiting for Mass in the Catholic Chapel at twelve at night. Our Church was very prettily ornamented and well lighted by Mr Salt, we had tea at Mr Kimballs before the service, and supper there afterward, Mrs Hale has a little girl, Mr Watson attended her, I want much to see her. Tom dined here on Christmas day we had a famous plum pudding, and treated ourselves with mulled wine in the evening.

Flora gets quite a romp, she throws herself over on the sofa till I am quite alarmed, she puts her hands over her head to peep at me in as saucy a manner as possible, and often takes up her frock or pinnafore to hide her face from me. She is delighted with music, and is almost wild to get to the Harp when I take off the cover. She has only one tooth yet.

30th – We had six from Belvedere on Monday, I wore, for the first time, Papa's handsome present, it was much admired, our friends did not leave us till eleven. Mrs Felton goes to Quebec tomorrow. Edmund and Tom are going tomorrow to Brompton to call upon Mr Campbell, so I hope I shall hear where he saw you and Papa. I fear I shall never have your next journal, the Post Office and many more buildings at New York are burned down, it was a dreadful fire, it is supposed some incendiaries have been at work.

Edmund, when he read this letter, said, with his usual good sense, that I should not have written to you on those very cold days, no one could feel comfortable then, and they occur so seldom, it is scarcely fair to give way to ones feelings on paper when suffering, as we cannot under excitement form a just idea of things; we have now the usual winter weather, and I am as contented with Canada as ever, and enjoy a drive in our comfortable sleigh. There was a fall of snow last night which will improve the roads when it is beaten down; we have had very little snow this winter, talking of snow, do send me the receipt for Snow cheese. I

thought often of dear old England on Christmas day and the many pleasant Christmas' I have spent at Oak Hill.

Edmund has made a nice box for our wood, it stands in the passage
and has a partition for green and dry wood, the box is six feet four long,
four feet high, three wide. My husband is now stitching by my side at
Toms bolsters, he has also began another rug in squares formed by red
cloth. I assure you we are very seldom idle, we have neither time nor inclination to be so. Pray send our best love to Sturges when you write to him –
Kiss Papa for me, love to all our relations, ever your attached child –

Lucy Peel.

No. 34

To Mrs William Birch
Dunstall Villa Jany 7 1836 –

My dear Rose

I am quite behind hand with my journal, I have not, till to day, had time to
write and it is more than a week since I sent off my last to Mamma. My
good husband assists me in working for Flora, we are making night Caps
and pinnafores; the last day I wrote Edmund and Tom were gone to call
upon Mr Campbell, they were pleased with him, I find he does not know
either Papa or Mamma, Charles was only a hunting acquaintance, he said
my brother was a beautiful rider and generally first in the field, he also
knows Robert John Peel, and praised him as a horseman. I believe Edmund
Peel of Sorel is almost certain to come and live about eight miles from us
next Spring, he is wishing to purchase Captain Colclough's Farm at Brompton, for which he is to give five hundred and fifty pounds, there are about
190 Acres, a small house and a good barn.

Last week we called at the Judges, Mrs Fletcher was in bed, I went up
to her, she said she was very unwell, I asked what was the matter, I don't
know she replied, I am very poorly, and there is no money coming to us.
Government owe them a thousand pounds. On tuesday last Edmund drove
me to see my friend Mrs Hale, she was up stairs but looked quite strong,
and happy as possible, she has a delightful English Monthly nurse from
Quebec, who wishes to come and settle in Sherbrooke if her husband can
find employment here, she is a superior person, gentle Ladylike manners
but no fine airs, waits upon herself. Mrs Hales baby is very plain. Yesterday
Mr Hale and Miss Ann Bowen called, Flora was greatly admired, Mr Hale
said he should not have known her she looks so rosy and healthy. After din-

ner we went to Toms and finished his Sofa, we stayed tea and had a lovely ride home by moon light.

We have had delightful, and very moderate weather ever since those *killing days* I so bitterly complained of to Mamma; there is something very sublime in a Moonlight ride through the woods, every thing in nature seems at rest, and your thoughts instinctively rise to heaven and the great maker of all that is noble and lovely. I really was sorry to find myself at home, but as I entered the house how quickly my feelings changed, fancy gave place to reality and I ran into the nursery to see if all was right with dear baby whom I found fast asleep in her cot, and she did not awaken till the next morning, she is now playing with her Papa, she gets more amusing every day. Mrs Charles Felton is dead, her husband will now have some chance of maintaining his family.

15 – Mr John Felton, Fanny and Isabella dined here last Saturday we kept Flora's monthly birth-day – On Tuesday Mr John Felton came with Fanny in his Sleigh to take me to make some calls, we went to Mrs Hales, she had been a drive, she looked very pretty and the baby is much improved, we called at her sisters Mrs Bells, she was not at home, I received your joint journal, the continued good accounts of dear Sturges delight us, what an advantage his drawing so well is to him. Thank dear Mamma for answering all my questions, at this great distance I like to hear of people I even did not care much about when in England. Every thing regarding my native Isle, or those that dwell therein, interests me.

Mr Watson has been to vaccinate Flora, she cried & kicked so much he did not do it effectually. I have been making silk shoes for Flora, those I have from England are much too large at present & here I must find the material & pay 2/6 besides, I begin to be quite expert at this work, and am now making leather shoes they are Deer skin – bound with purple ribbon; her socks I knit, I could not get any small enough. Edmund, I am sorry to say, is suffering with Rheumatism, he rubs with the Embrocation [a type of liniment, *GCD*] Papa sent, and brushes every night, the pain is in his back and left Hip, he finds that he cannot chop much now, I hope he will soon be well again.

27th – Flora has been vaccinated twice since I last wrote, I believe it will now take effect. Mr Watson is not a nice operator, he has a heavy hand & is slow. Mrs Hale was pleased with him at her confinement. Edmund was quite ill two days last week with a gathering in his mouth, he could not eat and was in great pain, he is now nearly well. Flora is quite healthy, her eye lashes are very long & like gold thread, she has but little hair at present, she gets more like Celia in all her little ways.

Yesterday we received Sara Janes and Mamma's journal and are much obliged for it, I will write next to Mrs Mayne. Give my kind acknowledgements to William for what he says of Flora, I believe to this day Mr Watson has not made up his mind to what her complaint was, he never gave any decided answer to any of our questions. We had a long letter last week from Mrs Peel, she, Mr Peel, George and Sidney are at Lytham for the winter. The works are sold at Church Bank & they appear delighted to be clear of all the cares and troubles of trade. Mrs Peel always writes most affectionately to me, the more I know of her the more highly I value her good opinion and I hope I shall always retain it.

Papas writing, tell him with my love, is I think like Edmunds, always coming but never makes it [*sic*] appearance, however if it be a trouble to him I would not have him write, I know he loves, and often talks about us. Mamma's praises, I feel, I do not altogether deserve, if I lived near her now she would find me a better daughter I think, I have a child of my own & know how much I owe to my mother, I think a child cannot do too much for a parent whatever inconvenience it may put them to, I can scarcely fancy anything more dreadful to a parent than the neglect of a child.

30th – Poor Mr Twis [Twiss] whom I named as a naval officer coming out to Canada last summer with his wife and child has just had a terrible loss, his stove pipe was red hot and the wall through which it passed not being sufficiently protected took fire, he was at Lenoxville – his wife, their baby and a friend a Mr Tarset, were in the house, in little more than an hour not a vestage of the place remained, everything was lost save what they had on; they brought out large stocks of clothes and linen, the flames spread so rapidly that nothing could be saved. Mr Tarset was twice nearly suffocated in trying to get his boxes out at the window, they were too heavy for him to lift. They are now at Captn Colcloughs where they will most likely remain the winter. Mr Twiss brought out four hundred pounds which he spent in land, stock and improving the house on his farm, he has now nothing but his half pay, but I hear that his father is very well off and lives in Cambridge, he is very penurious, but surely when he hears of his Son's losses he will assist him.

Flora has been suffering from her arm the two last days, she scarcely slept at all last night, I think the worst is over, she has cut another tooth. Does Mamma know that Mr Roebuck[4] formerly taught dancing at Quebec, some of the Bowens learned from him.

6th – Fanny & Louisa Felton spent Wednesday here, Fanny had been to a party at Mr Austins a few evenings before, they had music, singing and dancing. The Twiss' are having a new house raised, some people say they will in the end have but little loss, but Mrs Twiss is much depressed. Flora's arm is now quite well, when she and her papa are together I cannot tell which makes the most noise, she clings to him as fast as possible when I attempt to take her away.

Mr Doolittle's organ is at last arrived & he has had a man to put it up for him, I am expecting him to call to invite me to play upon it, I quite long to try it. How this country has improved in refinement since we came!! At that time the Cobblers Piano was the only one in the neighbourhood, and my Harp, the greatest possible wonder, now there are five Pianos –

The Judge has had a fit of the Gout, but is now well and gone on one of the circuits, I have not been at his house lately, we can never get away again when we find them at home. I suppose if Charles & Kate come to America they will visit us before they settle, even if the [sic] do determine to live in the States. They must come and see how happy and comfortable we are, Edmund thinks he & Charles would agree very well, both being quiet and domestic, and little inclined to interfere with the concerns of others, but I never for a moment allow myself to think it possible they will settle near us, it is too great a pleasure to expect.

Give our united love to our Parents and the Maynes and to dear good industrious Sturges, accept every good wish for you & those near and dear to you & believe me your very affectionate Sister

Lucy Peel

No 35

To Mrs Mayne –

Febr^y 15 – 1836

My dearest Sarajane

Your nice letter gave me much pleasure, you answer all my questions so openly, Mamma would not have told me so much about the Oldershaws. We have had a great deal of snow since I last wrote and it is now very deep, Mrs Felton came home last Tuesday. She called here on Wednesday, she looked very well & was in good spirits, Mr Felton going on as well as possible.

On Friday we went to Sherbrooke & on our return Mr & Mrs Austin called, accompanied by a Mr Mottram, a very fine, handsome young man come out to settle, Mrs Austin thinks him like Mamma's picture & he said it was just like his Mother – Mr Mottrams Father & Mother are coming out next Spring, they live in Bath, & this young Man has been brought up a Gentleman; I understand all the Ladies admire him exceedingly. I played to my visitors, & they flattered me by saying they could listen all day. Mr Austin said he wondered how he could be induced to marry a woman who was not musical, he was determined his next should play well, she laughed at his bandinage [*sic*] and appears a very amiable woman. Yesterday Tom dined here, he gets very impatient for the arrival of Sidney.

19th – We have been quite gay this week, and to night, as we sat alone by our fireside, we agreed we would not be such rakes often for all the world, I am convinced the longer you lead a happy quiet life the less you are disposed for gaiety. If we followed our own inclinations we should never visit, but we must give way a little to custom, it would be selfish not to do so.

On Monday we were at an evening party at Belvedere, Mrs Twiss is staying there, we had music, dancing, Waltzing, till after two in the morning, we did not leave till nearly one. I made myself useful by playing to the dancers – Mr Bowen and Mr Collard sang some very pretty duetts. Mr Twiss had seen Edmund before on board some Ship, though my good husband did not remember him, he seems to be a quiet domestic man.

On Thursday we drove to Sherbrooke & took Flora to see Mrs Good-hue who pronounced her a great beauty. On Friday we had an evening party, we dont give more than two a year & by their coming so seldom I believe they are thought more of. Our drawing room looked very pretty and we had a famous fire, which every one seemed to enjoy. The young people danced in the dining room, I had prepared it for them, we supped in the nursery, I gave them two dishes of beautifully cooked Turkey, two of Ham, Fish dressed with eggs, milk & butter, Tarts, Curd & Cream, Almonds & Raisins & figs – During the evening we all sang, even Edmund favored his visitors, and after supper the Gentlemen toasted he [*sic*] Host & Hostess in a very pretty chorus. Mrs Twiss told a Ghost Story, the party broke up about one.

I am quite tired to day, I am not able to bear much fatigue. I dread my approaching trouble more this time than last, then being childless, I felt I could endure any pain to be once more a Mother. Dear Sarajane the love of a Mother is beyond all belief, & the anxiety I feel for my child I find sometimes too powerful for happiness. We think Flora is about more teeth, she is so fretful, she cries after her papa whenever she sees him. I never saw so good a nurse.

26th – We have all colds & coughs, Flora's is the worst, we put her into warm water and gave her medicine, we did not like to take her out of the warm nursery, so we sat up with her all night. Edmund always shares my troubles with me, surely there never was such a husband, he has all the courage and firmness of a man united with the tenderness and thought of a woman. I am sure I never expected to be possessed of such a devoted husband, I can never love him enough for all his kindness.

On Tuesday we received a delightful journal from Mamma & you, the accounts of Sturges gave us great pleasure, he certainly is in a trying situation, and it requires sound judgement and good sense to think so humbly of ourselves as we ought, when so much courted & flattered as our brother appears to be, how dearly I should love to see him, and hear him sing. I will write to him with pleasure if you will send me his address. You all appear in good spirits & to be enjoying yourselves. I am glad you have my letter at last, but am quite angry you should rejoice at what I consider a misfortune, but Mamma's pretty compliment makes all right. You seem to forget that the more children we have the less likely we are to visit England. The idea of seeing Charles delights me, I can scarcely believe there is such a pleasure in store for me, we will make room for Kate & the children. My good husband will be ready to devote his time to Charles & will take him to see the different farms. I bought sixteen pounds of Venison yesterday for 2/9. Edmund is making a bedspread for Flora. I wish you may have thought of telling Mr & Mrs Peel that my brother is coming to Canada, I am sure they would be so glad for Sydney to accompany him, and it might be agreeable to both parties. We have made fifty pounds of beautiful soap, and have more than a hundred to make, I wish you had a box of it, I can sell it for 7 1/2 per lb in exchange for anything I may want at the Stores, or from the small farmers near.

March 8th – Flora ten months old to day, her cough is not yet well, Mr Watson has been twice to see her, & says how well she looks, her cold has not stolen one rose from her cheek, we are not at all uneasy as neither her chest nor her lungs are affected, and she coughs almost as strong as I could, she does not attempt to walk and Mr Watson begs I will not urge her, he says she will of her own accord when she feels able.

Her new bed is finished, all our own handy work, it is the prettiest little thing I ever saw, four feet long, three wide, and about five high with curtains all round looped up at each post, a nice mattress which we made and yesterday I made the sheets and pillow coat, a neat little white bed quilt which I got from Montreal makes every thing complete. Flora did not sleep in it much more than an hour last night, we must get her to it by degrees, she at present, I fancy, wants my face, which she has been accustomed to feel most of the night, a bad practise she got when ill, at which time I could not refuse her any comfort.

Fanny Felton spent the other morning with me, she had been at a party at her Uncle Witchers the night before, Mr Watson brought her; our horse is lame so I have not been out much lately. Mrs Kimble called to day, she greatly admired baby. If this letter arrive before you send off the box I should like to have some flower seeds sent.

12th – On Thursday we dined with Tom at three oclock upon Salmon, hashed venison & pudding, there was a party at Belvedere that evening, we were all invited. Tom went, we declined, I do not feel well enough for parties and have not a company figure just now. On Friday we went to Sherbrooke, I sat with Mrs Fletcher whilst Edmund marketted for me, he manages as well as any body, and is always ready to save me trouble.

We received your journal, poor dear little Mini! I cease to wonder but never to grieve at your dear husbands frequent attacks, and fear, with you, his life will be full of suffering. I am afraid I should be as selfish as you if placed in similar circumstances. Edmund sends love to Papa and many thanks for his intended kindness. I wish we could have the seed, time enough to sow this Spring. I think you will find dear Sarajane that you have not a more affectionate Sister than the one now addressing you, and if I lived nearer I would prove it. Pray send me word all about Mr Whatton, I never heard he was dead till your last letter, the journal before you mentioned having had a letter from poor Mrs Whatton, and we could not think why you called her poor.

We had a terrible fright last night, just as we were going to bed Ellen ran to tell us the stove pipe was on fire, we set all hands to work, I was undressed so could not assist. I sat in the nursery watching my darling Flora, and planning what things I could save if the house were burnt. There was a high wind which blew most of the sparks clear of the house as they came out of the chimney, as there was a little snow still on the roof there was not much danger in that quarter, Patrick kept watch on the roof all the time, the danger was up stairs where the Pipe was red hot and close to some dry timber which formed the ceiling, the women kept pouring water upon the pipe and ceiling & by those means kept the great heat under, it looked most formidable at one time, but thank heaven all is now right except some of the pipe being burned, Edmund is gone this morning to Sherbrooke for some new pipe, and we must be careful for the future to clean them more frequently.

Flora's cold is nearly well, and she really looks beautiful, I wonder whether Charles will admire her. Parke's wife has a little girl, he looks as proud as possible, yesterday when I asked how she was, he said he would not take a thousand pounds for her. We are much pleased that Sturges can give up pleasure for duty and laughed about his God cake. Our best love to dear Papa, Mamma and all friends. Flora sends cousin Mini a kiss.

ever your affect Sister
Lucy Peel.

I shall send a small parcel to England by a friend in May.

No 36

Dunstall Villa March 17th 36

This letter I shall address, dearest mamma, to you, I feel it is a long time since I wrote to you. We went to Sherbrooke, I called upon Mrs Fletcher, she was unwell, and low spirited about the Judge, who cannot get paid, and from whom some kind persons in the house of Assembly are trying to take his situation.[5] On Wednesday Mr & Mrs Hale and the two eldest children called, they were delighted with Flora, thought her a great beauty, and little Fanny wanted to take her home, Mr Hale said she was like his Uncle, Lord Dundas.[6] When they were gone Mr Watson & Mr Bowen called. Our horse is still lame, Edmund means to part with him and buy two Canadian horses to drive this summer, we require two for these heavy roads. We have had snow the two last days and a high wind, I never saw a more disagreeable winter.

24th – We have been to day to Belvedere and took Flora, the weather quite warm, the Feltons made a great fuss with baby, I never saw her look better. Mrs Felton wished us to remain dinner but I would not on Flora's account, she is too precious for us to run any risk with her. All the horses at Belvedere have the distemper so our friends cannot stir from home. We have another medical man come to live at Lenoxville, he is an Irishman, and married, he means to buy a farm, and to practice his profession if required. This is well, for Mr Watson has occasionally to go a great distance, we shall now not be left without a medical man at hand.

27th – On Tuesday I was overpowered with visitors, all the Feltons in succession, Mrs Twiss and Miss Weatherston. Tom and Edmund are gone to Church to day, it is very warm, we took Flora to Belvedere on Thursday, she looked very pretty in the Pelise & Bonnet, Mary Lyon sent. I will tell Mrs Salt what you say of her friends, her husband is alive, he is old and drinks terribly when ever his wife leaves him, he would have been starved to death this winter had it not been for James M'Cready who found him in a snow drift quite insensible one evening between here & Sherbrooke. Mr Salt has lived as servant to the Judge many years, he was Jack of all trades, even cooked their dinner occasionally, his wife was seven years servant to Mr Felton, they talk as if they had seen better days. Mr Salt could not make farming answer, all their children but one, are married, one to a Dutchman, a farmer at Sorel, another to an English Sailor who has a farm not very far from us, another to farmer at Melbourne. The youngest tells her mother she never will be married.

29th – Yesterday we went to Belvedere after dinner & remained tea. Mr Felton is returned home in excellent spirits, though his affair is not yet settled, the House is not sitting now, it is six months since Mr Felton was at home and we were quite glad to see him again. This morning Mr Campbell called, his Father is the Captain Campbell Papa knew, and this young man remembers hearing of the horse Minister, he saw Charles Meek as late as 31 – and knows many persons we do, he brought us up from Sherbrooke yours and Rosa's letter. I am sorry you have not time to work me a bell rope, remember if you buy one, I shall pay for it. I am surprised you do not remember the pretty little pasteboard things you used to make with reels of cotton all round, I thought they were your own invention.

Rosa gives a very good account of herself and children. Give my love to her and say, I am much obliged for the receipts, I shall try them all. I have made a white frock for my little niece Kate, to send by Mr Mottram, every stitch is my own, and the pattern also, I hope Rosa will like it. I have also made a pair of shoes for the baby that is coming, the same as Flora wore when first put into short petticoats, I have worked some more lace for you dear Mamma. I am sorry I cannot get the second part of the Arithmetic for Mini, it is not published.

Pray do not for a moment suppose I am tired of Canada, it would be a dreadful change to leave a house & farm of our own, give up horses, Cows, and carriages, for a humble cottage in Wales, where perhaps we could only afford some lean mutton once a week; No, dearest Mamma, though sometimes half frozen in the winter, I am very happy, and get more attached to this place every day. If you had seen my face of alarm the other day when Edmund received a letter from the Admiralty, fearing it was to order him home, you would have been quite satisfied of my contentment here. Fortunately the letter gave him two more years leave of absence from the 22d of May next, his birth day.

Mr Campbell appears an active industrious young man, he has not any servant, cooks his meals and keeps his house in order, chops his wood, and in short does every thing for himself, he made us laugh by telling us of a Mr White, a young Lawyer who lives near to him, he is so dreadfully afraid of chopping his legs and feet that he stands in a tub all the time he uses his axe. I am surprised Kate's nurse has left her, I hoped she would come out with her. You must be glad to have the Peels at Barton, where are the Webbs gone to live?

30th – Just as I had written the above, and it was our dinner time, Mr & Mrs Doolittle called, I asked them to stay and they did, we had soup, roast veal & stewed Kidneys, they appeared quite satisfied with their humble repast. After dinner I had Coffee for them. Flora is in high spirits, she really looks beautiful, I do not think any child can be prettier, tell Rosa I will show her against Kate any day. I hope to have a boy this time, my dear husband is anxious to have a Son and Heir to his *large Estate*. If it be a boy it is to be named Richard Edmund after the Papa and two Grandpapas, and he will be called Richard. Papa must hold himself in readiness to be one Godfather.

April 5th – On Saturday we went to call at Belvedere and took Flora & Ellen. Edmund and I tuned the Piano for them, they are having an evening party on Easter Monday, we decline going, Tom will be there. We took Flora to the Hales last week, their baby is plain but very strong and forward. To day we have been to Lenoxville to the Doolittles, their roads are so bad that we were two hours in going three miles; we found that Mr John Felton and Fanny had called in our absence, they left me some beautiful honey. We have one Lamb, Flora is quite delighted with it.

12 – Wednesday last was a lovely day, the snow so crisp we could walk upon it; Edmund had several large fires close to the house. Flora and I went to them, the dear child was so pleased that she did not like to leave them, & cried so much when taken into the house that I sent her out again. Mr Felton, Fanny, Louisa and Edward walked to invite us to go that day to dine at Belvedere to meet Judge Fletcher and his Lady, Mr Felton said so much we felt ourselves obliged to go; the Judge did not make his appearance having an attack of Gout, Mrs Fletcher was there and Mr Collard, I never saw the old Lady look better, she had not been to Belvedere of four years, she remained there till Saturday, she called upon me on Thursday and saw Flora for the first time, I thought she would never have done admiring her, she kept saying, Oh what a pretty child, a sweet little dear –

Edmund has been three days white washing & colouring our rooms, we had the house thoroughly cleaned, it looks so neat & smells so sweet now all is finished, it is really quite delightful. I am very busy with my new Sofa Cover and curtains, I want to have everything in order for Charles Meek, I hope he will like our little Villa. Flora will now always be on her feet, I think she will walk very soon.

13th – Yesterday I received your nice journal, we are sorry for the death of our Cousin, he was a very quiet amiable boy. I really am delighted you are sending the Bell Ropes you worked. I shall value them so much, I am even so selfish as to feel little annoyed to deprive you of them. I am afraid I trouble you all very much with such numerous commissions. Mr Mottram leaves on Friday, I expect he will call tomorrow for the parcel, it will be directed for you to be left in the care of Charles Lyon, so you can inform him about it. I shall send this off tomorrow by New York. We hear little of the Peels of Sorel, I understand they have sold their farm, to some loss, and have taken a house in Sorel. Do not be uneasy if my next journal does not arrive so soon as usual, I shall most likely keep it back that Edmund may give you his annual addition to it. Mrs Salt is not coming to nurse me, she is living at a great distance. Mr Watson has recommended an American nurse to me whom he highly approves. Edmund sends his best love with mine to you all. Flora is quite well, and having worn out all her Caps, goes without – Believe me your attached child –

Lucy Peel

Thanks for your advice, we value it upon all occasions.

Unnumbered Journal

Dunstall Villa April 22^d 1836

It is now more than a week my dearest Mamma since I sent off my last journal. Last friday Edmund drove me to Belvedere. Mr Felton and Fanny set off for Quebec the day before, we went to ask Mrs Felton and Mr John to dine with us the next day. Mr John gave me a Jar of honey – Mrs Felton was in good spirits, Mr Felton has a law suit against all persons who have attacked his character; I understand there is not any doubt but he will clear himself.[7] Our friends came on Saturday and Octavia with them, Tom could not dine here but came to Tea, we had a pleasant quiet day. I gave them Soup, Roasted Beef, Venison, Rice flummery & Angel pudding. Flora was very good – I have the mortification of seeing Ellen the favorite with Flora because I am not able to nurse her as I used to.

Yesterday was like spring, we had all the windows open and were without fires. Edmund was putting a fence on one side of the house to enclose some young trees, and he was in high glee to see the snow all gone except small patches here & there, but Oh! the changeableness of this curious & variable climate, this morning the ground was again covered with snow, & it blew a hurricane, the windows in our room were frozen. Edmund and I are much obliged for your advice, we do not I assure you, think ourselves wiser than any one else, and are quite willing to profit by the experience of those we esteem and love, besides, surely a mother may at all times give advice to her own children without offending, bad must that childs heart be who will not listen with attention and respect to one who loves her so dearly.

May 2d – A lovely morning, quite hot, Edmund and Patrick are ploughing, and David M'Cready is working in my flower garden. I hope to have the seeds in this week. My friend Eliza Felton is to be married the 15th of this month, quite a sudden thing, the Gentleman is a Mr Elvin [Aylwin],[8] a Lawyer at Quebec, I hope she will be happy for she is a good girl, she goes to New York as soon as she is married. There has been very little Sugar made here this year, every thing is scarce and dear, we have two men coming tomorrow to put the garden in order. Edmund hopes to grow grain enough this year, it is a terrible drawback being obliged to buy so much, we give 7/6 a bushel. Flora looks as blooming as possible, she can walk with holding one hand, and never seems tired, she is the best child at night I ever saw.

10th – Mr Watson called & lanced Flora's gums, the four top teeth are through. Tom dined here on Sunday to keep her birth-day. I dare say you all drank her health. I give my cook fifteen pounds a year, I think she deserves it for she is never idle a minute, she is very good tempered and obliging, she says she could do anything for me because I never grumble or speak crossly to her. We have very fine weather, Edmund is as busy as any three bees, we breakfast soon after seven & from then till dinner at two, he is out at work, and often till past eight at night. He comes home sadly tired but not stupid, for he looks happy and cheerful and tells me all he has done throughout the day, I am afraid he works rather too hard, however he cannot remain quiet when he sees so much to be done, his bodily strength is not equal to his active mind. My flower garden is now in nice order and all my seeds in the ground. Mrs Hale sent me a very kind note on Sunday saying, she was ready to come to me at a minute's notice when I am ill if she can be of the least use or comfort to me.

14th – On Wednesday we had a letter from Johnathan Peel saying, Sydney was to Sail on the 1st of April, the letter had a long passage, so Tom set off the next morning to meet his brother, perhaps he may not reach Quebec. We have five men working, and all to feed, you would be astonished to see all they eat, a large loaf is consumed at a meal, I hope we shall get rid of three Men to night, I want to have a quiet house before I am confined, things don't go right unless I can see after them.

My darling Flora is more engaging every day, she has six teeth and can walk alone, but is so upright & in such we dare not let her go without following with outstretched arms, she frequently falls backward, I wish you could see her kissing us when she wants any thing, or we give her what she likes, she is always chattering but the only words we can make out are, "too bad" and "Oh!" I was brewing yesterday, I hope the beer will be good. Edmund wants something better than water when he works so hard, and he never touches wine at home except on very particular occasions. Mr Feltons trial begins on the 24th of this Month at Sherbrooke, the Quebec Judges and Lawyers employed are coming up, I am quite anxious for the result. Finished by Mr Peel.

Dear Mother

When you see my writing you will anticipate what I am going to say, this good morning, of May 18th at 8 Oclock my dearly beloved Spouse and helpmate presented me with a Son & heir to all my extensive possessions in Canada. She went to bed the previous evening at 9 oclock, the Doctor arrived about eleven, gave Lucy some medicine & went to bed. I maintained my accustomed post at the bedside, at six in the morning I roused the Doctor, & after much suffering Lucy blessed me with a stout hearty boy – I feel thankful this is over. I suffered much to witness the agonies of one so dear to me, it is a most heart rending thing, a sort of thrill not to be described passes through me, such a scene would, I should think, reclaim all careless, inattentive husbands. Lucy has given you an account of our proceedings, the Farm progresses slowly. If I could borrow Lucy's gift of writing I should say more. Give my love to Mr Meek, I am much obliged for the seed he is sending me. To all my Barton Friends, not forgetting Sturges, give my love & believe me dearest Mother Yr affect Son.

E. Peel.

May 19 – Lucy has passed a good night, she is in good spirits. I shall persuade her not to get up so early this time, baby is well and much like what Flora was, only larger in limbs & features, has blue eyes & light hair. Flora is much pleased with her little brother & wants to pull his face. Lucy has a Yankee nurse who says her stomach is not constant and she must cook her own victuals. She came in the night to ask Lucy if she could get along with the baby, being translated if she could whilst she herself got some sleep; however she is a good nurse & knows her business. I hope you will be kind enough to let my Mother know of our happiness, when Lucy gets stronger she will write to her and you.

No 37[9]

My dearest Mamma

How much you would all rejoice, I well know, when you received my dear husband's letter informing you that we have a Son and indeed most thankful am I that this trial is over, I never felt so low upon a like occasion, and I shudder now, to think of what I have suffered. I have gained strength wonderfully since my confinement and now get up to breakfast. I assure you we have a very busy house for Flora cannot yet walk. Mr Watson has ordered her a warm bath every morning when the weather is a little warmer, she is rather jealous of the baby and would, I believe, pull his head off if allowed, our little son has a great deal of hair, I shall send a lock in this letter, he has small handsome features.

Mrs Ewen, my American nurse, is extremely kind and attentive to both the children, but she chews tobacco, and is too fond of sleep, her rest, as she calls it, she is often asleep in a morning when I am up and dressed, she makes us laugh at her strange expressions, she talks of going and *coiling* herself down with the baby, sometimes she says, she will nab down & take a little sleep, she guesses every other word, and will not eat a thing she does not cook herself, she says she has a very delicated stomach. She has only two meals a day, & has tea at both. She is good tempered and ready to do anything for me. Upon the whole I like her very well.

Tom has been a fortnight in Quebec to meet his Brothers who arrived last Sunday, I think we shall have them home to night. I am most impatient to have my box & to read my letters. I suppose Sydney will be the bearer of one of your journals, for this is May, and I have not received the one which ought to have left England in March.

June 2d – Our brothers arrived last Monday, I never saw any one so much improved as George, we were greatly surprised to see him, we like him exceedingly, and he stays with us as long as he remains in the Country, Edmund is quite pleased to have a companion when he is working, & George insists upon being made useful. Our kind Father, Mr Peel, sent

George on purpose to see if we were thriving and really happy, & to have the pleasure of talking with someone who had seen us.

7th – Last wednesday Mr & Mrs Hale & the two eldest children called in the afternoon, they drank tea here. Mr Watson is attending dear baby who is afflicted in the same way as Flora was but is not so ill, I never saw such a patient child he scarcely ever cries. I am now quite strong and never felt in better health. On Tuesday Mr Watson came again and brought us the dreadful letter containing the account of the death of both Edmunds parents. I think if it had been my own beloved parents instead of his I could scarcely have felt more wretched, for independant of my own grief I have to witness that of my dear husband and his three Brothers who all doated on their father & mother. Edmund bears up the best, he has been pretty well tried in the school of adversity, & though the loss of such near & dear friends is great, the loss of a child, dearest Mamma, is still greater. Our brothers have not known sorrow before, and this is a sad blow for them. George will return to England directly by New York, and I shall send this letter by him.

On Sunday Edmund, George, Flora and I walked to Toms, we brought him and Sydney here to dinner. To day Edmund, Flora & I have been to Sherbrooke in the Waggon to buy things we wanted, my little darling enjoyed the ride much, she looks lovely in her mourning, the bonnet you sent for me, just fits her, I have covered it with black silk and trimmed it with crape. George does not like this country, he has never been quite well since he came, he is anxious to return to see his Sister Mary. Sydney means to remain out and give the country a trial. George is to be Godfather to the baby, Papa the other, Mrs Hale Godmother, she was quite pleased when I asked her. I received Rosa's letter last Friday, thank her for it, thank God you are all well.

12th – On Tuesday Mr Doolittle called; Flora & I went with him to call at Belvedere, he drove us very carefully, and remained to tea with us on his return. Yesterday we drove to Sherbrooke, and had the pleasure of bringing up our box from England. I cannot tell you how much I am delighted with every thing, my commissions have been so well executed, and the presents are so pretty and useful. The Cap, dearest Mamma, is greatly admired, and Ellen is quite charmed with your gifts to her, she is a good girl and deserves them, she now does all the work of the house, washing and ironing besides, with the greatest good humour. My other servant is ill at home & I have Ellen's sister in the nursery, she is a nice steady little girl.

Tell Sarajane I think her presents very handsome. The white cloth I shall keep to make a winter dress for Flora, it will be beautiful when braided, the hat will only just fit, it must soon be given to Master Richard, the books will be a fine source of amusement to my children. As to Rosa's Shawl, I think I never saw anything so pretty, how kind of her to take so much trouble for me, Mr & Mrs Felton admired it exceedingly, the screens came without the least damage, but the toy with the bears was broken all to pieces, the bell ropes do not look any the worse for wear and I shall value them more than I can express. The Ceylon basket is very pretty, in short every thing is duly admired and appreciated. I have had two handsome presents from my brother Johnathan, a most beautiful shawl quite a new kind, and a dress, how generous our friends all are, he also sent Edmund a stock of worsted & Cotton Socks – Mr & Mrs Felton called yesterday, they talk of going soon to Quebec.

12 – Dear baby was christened yesterday, Edmund stood for Papa, we had only Mr & Mrs Hale, and Mr & Mrs Doolittle, they remained dinner and went home soon afterwards. Tom & Sydney came to tea, our Son is called Edmund Richard, we shall address him as Richard, because there are so many Edmunds. Flora is quite delighted with the musical pear, and I believe we are almost equally pleased with it. I am greatly disappointed to find by Charles letter that he does not think of coming to see us, I anticipated the greatest possible pleasure in having him.

13th – I have not yet told you that Flora can walk beautifully all over the house, she is so proud of herself she will not even be carried out of doors, this is very troublesome. She is quite delighted with the Soldier on horseback, indeed it makes us all smile to see him move his head. Our Man has been away owing to illness, we could not get another except for extravagant wages, so Edmund does all himself. My cook has left me, she is very ill, & I much fear will not be able to come again. I am going to Sherbrooke tomorrow to pick up one of the English Emigrants if I can, George leaves us tomorrow, he returns by New York.

I am so much occupied in the house, and my mind so full of sorrow for our late loss, I cannot think of anything to send but this letter. My next will be to Rosa, the pattern she sent me for trousers was what I wanted exceedingly as I shall make some for Flora against the winter. My nurse, Mrs Ewen is still here, I have been obliged to keep her till I can get another servant, this is very expensive, for I give her 2/6 a day, she has been here a month on Wednesday. Dear little Richard will now, I hope, soon be well, Mr Watson knew how to treat him at once & thereby saved much time, which is precious to one so young.

Edmund & George walked to Belvedere on Sunday afternoon, they returned to tea, Tom & Sydney joined us, I never saw any one so improved as George, I should scarcely have known him. He is very generous and kind hearted, we are quite sorry to part with him. He says, he thinks, on his return to England he must visit Barton to tell you about your children in Canada, I am sure you would be delighted to have a chat with him, and I should love to hear you question him.

I hope, when you heard of Mr & Mrs Peel's death, you did not entertain the belief that we shall return to England, there is no chance of this dearest Mamma. This kind of life suits Edmund, and I am nearly sure if he leave here it will be to go to sea, and never wish for that day until you wish to witness your child pining away for grief. We have a larger income now than we had, we must still be economical.

I am very glad to hear that William Birch has all the business, it was just it should be so, for he did all the work, he appears likely to have a large family – If I could keep the two children I have, without any more, how delighted I should be. Edmund sends his best love to Papa & thanks for his note and the seeds, he has not spirit to write in this letter, he grieves much, but silently, he cheers all his brothers. I, who know every shade, every line in his face can see how much he suffers. Adieu dearest Mamma, Papa, and all friends & believe me your attached child

L. P – –

No 38

To Mrs Birch –

June 26 – 1836

My dear Rosa –

It is now some time since I sent off my last journal to Mamma, until to night I really have not been able to spare a moment to write, my cook is still away & I have only Ellen and her little sister Eliza to assist me, I often have both children on my knee. Our little boy is now, I hope, quite well, he has been a great sufferer, I trust I shall soon see him fat, he is, as Mrs M'Ready says, "a real beauty," every feature is handsome.

Nothing particular has happened since George left us, Emigrants keep pouring in, and Sherbrooke is full of them, they make provisions very dear, beef has risen from 3^d to 6^d, and every thing else in proportion. I wish the company had taken a fancy to some other country, for it is not now the quiet place it was, we might, when we first came out, drive twenty times to Sherbrooke without seeing any one, now it is quite the reverse.

Mr & Mrs William Felton are at Belvedere, she has called here, she nursed Master Richard and took great notice of Flora, who amused her very much by warming flannels at the fire & taking them to her, she has seen me do this for baby, and she tries to do all she sees done. Charlotte Felton came to sit up with baby, I had been up three nights & felt quite tired. I had a journal from Mamma last Tuesday, in which I hear of the illness of your dear husband, I am most thankful he is out of danger, you must have suffered as much in mind during his sickness as he did in body, it is dreadful to see those we love in pain, how glad you must have been to get Sarajane's super excellent nursing for William. I hope the next letter I receive will give me the glad tidings that *your* troubles are over, and that you are as strong as I am, certainly I ought to be most thankful that I so soon recover after my confinements.

Edmund, Tom, Sydney & I went to Church this afternoon, Mr Austins brother preached, he has just arrived at Lenoxville from Demarara with his wife and family, he returns immediately but the rest remain the winter, his wife is very delicate, she looks like an Autumnal leaf. I wish you could see how beautifully Flora walks, and with what an air she carries herself. She looks the picture of health and beauty and meets with great admiration from every one. A Man in the store, the other day could not take his eyes off her, he followed her all about and at last told Edmund she was the prettiest child he ever saw, and that she was as bright as a dollar.

July 3d – A week since I last wrote, no additional help yet, I am as busy as ever, Mrs M'Ready is very kind & comes to nurse Master Richard whenever I want her, if it were not for this I could never leave the house. Baby is now quite well, and is really very handsome, some say he will throw Flora in the shade, I scarcely think this possible.

Last Thursday evening we drove to Belvedere and sat an hour, Mr & Mrs Aylvin [Aylwin] were there and a Mrs Du Cheni [Duchesne?], I never saw Eliza look so well, Mr Aylvin is plain, he appears to be very fond of his bride. Last night they called here, Eliza gave me a pressing invitation to visit them in Quebec next winter and take the children, if it were only a day's journey, I should like to go very much. On Tuesday last we had a visit from Mr Jones, he had business up here so came to call, he stayed dinner but refused the offer of a bed, he is much improved in manner, he likes Montreal and has good practice, his wife will go to England next Spring to see her Sister who is returning from India. I am sure

Edmund would have been greatly astonished if I had asked him to send me home to see Louisa.

11th – Mrs Felton & Charlotte called on Sunday, they thought baby very much grown. Mrs Ewen came to see baby, I thought she would have killed him with kindness, she said she never loved a child so much. Mr Charles Witcher is going to be married in a few days to Miss Elkins.[10] We have had very hot weather lately, every thing grows fast, our Wheat looks beautiful, I trust we shall have some worth speaking about this year. Edmund has been busy preparing land for Papa's winter wheat, I hope it will answer; my dear husband works early and late. One of the Emigrants, who had a wife & five children, lost himself in the woods, he was found the fourth day dead.

14 – On Tuesday we went to Sherbrooke & called at the Goodhues. Flora behaved very well, she is really beginning to be of some use to me. She brings any thing to me I ask for, she will rock little brother in his Cot, she will soon be very fond of him. Yesterday we went to Lenoxville, we called at Mrs Austins and Mr Doolittles to play upon the Organ. The Belvedere party were to drink tea with Tom last night, his drawing room looks exceedingly pretty, the Curtains are drab Moreen, bound with crimson, a present from Johnathan. I wish you could see the beautiful shawl he sent me, the same kind cost nine pounds at Quebec. Your knit shawl is admired by every one. Last night I tried to make out the stitch from your directions & you will be glad to know that I have succeeded. Mrs Du Chini thinks it quite elegant. We are going to Belvedere today, Mr & Mrs Aylvin [Aylwin] leave on Saturday.

My flowers begin to look very pretty, I wish I had more time to attend to them myself, I am obliged to get a boy to weed for me. We have not heard from Charles since his arrival at New York, this surprises us much. The last journal was wrapped up so large I had to pay more than five shillings for it, they judge by the size not the weight. I hear that Mrs Peel of Sorell is expecting her confinement immediately, Mr Jones attended her husband when he was ill in Montreal, he thinks him delicate. Edmund Peel has built a house in Sorel, the Man he sold his farm to has ran off without paying him.

You must not entertain any hopes of seeing us in England, I should dearly love to visit you but I know it would be wrong to spend our money in journeys, if we can save anything, which I hope & believe we shall out of our income, it must be saved for our children. We were 24 at tea at Belvedere last night, Mrs Felton looked well, she is always in spirits when her house is full of company, I played and no one would touch the

Piano afterwards, I am considered quite a musical wonder here, I can scarcely remember any thing on the Piano now. What a large little family you have, fortunately you have the means to make all comfortable & have servants to help you. Mr & Mrs Hale called the other evening. My best love to all friends, kiss the children for me & believe me your attached Sister

L. Peel –

No 39

Dunstall Villa July 20th 1836

My dearest Mamma

Last friday I had lots of callers, first Mr & Mrs William Felton, then Mr & Mrs Goodhue, then Mrs Felton, Charlotte, and Mr & Mrs Aylvin [Aylwin]. On Saturday all the Quebec party left Belvedere, Mr & Mrs Felton went also, and we are quiet again; Edmund is not sorry for this, nor I either. I have not time to attend to visitors, I have only Ellen and her little sister, every moment is employed, I frequently stitch away with one child on my knee. Our washing is very heavy. Flora requires change sometimes twice a day, she almost lives out of doors and walks all the time, I never saw a child so young such a woman, she understands everything I say to her, and it is quite pretty to see her when we do what she likes, she kisses us over and over again, she is very fond of her little brother. Oh how I wish you could see them both, there certainly never were two handsomer or nicer children. Our Man has again left us, he was too ill to work, it is most inconvenient as the grass is ready to cut. Sydney came on Tuesday morning to offer his assistance he has worked two days with Edmund. No letters yet, what can Charles Meek be about?

23d – I am now alone all day, Edmund & Sydney are gone over to assist Tom, and when his hay is finished they will come here to ours: We have had a most lovely summer so far, our place really looks beautiful, I wish you could fly over and sit with me in our pretty Veranda, what a nice chat we could have, I am sure you would not wish to leave us again whilst we have this delightful weather.

28th – Last Monday evening, my two dear children being asleep, I set off to meet Edmund on his return from haymaking at Toms, I had not proceeded far when I met two gigs containing Mr John Felton, Charlotte, Fanny and Maria they were coming to see me so I turned back & took Mr J. Feltons place, he walking by our side. Edmund soon joined us, and our friends remained till after ten, appearing to enjoy themselves, I gave them Raspberry and cream and Butter Milk Cakes; did you ever taste any, we think they are very like muffins, Butter milk pudding is very nice, it is made thus. Butter a basin, fill it with buttermilk boil it an hour it will then turn out quite stiff, either wine sauce or melted butter & sugar with it. Yesterday Fanny and Maria came in the waggon to take Flora, baby & me to spend the day at Belvedere, the children behaved very well and were much admired, we returned home to tea, Tom & Sydney came, I am happy to say I shall have Edmund home again on Saturday.

From Edmund, July 31st – Dear Father accept my thanks for your kind present of Seeds, some I ventured to put in this year though rather late in the season, all my land was disposed of with the exception of a small space in my garden in which I put the Peas, Beans, and a few drills of Barley as late as the 20th of June, they are looking strong and healthy, the Barley will ripen before the early frosts will do it any injury, 12 weeks is the average time it ripens in this Country, and is reckoned a certain crop but is very little grown; now the Brewery has commenced operations at Lenoxville there will be a demand for it, and I think it will be the best grain to grow.

All Spring Crops are the best adapted for this Country, at any rate in its present rough state with the stumps in, you cannot ridge & furrow the land sufficiently to drain off the melting of the snow in the Spring. It would be swamped, I have ploughed up, rooted out the stumps, and carried off the stone from a small piece ready to put in the winter wheat you sent me, the latter end of August is the time to put it in I believe, I must find out some person who has tried it for information. Winter Wheat is very uncommon here, besides the objection I mentioned it has a chance of being killed either by the early frosts before the snow has fallen or by the late frosts in the Spring after the snow is gone. Imagine the effect with the glass at Zero in the month of October or March upon a field of Wheat uncovered with snow. To give you an idea of the rapidity of vegetation, some Wheat I put in the 9th of May on land ploughed up last Sept, and crops ploughed this Spring will be ready for reaping three weeks from this.

August 7 – I am sure you will like to see my good husbands writing, he seldom favors you, I think he should now write in every sheet for my time is so fully employed, I have only Sunday to indulge in this way. Last tuesday Charlotte Felton, Maria, Flora and I went down to Sherbrook to gather currants at Mrs Kimballs nice garden, it is beautiful, very large and full of fruit and very tastefully laid out in terraces. I called at Mrs Bells, she has a Son & is doing well. Mrs Hale has been very ill, and is not yet out of danger, she poisoned herself with eating toad stools instead of Mushrooms. I have had Tom & Sydney here all week assisting Edmund, the hay is in and the Wheat will soon be ready, the weather continues lovely and I never enjoyed a summer more, the roads are now assuming the appearance of those in dear old England, thanks to the Company, which does everything in Style, sparing neither labour nor money, they spend a thousand dollars a day in Sherbrooke.

The Town swarms with Emigrants, five hundred more are coming up and buildings are raising their heads in all directions for their accomodation. Mr Watson has full occupation, he has to visit the sheds twice a day and receives five dollars a day for his trouble, there is I hear to be a Hospital built. Flora is now beginning to say a few words and is the most amusing child I ever saw. Master Richard is a perfect beauty, I wish you could kiss his fat cheek, I am sure you would be proud of your Canadian Grandchildren. I have not yet a journal from you, and begin to feel rather uneasy, Oh! When so far distant from those we love, how much we think about the merest trifle concerning them, I long to hear of Rosa's safe accouchment.

19th – I have not written for a very long time, Flora has been unwell and would be nursed all day, my little nurse was ill too, so you may suppose I have been fully employed, Fanny Felton remained two days to assist me, and then was obliged to return home as they had twenty men at work at Belvedere. Flora is now much better but still taking medicine, her illness proceeded from cold, I have received Sarajane's & Rosa's joint letter & am glad my parcel arrived safely; I am surprised you do not like the tea, we do very much. The people here talk as much about tea as they do of wine in England, it is quite amusing to hear Edmund & other Gentlemen descanting on the merits & demerits of this nice beverage.

We had a letter from our sister Anne the other day, she writes very sensibly and bears up under the present affliction nobly, you know dear Mamma what a superior woman she is. I was also delighted to have a letter from Charles & Kate, it had been a month on the road, Kate writes in bad spirits – poor thing she has suffered much, Charles seems to be in good spirits and says he is coming to Dunstall with Fanny and Lucy, my dear husband, who has the warmest heart in the world, has written to beg and desire they will all come and remain the winter with us, they will then see what a Canadian winter is, and if not very terrible, they may perhaps be induced to settle near as Kate seems to think the pleasure of being together would induce her to bear the cold. Land is very dear where Charles is, and here it is cheap at present, he does not intend to purchase till the Spring, so no time will be lost in coming here. I have a nice scheme if they come here, & I can't help thinking it will be realized, for we are prone to believe what we wish. I am quite impatient to embrace them all and am sure I can make them comfortable and make Kate better pleased with the Country and the *Yankees*. How nice for Flora to have her Cousins. You must not be uneasy if my next journal, which will be to Sarjane should be *after time*, for I may keep it back to tell you the Meeks are under my roof safe. Dear little Richard cries a great deal, but is as fat and handsome as the most unreasonable mother could wish.

27 – Edmund and I went to Sherbrooke on Tuesday, we called at Mrs Bells, her baby is a beautiful boy, I received your delightful journal from those dear kind friends, the Cresswells, pray send my love to Ellen and thank her for her addition to you letter, I like to hear my friends still love me. Dear Papa we were much gratified to see your hand writing, you had been silent a long time, but I well know you think of us every day.

It would indeed be delightful, dearest Mamma, to spend a winter amongst you all, but at present it is impossible, the expense would not suit us, we could not reach home again under two hundred pounds, besides we are hoping to have Charles and his family this winter. Edmund too, would not like to visit England so soon after the death of our dear & excellent parents, think what a dismal meeting it would be with all his relations so soon after such a melancholy event. I do live in hopes that we shall meet again my dear Mamma, and I am sure my kind husband will forward this plan when he possibly can, for he would do anything to make me happy, he devotes himself entirely to me and my children, thank heaven I possess all his heart, and I would rather die than give up one particle of it to another.

Mr & Mrs Felton & the girls drank tea here last night, also Tom & Sydney, the two latter came again to night to cut corn. Flora is better, Richard quite charming. You, dear Mamma, ought never to have your pen out of your hand, you write so delightfully, I like your last journal exceedingly. Kiss Papa for me, love to all friends. Yr attached

L. Peel

after a long lapse, dear father, I tie the broken thread of my narrative. You must not attribute my remissness to forgetfulness or to that foolish common place excuse, want of time, for I deem to those we love, time might be snatched from our sleeping hours were it requisite, the true cause is, want of ability, I am indeed a mere scribbler. This week I have ploughed up a piece of ground for your winter wheat in the English style of ridge and furrow, I cannot make the ridge round as I fancy I have seen it, botheration to it, the next time I will stick the plough in deeper at the centre than the sides, that is the only way I can think of. Charles will tell me when he comes. I anticipate his arrival with great pleasure and hope he will be induced to settle near us. I begin to reap tomorrow, the grain looks well with the exception of part which is laid. In my next I will send you word what the acre yields as this is considered a very good Canadian specimen, no sea room for your affect. Son.

E Peel.

No 40

To Mrs Mayne –
Dunstall Villa August 28 th/36

My dearest Sarajane

This journal is for you & I shall begin by telling you a long story about Mrs Hale being poisoned as I think the effects are curious, and William Birch may like to hear about it. Mrs Hales brother, Mr Bowen, took her some mushrooms, they went to cook them themselves, the Canadian Cook exclaimed against them, say [sic] they were not the right kind, Mr Bowen declared he had eaten the same several nights, so Mrs Hale, the two children, and even Madame *Juge* the cook eat of them. In a short time afterwards Mrs Hale, without any apparent cause, began to laugh in the most distressing manner till her sides ached so she was obliged to hold them, the rest of the party joked and said she did it on purpose. However such violent fits of laughing and crying succeeded each other she went to bed.

Mr Hale left her & when he entered the drawing room he found Mr Bowen in the same state, the two children and Madame Juge were soon taken in like manner. Mr Hale became alarmed & went up again to his wife, she lay quiet, he spoke to her and asked her to get up, she said she could not move and he found she had lost the use of both arms & legs, he sent off for Mr Watson but before he arrived Mrs Hale could only move her head and was quite stiff and nearly cold up to her neck, he gave emetics to all the party, and excepting my friend they soon all recovered, she remains in a doubtful state. She is very low & says she feels as if she were not herself, her friends fear she will go into a decline. I am very sorry for she is a nice kind domestic woman.

Sept 4th – Since I last wrote we have been busy arranging our house for the arrival of Charles. Flora is pretty well, Master Richard quite well, I am sure you would admire him greatly, every one calls him handsome. On Saturday we went to call at Belvedere, Mrs Felton has been unwell, she was pleased to see us. Last night we were surprised by a visit from Mr & Mrs Henry, they have not been here of two years, they had not seen either of my children, Flora was quite overlooked in their admiration of baby. Edmund has been making a new road up to the house which is a great improvement. Part of his Wheat is down but not carried yet.

11th – Last friday we drove to Lenoxville & saw all the great people as we returned through Sherbrooke, Lord Gosford is there, he is a mean looking man, nothing noble in appearance. We got a letter from Charles and Kate, they say they cannot resist accepting Edmunds kind & hearty invitation & will be here next week, they say they all yearn to be with us. I am delighted and am quite busy making ready, should you not like to see how happy we shall all be together. We should have passed a dull winter had they not come, for Tom is quite tired of the Country & will leave before the winter sets in. Sydney only intends remaining to see a little of the winter. If my brother pronounces against Canada and leaves us, I really think I shall try to prevail on Edmund to return to England if we can sell without loss. We shall be very sorry to lose Tom, he is so kind & obliging, if he had been my own brother he could not have been more attentive or willing to do any thing for me.

Oct 8th – What a long time it is since I last wrote, and I might fill a sheet if I expressed all I feel at having dear Charles & his family with us. Oh! Sarajane what an excellent man he is, I think I never knew a more delightful disposition, so gentle, so kind, such a husband and father. I am sure he deeply feels leaving his native land & all his friends, yet not a word of complaint escapes him, he is always cheerful, and assists Edmund in every possible way, indeed now my dear husband is ill, I know not what I should do without him. Yesterday he was reaping and tired himself sadly, to day he is gone many miles off to take some wheat to the Mill. I think Charles very like Papa in manner and figure, the shape of his face is just the same. Kate & I get on famously together, she assists me in all my household concerns. She is very fond of little Richard & nurses him very often. The children behave well & do all I wish them. Fanny is very useful in nursing the baby & helps to set the table for dinner & Tea.

Flora is at Belvedere with Ellen, the girls are delighted to have her, and I found I could not attend to my sick husband and two children in the night. Flora will not leave me if she can help it. Edmunds complaint is the Jaundice, he is much better but still very weak. Yesterday I took Fanny & Lucy to Belvedere, darling Flora was glad to see me, I thought she would never give over kissing me, she cried when I left her, I was tired with my walk. Mrs Felton is in Quebec.

I received Mamma's last journal after her return from Mr Creswells. The tidings of dear Sturges are delightful. I hope he will now be able to maintain himself. Kate and I are never tired of talking together about England and old friends. Tom & Sydney are gone to Niagara,[11] not very pleasant weather for their journey. You will have lots of letters by Tom when he goes to England. I shall not send a journal so often now Charles & Kate are here, for the news would be twice told, besides I have taken a great dislike to writing lately, and well as I love you all I have been several days in making up my mind to finish this journal, but pray write to me, I love to receive your letters.

12th – On Sunday Kate, the children & I went to Church. Edmund is much better, he drove me to Sherbrooke yesterday. Mr John Felton came to call upon Charles, Mr & Mrs Doolittle also, they stayed dinner. We have snow several inches deep, but it is not likely to remain. Charles has shot me several brace of Partridges, both he and Kate think they are delicious. Mr Watson gave me some beautiful potted fish, we had it for breakfast this morning & it was pronounced excellent. I never met with an Englishman who appeared so fond of Canada, he says he has not any wish to return home, I can scarcely believe him.

We have killed a Cow since Charles came and the Beef is capital, my brother says you do not often see better in England, we were very near selling it. I am glad we did not as we should thereby have lost considerably. I have nearly 40 lbs of Suet for candles from her. We shall kill a pig soon. Wheat is what we most fail in, the early frost killed nearly all ours, we have not more than 25 Bushels, but what we have is good.

The Feltons are very quiet, but they appear happy and are as kind to me as ever. I don't think Kate admires the appearance of any of them, at which I am surprised, the one I think most Lady-like she thinks the least so. Edmund agrees with me, and he is rather fastidious about our sex – Charles desires best love, he is expecting to hear from you and concludes you have his letter, Kiss dear Papa, Mamma, Mr Mayne & Mini for me, & with best love to Rosa & all dear to her

believe me your much attached
Sister –

Lucy Peel.

[Unnumbered Journal]

Dunstall Villa Dec[r] 5th

My dearest Mamma –

When you learn our intention to return home next Spring I am sure your heart will rejoice, for I now know a mother's feelings and am therefore aware of the anxiety you must experience to see us again. Edmund is, after four years hard labour, convinced that nothing is to be done by Farming in Canada; the land here produces too little to pay the labour requisite to cultivate it; My dear husband has worked much to the detriment of his good looks, and it is very discouraging, after such drudgery to find that nothing can be gained. Provisions & labour continue to rise and will still be upon the increase whilst the mania for Emigration continues, but many think this will not long be the case, it is thought that the Company is exceeding its means, and that such a great expenditure cannot last long, then, before the error is found out, is our time to sell to advantage, for the natural consequence of the failure of the Company would shortly be a decrease in the value of Land, we think we can live cheaper in England in a quiet way than here, fewer servants would be necessary, and these *helps*, run away with a great deal of money. From what I learn from Charles & Kate every thing is cheaper in England excepting Meat. Wood is quite as expensive as coal, we use so much. We now pay more than sixty pounds a year for Servants wages, besides the additional help we are some times obliged to procure, their keep we reckon at fifty more for four of them.

We intend to take the voyage without a servant, we shall have Sydney with us and I am sure he will make himself useful for he is the most amiable young man I ever saw. I dare say that Charles in his letters, has passed his opinion of this Country, and you know he can judge of these matters. I weep when I think we must leave the remains of our dear child, I cannot bear to dwell upon this subject, I never talk about her to any one but Edmund, not even to Kate has one word passed my lips, I feel my blood run cold when I think of her. I hope I shall be a comfort to you when I am at Barton: I dare say I shall miss many things in England which I have here, my Sleigh, waggon & pair of horses, my nice large house with every convenience, and a store room always full of useful things, but I shall have much in England to compensate for the loss of these. The Feltons are quite grieved at the thoughts of our departure, I am the only person Mrs Felton cares about out of her own family, I dread taking leave of her.

15th – Yesterday Edmund drove me to Belvedere to bring Fanny & Maria to spend the day and remain all night. In the evening we had Mr Bowen, Mr Watson and Mr Collard and our brothers. Kate was quite amused with Mr Collard & admired his & Mr Bowens singing, their voices accord well. I gave them supper and Punch – which they all enjoyed. We slept 15 in the house, this morning Edmund & I took the girls home. We found Mr Felton looking very ill.[12]

22d We remembered Louisa's birth day yesterday & Rosa's to day. I never saw such a climate as this, the day before yesterday we had beautiful sleighing, Edmund drove Kate, Flora, and me out, we went to call upon Miss Batt[?] but she was too unwell to see us. We hope she will buy some of our furniture, we shall begin selling soon, but I have left my subject, the weather, yesterday it rained & the snow disappeared and to day there is good sleighing again. Tomorrow, Charles will drive Kate & me to Lenoxville to call upon the Doolittles.

I hope dear old Sturges will be able to come & see us as soon after our arrival as possible, I long to see him. We shall go first to the Ethelstans, Edmund will have business in Lancashire. I shall write to Bessy by Tom, I shall ask her to look out for a nurse for me, Oh mamma if my little Richard keep up his good looks I shall indeed be proud to show him to you there never was a finer fellow, he sleeps much better at night. I quite long to see Rosa's children, Kate is always talking about them.

Charles has killed fifteen Hares on our *Estate* so we have pies & soup without end. Next Sunday Christmas day Tom & Sydney will be here. I shall give them Hare soup, a Turkey, a ham, a piece of boiled Beef and a plum pudding. I *guess* we shall not live so well in England, but I think when once there I shall not wish myself back in Canada. Excepting it be the day Edmund leaves me to tempt the waves, when I think of this I tremble for he has never left me yet, but the good of our children must be considered. When we live amongst you & you see what a husband and father Edmund is, you will not wonder at all the praise I bestow upon him, and the love I bear him. Edmund's love & mine attend you all, soon I hope we shall sit chatting together. Papa's stories will all be new after four years absence, & you must think of all your little tales for Flora, believe me your very affectionate child

Lucy Peel.

Notes

Notes to the Introduction

1 Harriet Blodgett, *Centuries of Female Days: Englishwomen's Private Diaries* (New Brunswick, NJ: Rutgers University Press, 1988), 24; Mary Quayle Innis, ed., *Mrs Simcoe's Diary* (Toronto: Macmillan, 1965); H.H. Langton, ed., *A Gentlewoman in Upper Canada* (Toronto: Clark, Irwin, 1950); Audrey Miller, ed., *The Journals of Mary O'Brien, 1828-1838* (Toronto: Macmillan, 1968); and Catharine Parr Traill, *The Backwoods of Canada* (Toronto: McClelland and Stewart, 1971).

2 Robert A. Fothergill, *Private Chronicles: A Study of English Diaries* (London: Oxford University Press, 1974), 7, 29; and Felicity A. Nussbaum, *The Autobiographical Subject: Gender and Ideology in Eighteenth-Century England* (Baltimore: Johns Hopkins University Press, 1989), 24.

3 Photocopies are available at the archives of the Eastern Townships Research Centre at Bishop's University.

4 Nussbaum, *Autobiographical Subject*, 28.

5 Margo Culley, Introduction, in *A Day at a Time: The Diary Literature of American Women from 1764 to the Present* (New York: Feminist Press, 1985), 4. On the general reticence of English women diarists, see Blodgett, *Centuries of Female Days*, 45-56.

6 Studies on Upper Canada that depend heavily on sources of this nature are Katherine M.J. McKenna, *A Life of Propriety: Anne Murray Powell and Her Family, 1755-1849* (Montreal: McGill-Queen's University Press, 1994); and Jane Errington, *Wives and Mothers, Schoolmistresses and Scullery Maids: Working Women in Upper Canada, 1790-1840* (Montreal: McGill-Queen's University Press, 1995). The only previously published volume of writing by English settlers in the Eastern Townships is the excellent *Lifelines: The Stacey Letters, 1836-1858* (London: P. Davies, 1976), edited by Jane Vansittart. They settled not far from Sherbrooke, where they remained all their lives, but unlike the Peels, the often impoverished Staceys did not socialize with the local elite.

7 The term "life writing" has recently been coined to break down the barriers between writing by "literary" individuals and "ordinary" individuals. Marlene Kadar, "Coming to Terms: Life Writing – from Genre to Critical Practice," in

Marlene Kadar, ed., *Essays on Life Writing: From Genre to Critical Practice* (Toronto: University of Toronto Press, 1992), 5-7, 10.

 8 Blodgett, *Centuries of Female Days*, 5, 7.

 9 Fothergill, *Private Chronicles*, 32-35.

10 Blodgett, *Centuries of Female Days*, 166.

11 Blodgett, *Centuries of Female Days*, 78-79.

12 Helen M. Buss, *Mapping Our Selves: Canadian Women's Autobiography in English* (Montreal: McGill-Queen's University Press, 1993), 37.

13 "Peel, Sir Robert (1750-1830)," and "Peel, Sir Robert (1788-1850)," *Dictionary of National Biography* (London: Oxford University Press, 1963-4); and genealogical information kindly provided by C.H. Kinder of South Walsham, England.

14 Sherbrooke Registry Office, Register A, vol. 6, p. 32, no. 2023, 3 Sept. 1832, William B. Felton to Edmund Peel, sale of Ascot, S.E. 1/4 l.13, r.9; p. 37, no. 2028, 5 Sept. 1832, Mrs Eleanor Burns to Edmund Peel (as represented by William Henry via a power of attorney), sale of Ascot, W 1/2 l.13, r.9; vol. 8, p. 322, no. 348, 21 Oct. 1833, William B. Felton to Edmund Peel, sale of Ascot, N.E. 1/4 l.13, r.9

15 See, for example, the entry for 21 August 1833 in journal 5. Another opaque reference (March 29, 1836) suggests that he may have once been in the military, where he was known as "the horse Minister."

16 Amanda Vickery, *The Gentleman's Daughter: Women's Lives in Georgian England* (New Haven, CT: Yale University Press, 1998), 13, 36-37.

17 Referring to the English settlers in the United States, Charlotte Erickson writes that this myth resulted in an "element of non-rational behavior in the emigrants' decision-making," by which she means essentially an avoidance of the commercial market. "Agrarian Myths of English Immigrants," in O. Fritiof Ander, ed., *In the Trek of the Immigrants* (Rock Island, IL: Augustan College Library, 1964), 61.

18 J.I. Little, *State and Society in Transition: The Politics of Institutional Reform in the Eastern Townships, 1838-1852* (Montreal: McGill-Queen's University Press, 1997), 18.

19 While British travellers generally cautioned English gentlefolk against emigrating to Upper Canada, some advised them to settle in remote sections of the colony where they could avoid the American settlers. Gerald Craig, ed., *Early Travellers in the Canadas* (Toronto: Macmillan, 1955), xxx-xxxi.

20 After the London-based British American Land Company purchased all the Crown reserves (250,000 acres) and unsurveyed Crown land (600,000 acres) in the southern part of the region in 1833, its promotional literature was targeted largely at the gentry class of settlers. See J.I. Little, "Canadian Pastoral: Promotional Images of British Colonization in the Eastern Townships of Lower Canada during the 1830s," forthcoming.

21 On this theme, see John Barrell, *The Idea of Landscape and the Sense of Place, 1730-1840: An Approach to the Poetry of John Clare* (London: Cambridge University Press, 1972); Raymond Williams, *The Country and the City* (London: Chatto and Windus, 1973), ch. 12; Denis E. Cosgrove, *Social Formation and Symbolic Landscape* (London: Croom Helm, 1984); and Anne Bermingham, *Landscape and Ideology: The English Rustic Tradition, 1740-1860* (Berkeley:

University of California Press, 1986). For the Canadian context, see I.S. MacLaren, "The Limits of the Picturesque in British North America," *Journal of Garden History* 1, 2 (1985): 97-111; and Jason Patrick Bennett, "Apple of the Empire: Landscape and Imperial Identity in Turn-of-the-Century British Columbia," *Journal of the Canadian Historical Association* 9 (1998): 63-92. Bartlett included eighteen views of the Eastern Townships in his popular *Canadian Scenery*, published in 1842. See Victoria Barker, "L'art et les artistes des Cantons de l'est, 1800-1950," in *L'art des Cantons de l'est, 1800-1950* (Sherbrooke: Université de Sherbrooke, 1980), 10-12.

22 Barrell, *Idea of Landscape*, 57; and Janet Wright, *Architecture of the Picturesque in Canada* (Ottawa: Parks Canada, 1984), 12.

23 W.J. Keith, *Literary Images of Ontario* (Toronto: University of Toronto Press, 1992), 22. F.K. Stanzel has pointed out, however, that while Catharine Parr Traill was attracted to the picturesque, Susanna Moodie was more drawn to the sublime. "Innocent Eyes? Canadian Landscape as Seen by Frances Brooke, Susanna Moodie and Others," *International Journal of Canadian Studies* 4 (fall 1991): 101-105. See also Patricia Jasen, *Wild Things: Nature, Culture, and Tourism in Ontario, 1790-1914* (Toronto: University of Toronto Press, 1995), 9-10; Susan Glickman, *The Picturesque and the Sublime: A Poetics of the Canadian Landscape* (Montreal: McGill-Queen's University Press, 1998), ch. 4; and Roderick Nash, *Wilderness and the American Mind*, 3rd ed. (New Haven CT: Yale University Press, 1982), ch. 3.

24 For critiques of the garrison mentality thesis proposed by Northrop Frye, Margaret Atwood, Gaile McGregor, John Moss, and other literary critics, see Glickman, *The Picturesque and the Sublime*, Mary Lu MacDonald, "The Natural World in Early Nineteenth-Century Canadian Literature," *Canadian Literature* 111 (winter 1986): 48-65; and Helen M. Buss, "Women and the Garrison Mentality: Pioneer Women Autobiographers and Their Relation to the Land," in Lorraine McMullen, ed., *Re(Dis)Covering Our Foremothers: Nineteenth-Century Canadian Women Writers* (Ottawa: University of Ottawa Press, 1990), 123-36.

25 William Gilpin, *Remarks on Forest Scenery and Other Woodland Views* (1791). Quoted from Stanzel, "Innocent Eyes?" 105. It would take Catharine Parr Traill considerably longer to become reconciled to the view of "odious stumps," and Edmund did remove all those within view from the house. Stanzel, "Innocent Eyes?" 104-105, claims that it would not be until Emily Carr painted *Stumps and Sky* in 1934-35 that they would be artistically appreciated.

26 Wright, *Architecture of the Picturesque*, 15. See also Barrell, *Idea of Landscape*, 48-50; Michael Bunce, *The Countryside Ideal: Anglo-American Images of Landscape* (London: Routledge, 1994), 79-81; and Tom Gerry, "Extremes Meet: Elizabeth Simcoe's Birchbark Landscapes," *Queen's Quarterly* 106 (1999): 590.

27 The descriptions of Anna Jameson and Susanna Moodie were more influenced by Thomson. Stanzel, "Innocent Eyes?" 98-99, 103.

28 Jasen, *Wild Things*, 25.

29 See Edward Dahl, *"Mid Forests Wild": A Study of the Concept of Wilderness in the Writings of Susanna Moodie, J.W.D. Moodie, Catharine Parr Traill and Samuel Strickland, c. 1830-1855* (Ottawa: National Museums of Canada, 1973).

30 See, for example, Marcia Kline, *Beyond the Land Itself: Views of Nature in Canada and the United States* (Cambridge: Harvard University Press, 1970).

31 Bunce, *Countryside Ideal*, 32, 34.

32 Jean-Pierre Kesteman, Peter Southam, and Diane Saint-Pierre, *Histoire des Cantons de l'Est* (Sainte-Foy: Les Presses de l'Université Laval, 1998), 160.

33 Kenneth Kelley, "The Transfer of British Ideas on Improved Farming in Ontario during the First Half of the Nineteenth Century," *Ontario History* 63 (1971): 103-11.

34 Even though the company invested a considerable fortune in building roads and mills, the British influx ended with the Rebellion in 1837 and failed to recover fully thereafter. While 33 percent of Upper Canada was British-born as of 1842, the Eastern Townships had only half that ratio in 1844, which was in the peak decade of British immigration. The Eastern Townships ratio is based on the population of the six counties that constituted the bulk of the region. (*Journals of the Legislative Assembly of Lower Canada*, vol. 5 (1846), appendix D.) On Upper Canada, see J.K. Johnson, *Becoming Prominent: Regional Leadership in Upper Canada, 1791-1841* (Montreal: McGill-Queen's University Press, 1989), 136.

35 Jean-Pierre Kesteman has calculated that during the two decades from 1823 to 1843 accumulated investment in the St Francis District was only $14,000, while during the following ten years this figure increased fifteen-fold to $218,000. "Une bourgeoisie et son espace: Industrialisation et développement du capitalisme dans le district de Saint-François (Québec), 1823-1879" (PhD diss., Université du Québec à Montréal, 1985), 282, 284.

36 Bunce, *Countryside Ideal*, 34.

37 Dahl, *Mid Forests Wild*, 11.

38 Pratt uses the term "to refer to the space of colonial encounters, the space in which peoples geographically and historically separated come into contact with each other and establish ongoing relations, usually involving conditions of coercion, radical inequality, and intractable conflict." Mary Louise Pratt, *Imperial Eyes: Travel Writing and Transculturation* (London: Routledge, 1992), 6.

39 Sara Mills, "Knowledge, Gender, and Empire," in Alison Blunt and Gillian Ross, eds., *Writing Women and Space* (New York: Guilford Press, 1994), 42.

40 The following section on the Feltons is largely from J.I. Little, "British Toryism Amidst 'A Horde of Disaffected and Disloyal Squatters': The Rise and Fall of William Bowman Felton and Family in the Eastern Townships," *Journal of Eastern Townships Studies* 1 (1992): 13-42.

41 *British Colonist*, 26 Jan. 1826.

42 On Fletcher, see Christine Veilleux, "Fletcher, John," *Dictionary of Canadian Biography* (hereafter *DCB*), vol. 7, 300; and Little, *State and Society*, 52, 79-80, 97.

43 Vickery, *Gentleman's Daughter*, 196. See also Leonore Davidoff, *The Best Circles: Society Etiquette and the Season* (London: Croom Helm, 1973).

44 See J.I. Little, "Imperialism and Colonization in Lower Canada: The Role of William Bowman Felton," *Canadian Historical Review* 66 (1985): 536-7; J.I. Little "Felton, William Bowman," *DCB*, vol. 7, 283.

45 Blodgett, *Centuries of Female Days*, ch. 4. For more on this theme in the Peel journal, see J.I. Little, "Gender and Gentility on the Lower Canadian Frontier: Lucy Peel's Journal, 1833-36," *Journal of the Canadian Historical Association,* 1999 issue forthcoming.

46 On the importance of the addressee, see Bina Friewald, "'Femininely Speaking': Anna Jameson's *Winter Studies and Summer Rambles in Canada,*" in Shirley Neuman and Smaro Kamboureli, eds., *A Mazing Space: Writing Canadian Women Writing* (Edmonton: Longspoon/NeWest, 1986), 64-65, 73.

47 On motivations and justifications for women's diary keeping, see Blodgett, *Centuries of Female Days*, ch. 2.

48 Alan Macfarlane, *Marriage and Love in England: Modes of Reproduction, 1300-1840* (Oxford: Oxford University Press, 1986), 331-4; Vickery, *Gentleman's Daughter*, 39-41.

49 Buss, *Mapping Our Selves*, 44. Buss's comment follows from the silences she notices in Elizabeth Simcoe's journal, though she points out earlier (pp. 40-41) that Simcoe avoided certain subjects because her journal was read by her four young daughters in England. Blodgett, too, discusses "the burden of male language," though she provides several examples where female diarists discussed their pregnancy and childbirth. *Centuries of Female Days*, 53-55, 169-75, 178-79.

50 Errington, *Wives and Mothers*, 58-62. John Tosh states that middle-class husbands were normally present during delivery in Victorian England. *A Man's Place: Masculinity and the Middle-Class Home in Victorian England* (New Haven and London: Yale University Press, 1999), 81-82.

51 Tosh, *A Man's Place*, 39-41, 86-87. On attitudes to children in middle-class English women's diaries, see Blodgett, *Centuries of Female Days*, 185-92.

52 On this theme, see Tosh, *A Man's Place*, 100.

53 Tosh, *A Man's Place*, 36, 41; David Newsome, *The Parting of Friends: A Study of the Wilberforces and Henry Manning* (London: John Murray, 1966), 27-56; Ian Bradley, *The Call to Seriousness: The Evangelical Impact on the Victorians* (London: Jonathan Cape, 1976), ch. 10. The evangelical influence in general should not be overstated, for it was the Church of England's longstanding mistrust of dramatic conversions that made a nurturing Christian upbringing so important. This very point was being forceably made in the Eastern Townships at this time by the newspaper columns of Frelighsburg's Reverend James Reid. See J.I. Little, "The Fireside Kingdom: A Mid-Nineteenth-Century Anglican Perspective on Marriage and Parenthood," in Nancy Christie, ed., *Households of Faith* (Montreal: McGill-Queen's University Press, forthcoming).

54 Carroll Smith-Rosenberg, "The Female World of Love and Ritual: Relations between Women in Nineteenth-Century America," *Signs: Journal of Women in Culture and Society* 1, 1 (1975): 28. This is the interpretation adopted by such Canadian studies as Margaret Conrad, Toni Laidlaw, and Donna Smyth, eds., *No Place Like Home: Diaries and Letters of Nova Scotia Women, 1771-1938* (Halifax: Formac, 1988).

55 Blodgett, *Centuries of Female Days*, 95, states that private diarists responded "to the opportunity to be freely captious about patriarchal ways largely by ignoring it."

56 This image of congenial genteel domesticity is also strongly supported by the voluminous correspondence between the Peels' friends, Edward and Eliza Hale. McCord Museum, Hale Family Papers, 1828-1913.

57 On the relationships within one family of American origin in the Eastern Townships, see J.I. Little, ed., *The Child Letters: Public and Private Life in a Canadian Merchant-Politician's Family, 1841-1845* (Montreal: McGill-Queen's University Press, 1995). It is suggestive that the later Anglo-Indians would deny natives their political rights due to the degraded plight of native women. Mills, "Knowledge, Gender, and Empire," 41.

58 L. Stone, "Family History in the 1980s: Past Achievements and Future Trends," *Journal of Interdisciplinary History* 12 (1981): 73-74.

59 On the role of the neighbour's girl as domestic servant, see Errington, *Wives and Mothers*, ch. 5.

60 Leonore Davidoff and Catherine Hall, *Family Fortunes: Men and Women of the English Middle Class, 1780-1850* (Chicago: University of Chicago Press, 1987); Nancy Cott, *The Bonds of Womanhood: "Women's Sphere" in New England, 1780-1835* (New Haven, CT: Yale University Press, 1977); and Mary Ryan, *Cradle of the Middle Class: The Family in Oneida County, New York, 1790-1865* (Cambridge: Cambridge University Press, 1981).

61 Philip Greven, *The Protestant Temperament: Patterns of Child-Rearing, Religious Experience, and the Self in Early America* (New York: Alfred A. Knopf, 1980). The family correspondence of the eighteenth-century French-Canadian elite supports Greven's argument. See Lorraine Gadoury, *La famille dans son intimité: Échanges épistolaires au sein de l'élite canadienne du XVIIIe siècle* (Montreal: Editions Hurtubise, 1998).

62 Vickery, *Gentleman's Daughter*, 59-60.

63 Literary scholars, in particular, have stressed the transforming impact that British North America's settlement frontier supposedly had on higher status women. See Buss, *Mapping Our Selves*, ch. 1; Marion Fowler, *The Embroidered Tent: Five Gentlewomen in Early Canada* (Toronto: Anansi, 1982), 10; and D.M.R. Bentley, "Breaking the 'Cake of Custom': The Atlantic Crossing as Rubicon for Female Emigrants to Canada?" in *Re(Dis)Covering Our Foremothers*, 91-122. Patrick Dunae, on the other hand, states that genteel women were considered to be a burden on the frontier. *Gentlemen Emigrants: From the British Public School to the Canadian Frontier* (Vancouver: Douglas and McIntyre, 1981), 28.

64 Anthony Fletcher, *Gender, Sex, and Subordination in England, 1500-1800* (New Haven, CT: Yale University Press, 1995), 395, 400. See also Blodgett, *Centuries of Female Days*, 195-202.

65 Nussbaum, *The Autobiographical Subject*, xiv, xxi, 136. While Blodgett states that most of the English women whose diaries she studied "adjust to what their contemporary life allows them and observe the codes," she also claims that "the very nature of the diary as a personal record counters the limiting and devaluing of the female self entailed by accommodation to a male-dominated culture." *Centuries of Female Days*, 4, 97.

66 Vickery, *Gentleman's Daughter*, 226, 228, claims that the female public world of the Georgian era "was both larger and much less menacing than historians have often allowed." On this theme in Upper Canada, see Errington, *Wives, Mothers*, ch. 7.

67 Mills, "Knowledge, Gender, and Empire," 47.
68 ETRC, Peel Papers, C.H. Kinder to Monique Saumier, n.d.; C.H. Kinder to J.I. Little, South Walsham, England, 22 June 1999.
69 See Little, *State and Society*.

Notes to Book One

1 Drogheda lies on the east coast of Ireland, about halfway between Dublin and the Ulster border.
2 Holyhead is on the northern Welsh coast directly across the Irish Sea from Dublin.
3 A yellowish flour prepared from the pith of palm trees; it serves as a staple food in the southwest Pacific. *The New Grolier Multimedia Encyclopedia* (hereafter *NGME*).
4 A strong wooden or iron shutter fixed outside a cabin window or porthole in a storm, to prevent water from entering. *Oxford English Dictionary*, 2nd ed. (Oxford: Clarendon Press, 1989) (hereafter *OED*).
5 "The body; the abdomen; esp. when large and prominent," *OED*.
6 Bilson states that at Quebec, as well, "cabin passengers were not required to land or clean their baggage because they had not been subjected to the same squalid conditions as their fellow passengers." Geoffrey Bilson, *A Darkened House: Cholera in Nineteenth-Century Canada* (Toronto: University of Toronto Press, 1980), 9.
7 Lucy numbered only the journals she sent to her own family.
8 On the Hudson River as a tourist destination, see Patricia Jasen, *Wild Things: Nature, Culture, and Tourism in Ontario, 1790-1914* (Toronto: University of Toronto Press, 1995), 58.
9 Presumably referring to Weehawken, New Jersey.
10 Ossining in Westchester County, New York, became the site of Sing Sing prison in 1825.
11 *The Sketch Book of Geoffrey Crayon, Gent* (1819-20) by American writer Washington Irving included the tales "The Legend of Sleepy Hollow" and "Rip Van Winkle."
12 Morgan Lewis (1754-1844) was deputy quartermaster general for the New York department during the American Revolution, and chief of staff with Gates at Ticonderoga and at Saratoga. He served as chief justice of the New York Supreme Court from 1801 to 1804, when he became state governor. He lost the election of 1807, and during the War of 1812 he was quartermaster general and major general in service on the Niagara frontier. In 1814 he was in command of the region around New York City, *NGME*.
13 Lewis was connected with the extensive Livingston estates, *NGME*; Harry B. Yoshpe, *The Disposition of Loyalist Estates in the Southern District of the State of New York* (New York: AMS Press, 1967), 67-68.
14 On the various theories concerning this case, see http://4speaks.com/fkm-crea.htm.
15 Whitehall, New York, is on the Vermont border, directly south of Lake Champlain.

16 William Hamilton became the region's first customs officer in 1821, but he appears to have had little success in curbing smuggling from Vermont. J.I. Little, *State and Society in Transition: The Politics of Institutional Reform in the Eastern Townships, 1838-52* (Montreal: McGill-Queen's University Press, 1997), 102.

17 The original transcriber clearly had trouble deciphering this word, whose spelling is not clear in the transcript, but Lucy was obviously referring to Lake Magog.

18 The 1831 census for Ascot Township lists Guy C. Colclough with fifteen improved acres, eight members of his household, six cattle, two horses, and five hogs. In 1836 a report stated that Captain Colclough, who had become an agent of the British American Land Company, was "an intelligent and agreeable man, always most willing to afford assistance and information, to those destined to the Eastern Townships." "Statement Made to a Special Court of the Directors of the British American Land Company . . . by Mr Frederick Templeton," in *Report of the Court of Directors of the British American Land Company to the Proprietors, 19 June 1834* (London: W.J. Ruffy, 1834).

19 Although the name Theney is used for the first part of the journal, it is clear that Lucy is referring to William Henry, who purchased part of Edmund's land for him in October 1832, and whose name is used in place of Theney in the later entries. It is quite likely that the original transcriber made the mistake in spelling. Lucy later mentions that William Henry was the son of the noted fur trader Alexander Henry; he is also referred to in this journal as a surveyor and former fur trader himself. David S. Armour, "Henry, Alexander," *Dictionary of Canadian Biography* (hereafter *DCB*), vol. 6, 316-18.

20 Referring to William Bowman Felton, the chief landowner and holder of political power in the region. For more information on him, see "Felton, William Bowman," *DCB*, vol. 7, 281-83; J.I. Little, "Imperialism and Colonization in Lower Canada: The Role of William Bowman Felton," *Canadian Historical Review* 66 (1985): 511-40; J.I. Little, "British Toryism amidst 'a horde of disaffected and disloyal squatters': The Rise and Fall of William Bowman Felton and Family in the Eastern Townships," *Journal of Eastern Townships Studies* 1 (1992): 13-42.

21 John Felton had served as a lieutenant in the Royal Navy during the Napoleonic Wars. He was dismissed in 1809 when the French vessel under his charge was wrecked, but he was reinstated before being paid off at the onset of peace in 1815. He served for thirty-seven years as the local Crown lands agent in Sherbrooke, resigning only in 1865 due to failing eyesight and the shrinking of his jurisdiction. McCord Museum, Morris Papers, M215 85, folder I, Genealogical and Biographical Notes; Testimonial from the citizens of Sherbrooke to Captain Felton [1865]; Captain John Felton to Hon. A. Campbell, Sherbrooke, 1 March 1865.

22 Various spellings appear throughout the journal. The Feltons spelled it Belvidere.

23 The controversial John Fletcher was judge of the King's Bench for the St Francis District. For more information, see Christine Veilleux, "Fletcher, John," *DCB*, vol. 7, 300; and Little, *State and Society*, 52, 79-80.

24 For more information on Charles Whitcher, see Little, "British Toryism," 27-29; and Little, *State and Society*, 23, 24, 48, 54, 55.

25 For those imbued with an appreciation for the picturesque landscape the veranda served as a bridge between interior and exterior space, as well as providing an ideal spot from which to enjoy the vistas. Jane Wright, *Architecture of the Picturesque in Canada* (Ottawa: Parks Canada, 1984), 55-57.

26 The eldest was not named John, but William, and Lucy neglected to mention Matilda.

27 Postage stamps were introduced to the Province of Canada in 1851, but people resisted using them. William Smith, *The History of the Post Office in British North America, 1639-1870* (London: Cambridge University Press, 1920), 275-76.

28 Wright states that only with the small residential building in a rural or suburban setting, commonly referred to as a villa or cottage, "could the fusion of architecture and landscape into a Picturesque whole be achieved." *Architecture of the Picturesque*, 17, 25-26.

29 The deeds of sale reveal that the cost for the 150 acres in 1832 was £112. Sherbrooke Registry Office, Register A, vol. 6, p. 32, no. 2023; p. 37, no. 2028.

30 Battledore and shuttlecock is an old-fashioned game resembling badminton, played by two persons. The battledore is a small racket used to hit a shuttlecock back and forth. *The Gage Canadian Dictionary* (1993; hereafter *GCD*).

31 Cousin of Lucy's husband, Edmund.

32 A quarantine station had been established at Grosse Ile in 1832. Bilson, *A Darkened House*, 9.

33 *Orlando Furioso* is a Renaissance romance by Ludovico Ariosto in forty-six cantos. It makes use of a later interpretation of the French medieval hero, Roland, whom the Italians called Orlando, *NGME*.

34 The pro-Reform Sherbrooke lawyer, Ebenezer Peck, topped the polls in the constituency of Stanstead in 1829. By the 1840s he was teaching the "Canadian" theory and practice of party organization to the Illinois Democrats. J.I. Little, *The Child Letters: Public and Private Life in a Canadian Merchant-Politician's Family, 1841-1845* (Montreal: McGill-Queen's University Press, 1995), 11-12, 19.

35 On the circuit court, see Little, *State and Society*, 51, 79-81.

36 William Wilson's name does not appear in subsequent entries as a physician for the Peels, but the Hale Papers at McGill University include a number of letters between him and Edward Hale concerning the health of the latter's family.

37 Wilson's letter to England in January 1834 was printed in the British American Land Company's *Report of the Court of Directors*, 11-12.

38 Lord Aylmer served as the increasingly unpopular Governor of British North America from 1830 to 1835. See Philip Buckner, "Whitworth-Aylmer, Matthew, 5th Baron Aylmer," *DCB*, vol. 7, 904-908.

39 Joseph-Rémi Vallières de Saint-Réal was born in 1787 and studied law with Edward Bowen, taking over his cases when Bowen became a judge in 1812. Vallières had a highly successful law practice and speculated in land, as well as investing in a variety of businesses. A bon vivant, he served for many years in

the House of Assembly where he was a moderate member of the nationalist Canadian Party and vied with Papineau for its leadership. He was appointed provincial judge for Trois-Rivières in 1829, and to the district's King's Bench a year later. He was dismissed in 1838 for granting a writ after Lord Durham had suspended *habeas corpus*, but was reinstated with back pay by Governor Poulett Thomson in 1840. In 1842 he became the first Canadian to hold a chief justiceship; he died in 1847. James Lambert and Jacques Monet, "Vallières de Saint-Réal, Joseph-Rémi," *DCB*, vol. 7, 876-81.

40 According to the tenets of picturesque architecture, the location of the house was as important as the design: "Especially popular were those well-wooded, elevated spots, preferably on the edge of steep embankments providing broad vistas of the countryside." Wright, *Architecture of the Picturesque*, 57-58.

41 On postal communication with England, see Jane E. Harrison, *Until Next Year: Letter Writing and the Mails in the Canadas, 1640-1830* (Hull, QC: Canadian Museum of Civilization; Waterloo: Wilfrid Laurier University Press, 1997), ch. 3.

42 Probably the lawyer whose wife Lucy became friends with. She describes the house and garden in more detail on 11 Sept. 1834. The name is also spelled Kimball in the journal. In 1831 Sherbrooke lawyer George Kimball testified before the Assembly committee's inquiry into the conduct of Judge Fletcher that the judge was motivated by three dominant principles: fear, vengeance, and prejudice. Kimball moved to Wisconsin in 1837. Maurice O'Bready, *De Ktiné à Sherbrooke: Esquisse historique de Sherbrooke, des origines à 1954* (Sherbrooke: Université de Sherbrooke, 1973), 74; Jean-Pierre Kesteman, Peter Southam, and Diane Saint-Pierre, *Histoire des Cantons de l'Est* (Sainte-Foy: Institut québécois de recherche sur la culture, 1998), 123.

43 "In the prophecy recorded in Ezekiel 38-39, Gog, ruler from the land Magog, is to be destroyed when he attacks Israel. Symbolic of the conflict between good and evil, the theme reappears in Revelation 20:8, where Gog and Magog are both agents of Satan," *NGME*.

44 The Felton's eldest son was William Locker Pickmore. He studied law at Quebec in the firm of Andrew Stuart and Henry Black before being admitted to the bar in November 1834. He would practise law in Sherbrooke after 1837, serve as an active municipal councillor during the 1840s, and win a seat in the Legislative Assembly in 1854 See Maurice O'Bready, "Felton, William Locker Pickmore," *DCB*, vol. 10, 281-82; and Little, *State and Society*, 155.

45 This reference is to Edward Hale, not the carpenter Hale mentioned earlier in the same entry. After the Rebellion of 1837, Edward Hale would succeed William B. Felton as the most influential individual in the region. For more information on him, see Little, *State and Society*, 25-32, 34, 36-39, 55, 75, 85, 126, 131-38, 154-55, 179, 206; and Louis-Phillippe Audet, "Hale, Edward," *DCB*, vol. 10, 326-27.

46 Lord Aylmer added to his unpopularity by refusing money to Montreal during the cholera epidemic of 1834 and retreating to his cottage at Sorel during the height of the outbreak. Buckner, "Whitworth-Aylmer, Matthew, 5th Baron Aylmer," 907.

47 The St Francis King's Bench did not have full criminal jurisdiction until 1843. Little, *State and Society*, 64. On the nature of the counterfeiting economy

north of the Vermont border, and the state's attempts to suppress it, see Little, *State and Society*, 30, 50, 52, 55-57, 70, 76, 239.

48 After serving as MLA for the county of William Henry from 1809 to 1812, Edward Bowen became judge at the Court of King's Bench at Quebec. With his other official positions, he received a stipend of over £1,000 a year, as well as generous land grants from the government, but from 1814 he complained continually about his financial difficulties. He entered the Legislative Council in 1824, and served as its president *pro tempore* in 1834. See Jean-Pierre Wallot, "Bowen, Edward," *DCB*, vol. 9, 74-75.

49 In August 1835, W.L.P. Felton married Clara Lloyd, daughter of Thomas Lloyd, a surgeon in the English Army. O'Bready, "Felton, William Locker Pickmore," 281.

50 Fanny Kemble (1809-93) was the eldest daughter of Charles Kemble, a noted Shakespearean actor and manager of Covent Garden from 1817 to 1832. Fanny began to act at Covent Garden in 1829 to save her father from bankruptcy. She became an accomplished performer in both comedy and tragedy, and toured the United States with her father in 1832-4. She then married the owner of a plantation and retired from the stage, later becoming an outspoken abolitionist and, after her divorce, pursuing a career as a writer of plays, journals, and poems, *NGME*.

51 This is the only reference to a Mary Jane. Possibly it should be to Sarah Jane, Lucy's sister.

52 Subsequently referred to as M'Ready, or various spellings thereof. The 1831 census for Ascot lists a John McCurdy with a household of nine, twenty improved acres on a hundred-acre farm, five cattle, and four hogs.

53 Aside from the possible necessity of making such articles himself, Edmund probably shared the English settler's common belief that homemade articles had an inherent superiority over any that were purchased. Charlotte Erickson, "Agrarian Myths of English Immigrants," in O. Fritiof Anders, ed., *In the Trek of the Immigrants* (Rock Island, IL: Augustana College Library, 1964), 75.

54 Charles Felton, brother of William Bowman and John, was the district prothonotary, and apparently outside the elite circle because of the embarrassment caused by his constant indebtedness. See Little, "British Toryism," 29.

55 The 1831 manuscript census for Ascot Township lists Sewell Haskett as carpenter with seven members of his household living on four acres of improved land.

Notes to Book Two

1 Charles Frederick Henry Goodhue was the son of a prominent physician in Vermont and Massachusetts. A year after Ascot's bankrupt township leader, Gilbert Hyatt, lost his land and mills to the Hart brothers of Trois-Rivières in 1811, they were purchased by Goodhue for $880. Goodhue then sold the mills and mill sites to Felton who leased them back to Goodhue in 1820. Goodhue served as Member of the Legislative Assembly from 1830 to 1834. Jean-Pierre Kesteman, Peter Southam and Diane Saint-Pierre, *Histoire des Cantons de l'Est* (Saint-Foy: Institut québécois de recherche sur la culture,

1998), 146, 154, 164, 207, 208; J.I. Little, "Imperialism and Colonization in Lower Canada: The Role of William Bowman Felton," *Canadian Historical Review* 66 (1985): 514 n. 14; Frederick H. Armstrong, "Goodhue, George Jervis," *Dictionary of Canadian Biography* (hereafter *DCB*), vol. 9, 323-24.

2   This sale took place on 21 October 1833 for the sum of £37 10s. Sherbrooke Registry Office, Register A, vol. 8, p. 322, no. 348.

3   On the British American Land Company, see J.I. Little, *Nationalism, Capitalism, and Colonization in the Upper St Francis District* (Montreal: McGill-Queen's University Press, 1989), ch. 2.

4   Lucius Doolittle was born in Vermont in 1800, moved to the Eastern Townships as a youth, where he was engaged in business with an uncle, and began to prepare for ordination in the Anglican Church at the age of eighteen. He entered the University of Vermont in 1824, left to study theology with the missionary in the village of Hatley near Sherbrooke in 1827, and was ordained two years later. Posted to Lennoxville in 1833, he served there the rest of his working life. Like many prominent local figures, Doolittle served as land agent for absentee proprietors, including the Bishop of Quebec, and he was himself comfortably established by 1840. The boys' school that he established in 1836 evolved into Bishop's College School, and he was intimately associated with Bishop's University, chartered in 1843. "Doolittle, Lucius," *DCB*, vol. 9; Christopher Nicholl, *Bishop's University, 1843-1970* (Montreal: McGill-Queen's University Press, 1994), 17-18.

5   Anna Maria Valls was from Port Mahon on the Island of Minorca.

6   Eliza would not marry John Davidson, whose father, John, was the brother-in-law and partner of John Caldwell, a major landed proprietor, lumber and flour mill operator, and shipbuilder who defaulted as the colony's receiver-general in 1823. The younger Davidson, who served as superintendent of Crown forests, would succeed Eliza's father as Lower Canada's commissioner of crown lands in 1837. Little, "Imperialism and Colonization," 531; André Héroux, "Caldwell, Sir John," *DCB*, vol. 7, 133-36.

7   George Moffatt and Peter McGill were very influential Montreal merchants and politicians who were major investors in the British American Land Company. See Robert Sweeney, "McGill, Peter," *DCB*, vol. 8, 540-44; and Gerald Tulchinsky, "Moffatt, George," *DCB*, vol. 9, 553-56.

8   A reference to the British American Land Company.

9   There is no mention of a John Colville in the *Dictionary of National Biography*, and John Coleborne, the governor of Upper Canada, had not been knighted at this point.

10 The Anglican bishop of Quebec at this time was Charles James Stewart. See Thomas R. Millman, "Stewart, Charles James," *DCB*, vol. 7, 825-28.

11 The Catholic archbishop of Quebec at this time was Joseph Signay. On the role of the Catholic Church in the region at this time, see J.I. Little, "The Catholic Church and French-Canadian Colonization of the Eastern Townships, 1821-51," *University of Ottawa Quarterly* 52, 1 (1982): 142-65.

12 William F. Buchan, identifying himself as a member of the College of Surgeons and late president of the Hunterian Society of Edinburgh, wrote the lengthy pamphlet *Remarks on Emigration: more particularly applicable to the Eastern Townships, Lower Canada*, 2nd ed. (Devonport: Soper and Richards;

London: Baldwin and Cradoch, 1842). In contrast to most of the region's promotional pamphlets published at this time, which spoke primarily to the gentry, Buchan claimed to be addressing "the class of persons with . . . limited means, and labourers with none." He assured them that the "forms and absurd refinements of a more settled country" were not to be found in the Eastern Townships, where the high demand for labourers meant that they were "united more strongly and closely to the more wealthy class" (pp. 59-60).

13 Vaccination was used to prevent smallpox in Lower Canada after 1801, and became a government program in 1815. Jacques Bernier, *La medecin au Quebec: Naissance et évolution d'un profession* (Quebec: Les Presses de l'Université Laval, 1989), 116-17.

14 Also spelt Buchanan; the following letters indicate that this is Charles Buchanan, not the Quebec immigration agent, Alexander Carlyle Buchanan.

15 The name given at the beginning of the eighteenth century to the finest kinds of Chinese black tea, but the quality now known as "Bohea" is the lowest, being the last crop of the season, *OED*.

16 This term would be most appropriate for pigs since a gutter snipe is a gatherer of refuse from street gutters, (*OED*), but a pig's neck and head is not designed to keep on a wooden collar.

17 Members of the Patriote party opposed Samuel Gale's appointment to the King's Bench in Montreal in August 1834 because of his testimony before the British House of Commons committee inquiring into the government of Canada in 1828. Gale represented the interests of the Eastern Townships, asking that the region be given representation in the Legislative Assembly (which was granted a year later), that British immigration be encouraged to the region (which also took place a year later), and that Lower Canada be united with Upper Canada. Lord Aylmer was chastised by the colonial secretary for appointing a political partisan to the bench, but he persisted and Gale remained judge despite fresh protests from the Assembly. J.-C. Bonenfant, "Gale, Samuel," *DCB*, vol. 9, 296-97.

18 Sherbrooke acquired its own Catholic missionary, John Baptist McMahon, in 1834. On his rather troubled tenure there, see J.I. Little, "Missionary Priests in Quebec's Eastern Townships: The Years of Hardship and Discontent, 1825-1853," Canadian Catholic Historical Association *Study Sessions* 45 (1978): 27-30.

19 John Moore had a large farm in Eaton Township, and served as secretary for the British American Land Company. He would alienate the local elite by becoming more liberal in politics during the early 1840s. Little, *State and Society*, 20, 29-31, 36-38, 40.

20 On Gugy's controversial political career in Sherbrooke, see ibid., 28-30, 40, 45.

21 With his brother Daniel, the American-born printer and journalist, Calvin Tolford launched the *St Francis Courier and Sherbrooke Gazette* in 1831. In 1832 it opposed the establishment of the British American Land Company and began to support the reformist ideas of Papineau. Jean-Pierre Kesteman, Peter Southam, and Diane Saint-Pierre, *Histoire des Cantons de l'Est* (Sainte-Foy: Institut québécois de recherche sur la culture, 1998), 210.

22 J.W. Hallowell had been practising law in Sherbrooke since 1824. He would become the district bankruptcy commissioner in 1847. See Little, *State and Society*, 79, 81-82.

23 Sir Edward Bulwer Lytton's *Pilgrims of the Rhine,* published in 1834, is described by the publisher as "a mystical narrative of the romance of youth." Lytton was a prolific novelist, publishing four historical novels between 1832 and 1834 alone. These were well researched and carefully constructed, but he failed to achieve critical acclaim. Lucy Peel's reaction was doubtless influenced by the charges that his works were immoral, and by his pro-reform political stance. L.S. Lytton, "Lytton, Edward George Earle Lytton Bulwer," *Dictionary of National Biography*, vol. 12, 380-87.

24 It was not uncommon for infants to die of diarrhea in the nineteenth century. Those who did were in a state of severe dehydration, as Celia clearly was. Jacalyn Duffin, *Langstaff: A Nineteenth-Century Medical Life* (Toronto: University of Toronto Press, 1993), 110-11. The infant mortality rate was 150 to 250 per thousand births for Western pre-industrial populations. Infants less than a year old were particularly at risk when being weaned because of the poor quality of the water and hygiene, and because of the loss of antibodies found in mothers' milk. Lucy mentions planning to wean Celia on 5 May, when she was only five months old, and Flora, her rather sickly second child, appears to have been weaned still earlier. R.E. Jones, "Infant Mortality in Rural North Shropshire," *Population Studies* 30 (1976): 305; Jean-Louis Flandrin, *Families in Former Times: Kinship, Household and Sexuality* (Cambridge: Cambridge University Press, 1979), 206, 208; R.V. Short, "Breast Feeding," *Scientific American* 250, 4 (1984): 41.

25 John Henry Mansur, *Henri Quatre: or, The days of the League*, 3 vols. (London: Witaker and Company, [1835]).

26 William IV dismissed his Whig ministers in late 1834, and Sir Robert Peel became the Conservative prime minister with a minority of seats after the subsequent election.

27 On midwives and "grannies" in Upper Canada, see Jane Errington, *Wives and Mothers, School Mistresses and Scullery Maids: Working Women in Upper Canada, 1790-1840* (Montreal: McGill-Queen's University Press, 1995), 59, 62-63, 70-71, 128.

28 Captain Frederick Marryat (1792-1848) was a popular and prolific author whose *Japhet, In Search of a Father* had recently been published.

29 Alexander Henry's *Travels and adventures in Canada and the Indian territories, between the years 1760 and 1776* was published in 1809. David A. Armout, "Henry, Alexander," *DCB*, vol. 6, 316-18.

30 William Bell, who married Edward Hale's sister-in-law, served as clerk of the Provincial Court. Little, *State and Society*, 32.

31 Edward Hale would ensure that his brother-in-law, George Frederick Bowen (son of Judge Bowen), became clerk of the district court, then bankruptcy commissioner, and, finally, sheriff of the St Francis District. See ibid., 31-32, 62, 65, 69, 74, 76, 81.

32 Presumably a rough fence made of brushwood and stumps rather than rails. On pioneer fences, see Edwin C. Guillet, *The Pioneer Farmer and Backwoodsman*, vol. 2 (Toronto: University of Toronto Press, 1963), 13-23.

33 Note that number 26 is missing, with its presumed description of the second baby's birth, though the only days not covered in the journal entries are 3 – 13 May.

34 A solution of opium in alcohol, used to lessen pain. During the later nineteenth century, opium became the most commonly recorded drug in one long-serving Ontario doctor's practice. Dr Langstaff of Richmond Hill used it for pain relief, sedation, control of diarrhea, and suppression of cough. Laudanum appeared less often in his records, and in some cases seems to have been administered by the patient before the doctor arrived. Duffin, *Langstaff*, 75-76.

35 Erysipelas is defined as "a febrile disease characterized by inflammation and redness of the skin and subcutaneous tissues." Benjamin F. Miller and Claire Brackman Keane, *Encyclopedia and Dictionary of Medicine and Nursing* (Toronto: W.B. Saunders, 1972), 331. See also Duffin, *Langstaff*, 106-108.

36 Perhaps referring to Colonel Duncan McDougall, a former inspecting field officer of the Nova Scotia militia who competed with the British American Land Company for wild land purchases adjacent to the company's unsurveyed St Francis Tract. In 1837, McDougall promoted a colonization scheme to settle 5,000 families on 150,000 acres free of charge. See Little, *Nationalism, Capitalism, and Colonization*, 48-49.

37 "A group of persons and accessories, producing a picturesque effect." In the theatre it is a "representation of the action at some stage in a play, created by the actors suddenly holding their positions or 'freezing,' especially at a moment critical to the plot, or at the end of the scene or act," *OED*.

38 In 1837, Thomas Austin would become associated with G. Slack to establish the Lennoxville Brewery with a capacity of 280 gallons. The enterprise would fail in 1842. Jean-Pierre Kesteman, "Une bourgeoisie et son espace: Industrialisation et développement du capitalism dans le district de Saint-François (Québec), 1823-1879" (PhD thesis, Université du Québec à Montréal, 1985), 184.

39 Also spelled later as "Twiss."

40 Captain R. Hayne was supervising the survey of the land company's St. Francis Tract. Little, *Nationalism, Capitalism and Colonization*, 41.

41 William Cobbett (1762-1835) was an essayist, politician, and agriculturist who devoted himself to the reform cause after 1804. He published the *Weekly Political Register* from 1802 until his death more than thirty-three years later. By the 1830s he was the leading reform journalist in Britain. E.S. Cobbett, "Cobbett, William," *Dictionary of National Biography*, vol. 4, 598-601.

42 For a brief overview of upper-class cultural life in Quebec at this time, see John Hare, Marc Lafrance, and David Thierry-Ruddell, *Histoire de la Ville de Québec, 1608-1871* (Montreal: Boréal Express, 1987), 249-53. On the British garrison, see Christian Rioux, *The British Garrison at Québec* (Ottawa: Parks Canada, 1996).

43 The full name is muskellunge, a large, freshwater fish of the pike family, *GCD*.

44 A farmer as well as a mason, Henry Beckett began to manufacture bricks and erect buildings in Sherbrooke in 1823. The Beckett brickworks, as well as a stone quarry, were still in operation in 1870. Kesteman, "Une bourgeoisie," 267.

45 A commonly used medicine since the eighteenth century, composed of ipecac and opium. Dangerous for small children when dosages were not carefully controlled. Unlike Taylor's powder, it is listed as a part of the pharmacopoeia used by the nineteenth-century Ontario doctor, James Langstaff. Mary Schaeffer Conroy, *In Health and Sickness: Pharmacy, Pharmacists, and the Pharmaceutical Industry in Late Imperial, Early Soviet Russia* (New York: Columbia University Press, 1994), 209-10; Duffin, *Langstaff*, 274-75.

Notes to Book Three

1 The Assembly's 1835-6 inquiry into Bowen's conduct as a judge was never completed. For details on the case see Robert Christie, *A History of the Late Province of Lower Canada*, vol. 4 (Quebec: John Lovell, 1853), 208-10.

2 Bathurst was Colonial Secretary in the Liverpool administration from 1812 to 1827. Peter Burroughs, *The Canadian Crisis and British Colonial Policy, 1828-1841* (Toronto: Macmillan, 1972), 119.

3 Although Felton claimed that the lots in question were ones he had set aside as his commission for sale of other Crown lots, the Assembly's Standing Committee on Grievances, chaired by Sherbrooke's B.C.A. Gugy, found him "guilty of oppression, speculation and extortion." In the spring of 1836 Lord Gosford ordered the attorney general to launch a formal charge of fraud, but the case was dropped on a legal technicality. Gosford, nevertheless, insisted that the "moral character of the question" remained the same, and Felton was dismissed from office in August.

4 Born the son of a civil administrator in India in 1802, John Arthur Roebuck lived with his family in Upper Canada from the age of thirteen to twenty-two. He then returned to England and entered the Inner Temple, being called to the bar in 1831. A disciple of Jeremy Bentham, he became MP for Bath in 1832. In 1834 he moved in the House of Commons for the appointment of the committee that inquired into the affairs of Canada that year, and in 1835 he became agent in England for the Lower Canadian Legislative Assembly, acting in effect as Papineau's personal representative. "Roebuck, John Arthur," Peter Burroughs, *Dictionary of Canadian Biography* [hereafter *DCB*], vol. 10, 626.

5 Fletcher's dismissal was recommended by the Assembly's commissions of inquiry in 1829, 1831, 1832, and 1836, when Lord Gosford was asked to make a decision in the case. When the attorney general and solicitor general both informed him that Fletcher had not legally overstepped his powers in his campaign against his local critics, Gosford referred the matter to the Privy Council in London. Here the matter lay, and Fletcher continued exercizing his judicial functions until his death in 1844. Christine Veilleux, "Fletcher, John," *DCB*, vol. 7, 300.

6 Edward Hale's biographies mention no kinship with Lord Dundas, so the family link was presumably by marriage.

7 The surveyor-general, Joseph Bouchette, would win a libel suit against Felton in 1836, but, if Lucy was right about the above-mentioned court case, it had

presumably not been settled when Felton died later in the year. J.I. Little, "Felton, William Bowman," *DCB*, vol. 7, 283.

8 Thomas Cushing Aylwin (1806-71) was a skilful criminal jurist who entered political life on the side of the Patriotes, defending those imprisoned during the rebellion, and being elected to the Legislative Assembly in 1841, 1844, and 1847. In 1848 he became a judge in the Queen's Bench of the St Francis District, shortly before Eliza, his second wife, died of cholera. Eliza's marriage may not have been happy, for in 1843 Marcus Child of Stanstead wrote that she "looked more like a ghost — than a lady. I spoke with her for some time — she was from Sherbrooke and remembered travelling to Quebec with our party in 1834 — She was then going into the world, young and full of expectation — now she is but the shadow of herself — and I think not long for this world — She is a good woman and has a good name among the poor in Kingston." J.I. Little, ed., *The Child Letters: Public and Private Life in a Canadian Merchant-Politician's Family* (Montreal: McGill-Queen's University Press, 1995), 115; and Andre Garon, "Aylwin, Thomas Cushing," *DCB*, vol. 10, 24.

9 The number should be 38.

10 The name should be William Whitcher, the son of Sheriff Charles Whitcher. His future wife was daughter of the British-born Sherbrooke lawyer Christopher Pferinger Elkins. J.I. Little, *State and Society in Transition: The Politics of Institutional Reform in the Eastern Townships* (Montreal: McGill-Queen's University Press, 1997), 80-81.

11 On Niagara Falls as an early tourist mecca, see Patricia Jasen, *Wild Things: Nature, Culture, and Tourism in Ontario, 1790-1914* (Toronto: University of Toronto Press, 1995), ch. 2.

12 Felton died on 30 June 1837.

Index to Letters

(References to members of the Peel and Meek families were too numerous to include)

Albany, N.Y., 31

Americans, description of, 25, 28, 32, 45, 85, 90-91, 93, 110, 116, 120, 122, 137-38, 141, 178, 193

Austin, Thomas and Mrs, 155, 175, 182, 223 n. 38

Aylmer, Lady, 48, 91-92, 113-14

Aylmer, Lord, 48, 53-54, 123, 137, 217 n. 38, 218 n. 46, 221 n. 17

Aylwin, T.C., 191, 197, 225 n. 8

Barnard, Dr, 80, 81, 100

Beckett, Henry, 168, 223 n. 44

Bell, William, 144, 157, 222 n. 30

Belvidere, 39, 40, 55, 85, 86, 216 n. 22

Bowen, Frederick, 144, 145, 151, 158, 184, 222 n. 31

Bowen, Judge Edward, 57-58, 178, 219 n. 48, 224 n. 1

Bowen, Lucy, 127, 157, 159, 160

British American Land Company, 96, 106, 154, 196-97, 201, 206

Buchan, William F., 109, 117, 220 n. 12

Buchanan, Charles, 114-17 *passim*

Burlington, Vt, 35

Campbell, Mr, 157, 164, 166, 180, 188-89

candle making, 142

carriages, description of, 29, 33, 140

childbirth. *See* pregnancy

cholera, 115, 124

Christmas, 89, 179

Colclough, Captain Guy and Mrs, 36, 38, 90, 97, 111, 137, 216 n. 18

Colclough, Major and Mrs, 36, 38-39, 97, 112

crime / law, 25-26, 55, 60-61, 113, 144, 163, 167, 217 n. 35

Crispo, Lieutenant, 175

David siblings, 155, 159

death / mourning, 85, 130-35, 138, 140, 145, 147, 148, 159-60, 161, 194, 195, 196, 206, 220 n. 24

Doolittle, Rev. Lucius and Mrs, 79, 93, 112, 116-17, 135, 160, 161, 166, 220 n. 4

Drummond (carpenter), 143

duelling, 139

Dunstall Villa, 41, 46-49 *passim*, 57, 58-59, 83, 88-89, 91, 111, 143, 147, 150, 164, 189-90, 200

economy and prices, Sherbrooke area, 42, 43, 51, 61, 62-63, 65, 68, 79, 88, 91, 95-105 *passim*, 109, 114, 118, 119, 120, 125, 128, 139-40, 142, 143, 158, 159, 168, 175, 185, 191, 195, 196, 206

economy, settler, 29, 43, 64, 65, 74-84 passim, 87, 92, 94, 98, 99, 106, 110, 111, 114, 120, 125,

128, 146-47, 161, 181, 185, 200, 205, 206
erysipelas, 151, 223 n. 35
Ewen, Mrs, 192-93

Felton, Anna Maria, 42-43, 54, 62, 85-86, 90, 98, 102, 112-13, 125-26, 134, 207,
Felton, Charles and Mrs, 67, 163, 181, 219 n. 54
Felton, Charlotte, 41, 124-25
Felton, Eliza, 42-43, 63, 129, 173, 179, 191, 225 n. 8
Felton, Fanny, 124-25, 142
Felton, John, 39, 55, 59, 96, 216 n. 21
Felton, Maria (daughter), 57
Felton, Narbon, 58, 67, 89, 96
Felton, William B., 39, 40, 41, 86, 112, 177-79, 188, 190, 192, 216 n. 20, 224-25 n. 7
Felton, William L.P., 57, 58, 219 n. 49
fire, 72, 86, 91, 94, 112, 124, 149, 163, 164, 166, 182, 186, 189
Fletcher, Judge John and Mrs, 39-40, 45, 47, 79, 81, 85, 95, 97-98, 115, 124, 132, 174, 183, 189, 216 n. 23, 224 n. 5
Fort Ann, N.Y., 33

gardens / orchards, 49-50, 51, 64, 68, 103-105 *passim*, 109, 112, 116, 117, 151, 200-201
Goodhue, Charles F.H. and Mrs, 61, 74, 106, 141, 184, 219 n. 1
Gosford, Lord, 163, 177-78, 204

Hale (carpenter), 43, 48, 52-53, 60-61
Hale, Edward, 53, 175, 218 n. 45
Hale, Eliza, 58, 62, 95, 107, 114, 134, 140, 144, 154, 175, 201, 203-204
Hamilton, William, 36, 93, 216 n. 16
Haskel (carpenter), 53, 54, 56, 67, 219 n. 55
Hayne, Captain, 158, 159, 223 n. 40
Henry, Mrs William (Charlotte), 89, 91, 92, 137-38

Henry, William, 39, 40, 112-13, 121-22, 143, 216 n. 19
hotels / inns, 27, 28, 31-36 *passim*, 104, 110, 137-38
housekeeping, 50, 62, 64, 65-66, 75, 84, 118, 143-44. *See also* servants
Hudson River, 30-31

Indians, 33, 36, 48, 81, 104, 120, 121-22, 143

Kimball, George and Mrs, 51, 61, 117, 135, 200-201, 218 n. 42

Lake Champlain, 34-35
Lewison, Sarah, 62, 65, 67

Macarty, Patrick, 175
mail delivery, 32, 35, 40, 49, 109, 217 n. 27
McDougall, Col., 155, 156, 223 n. 36
McReady, Ellen, 65-67 *passim*, 75, 81, 89, 142, 191, 194
McReady, Mr and Mrs, 65, 80, 81, 91, 101, 102, 157, 167, 188, 197, 219 n. 52
meteorite, giant, 106
midwives / nurses. *See* Ewen, Mrs; Goodhue, Mrs; and Salt, Mrs
Montizambert, Mr, 159, 160
mosquitoes / black flies, 44, 46, 108, 116, 121, 151
music, 28, 39, 41, 42, 44, 52, 57, 63, 84, 91, 94, 95, 99, 100, 103, 104, 107, 108, 116, 118, 146, 150, 152, 158, 159, 169, 178, 179, 182, 183, 184, 198-99

Nelson, Miss (Judge Vallières' adopted daughter), 48, 57, 127
New York City, 26-29

Parkes, 59, 76-77, 80, 175, 187
Peck, Ebenezer and Mrs, 47, 139-40, 217 n. 34
Peel, Edmund (Sorel cousin) and Mrs, 44, 45-46, 53-54, 59, 90, 95, 109, 113-15 *passim*, 124, 144, 153, 163, 180, 190, 198

politics, 127, 137, 139, 158, 159, 177-78. *See also* Lord Aylmer and Lord Gosford
pregnancy / child-birth, 53, 54, 75-76, 80, 81-82, 87-88, 111, 133, 148, 149, 165, 166, 184, 185, 189, 192-93, 196

religion, 161-62. *See also* Doolittle, Rev. Lucius
Roebuck, John Arthur, 182, 224 n. 4

Salt, Mrs and Mr, 81, 82, 142, 149, 179, 187-88
Sandy Hill, N.Y., 32-33
servants, 28, 31, 62-67 *passim*, 86, 88, 89, 118, 136, 160, 166-67, 175, 178, 180, 192-99 *passim. See also* Lewison, Sarah; Macarty, Patrick; McReady, Ellen; Parkes; Salt, Mrs
Sherbrooke, 36, 86, 89, 110, 196-97, 201
sleighs, 78, 128-29, 139
Stewart, Bishop Charles, 108, 109, 220 n. 10
St Francis River, 36, 39, 51, 53

Stanstead, 35
steamboats, 30, 34

Tolford, Calvin, 127, 221 n. 21
travel, trans-Atlantic, 23-27; New York – Sherbrooke, 30-36
Troy, N.Y., 32
Twiss, Mr, 155, 182-83, 184

vaccination, 112, 113, 181-83 *passim*, 221 n. 13
Vallières, Judge Joseph-Rémi, 48, 142, 217 n. 39

Watson, Dr, 151, 152, 155-56, 162, 163, 166-76 *passim*, 181, 185, 186, 187, 190, 191, 192, 195, 201, 205
weaning, 105, 107, 108
Whitcher, Charles and Mrs, 40, 54, 55, 116, 217 n. 24
Whitehall, N.Y., 33, 34
wildlife, 48, 56, 62, 85, 116, 122, 161, 205
Wilson, Dr William and Mrs, 47, 50, 51, 62, 96, 131, 217 n. 36 and 37

DATE DUE